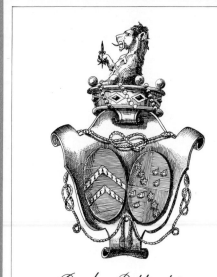

# ELEGANT WITS AND
# GRAND HORIZONTALS

BOOKS BY
CORNELIA OTIS SKINNER

*Tiny Garments*

*Excuse It, Please!*

*Dithers and Jitters*

*Soap Behind the Ears*

*Our Hearts Were Young and Gay*
with Emily Kimbrough

*Family Circle*

*That's Me All Over*

*Nuts in May*

*Bottoms Up!*

*The Ape in Me*

*Elegant Wits and Grand Horizontals*

# ELEGANT WITS
## AND
# GRAND
# HORIZONTALS

---

*A sparkling panorama of "La Belle Epoque":
its gilded society, irrepressible wits and
splendid courtesans*

BY

## CORNELIA OTIS SKINNER

*illustrated with photographs*

The Riverside Press Cambridge
HOUGHTON MIFFLIN COMPANY BOSTON
1962

*For Marina*

# PREFACE

---

THIS IS a book which deals with certain aspects of a city during a particular period of its long and rich life. The city is Paris and the period is the final decade of the last century, that era of elegance, animation, blitheness and security which is known in France as La Belle Epoque. Ever since I went there as a girl to study for the stage, many more years ago than I'd dream of admitting, Paris has never ceased to beguile me. *Beguile* is an all too inadequate verb for expressing an emotion which, in me, is a mixture of admiration, stimulation, exasperation and abiding love. Interest in the period began when I started working on a solo musical show called *Paris '90,* a one-woman revue with score and lyrics by Kay Swift, scenic effects by Donald Oenslager, costumes by Helene Pons and the script by me. It consisted of fourteen sketches in each of which I portrayed a different character, all representative of varying facets of the Gallic 1890's.

Before starting the script, I had made a trip to Paris where I spent many hours ferreting out information . . . browsing in bookshops, interviewing persons who either had known that era or were authorities on its history, looking up locales and undergoing the frustrating red-tape intricacies attendant upon doing any research in the Bibliothèque Nationale. The result was an accumulation of material only a lesser portion of which was used in the show. For a number of years a surplus collection of books, notes and filing cards on the subject lay unconsulted in the bottom drawers of a bureau in my "study," which is another name for our one and only guest room. In anticipation of the arrival of visitors who were due to stay with us for some time, I began clearing out the bottom drawers and was halted soon after the start of that laudable chore by one of those compulsive reading attacks which stop short in their labors all clearer-outers of books, notes and filing cards from bureau drawers. My interest in the Paris of the *Belle Epoque* which had remained dormant for a good six years awoke with a leap. To my economical mind, it seemed a crying shame to let all this material go to waste. Accordingly, I economized by making another trip to Paris and gathering further material from bookshops, authorities on the period, and library research.

During this stay, however, I was spared the red-taperies of research in the Bibliothèque Nationale through the kind offices of Dr. Paul-Emile Seidmann who put me in touch with Monsieur Renoult, the distinguished director of the Mazarine Library of the Institut de France. He, in turn, put me in touch with the chief librarians of a few less awesomely complicated fountain-heads of information than the Nationale, namely, the Bibliothèque de l'Arsenale, the Bibliothèque Sainte-Geneviève, and particularly the Bibliothèque de la Ville de Paris. The librarians in these learned establishments were wonderfully cooperative, as the French always are provided one approaches them armed with the proper credentials, and guided me to a wealth of books, periodicals and pamphlets which, given time, I might well be reading yet.

Actually, I must admit that most of the books I consulted over there are to be found right in my own front yard, if I may claim as front yardage that section on the west side of Fifth Avenue between Fortieth and Forty-second streets where stands the New York Public Library. As a patriotic New Yorker, I am willing to grant that research in that superb bibliographical treasury can be done with far greater ease and effortless efficiency than in any Paris library, with the exception of the American one on the Champs Elysées in which the obtaining of a book is uncomplicated to the point of seeming, in Paris, to be practically illegal. But as a dedicated Francophile, I find that there is something about the very frustrations involved in any research in France's capital that adds value to the ultimate discoveries.

Furthermore, in Paris I was able to meet a number of men and women who were familiar with the period and to get from them first hand, or at all events, a closely accurate second hand, much information. Of these persons, I should like to pay grateful thanks to three in particular. First of all, to Marie-Jeanne Courteline, the widow of that beloved and prolific author Georges Courteline whose deliciously funny plays and short novels have earned him the name, according to the *Oxford Companion to French Literature,* of "probably the greatest humorous writer of modern France." Mme. Courteline lives at 43 Avenue de Saint-Mandé where she and her husband spent the years of their married life. There is a plaque to his memory on the building, and in the square outside a bronze bust which during the Occupation, courageous and clever friends were able to conceal from the Germans — who were purloining every malleable public monument in France to melt into weapons. Mme. Courteline keeps her apartment exactly at it was during her husband's lifetime and holds a little court for his pleiad of friends and admirers who call daily to pay respects to the memory of the author and devoted homage to his widow. Under the stage name of Marie-Jeanne Brécourt, she had been an excellent comedienne in her day. She and Courteline first met when she was performing in his *Joyeuses Commères de Paris.* The dear lady received me several times. She talked long and enchantingly of her husband and his friends, most of whom were celebrated *boulevardiers,* of the Paris theatre at the turn of the century and of the playwrights and men of letters she had known. Marie-Jeanne Courteline is a lively and adorable person of cheery wit and outgoing warmth.

Another gracious lady who also dates back to the Belle Epoque and who has my thanks and true affection is Mademoiselle Cléo de Mérode, the dancer whose flawless beauty was once the toast of three continents. In all the capitals of Europe audiences gazed spellbound at her delicate loveliness, gentlemen adorers trailed her footsteps and critics were lyrical in their praises. One even headed a review of her ballet *Phryné,* "Gloria in excelsis Cléo!" She was famous not only for her looks and her dancing, but for the distinctive manner in which she always wore her hair . . . parted in the middle and brought down over her ears in classic severity. The style caught on for a time as the *bandeau à la Mérode* and other women copied it but with little success, for only a ravishing creature could get away successfully with such stark simplicity. There had once been a rumor that Cléo de Mérode combed her hair over her ears either because she didn't have any or because they were deformed. This is completely untrue, as untrue as was that other rumor which crops up again and again coupling her name with that of Leopold of Belgium. This too was as slanderous as it was false. That amorous monarch was in the audience one night when she danced at the Opéra and, like every man who set eyes on her, was quite overcome by her grace and beauty. During the intermission, he went backstage to the Dancers' Foyer to congratulate her. He took her off to one side and talked with her in a somewhat protracted interview. The white-bearded king had the international reputation of being an incorrigible old satyr and the public jumped to its usual salacious conclusions. In her autobiography *Le Ballet de ma Vie,* Cléo admits to only two love affairs both of which were apparently idyllic, one with a French count, the other with a Spanish marquis (she discreetly withholds their names). Each of these suitors must have had far greater charm than Leopold. Any man who would sleep with his beard carefully tied up in a chiffon bag to preserve its silkiness could never have been the type to win her heart. One has only to meet this quiet gentlewoman of exquisite refinement to realize how far removed she must always have been from the brazenly spectacular professionals *"de chez Maxim's."* To this day she has preserved her delicate freshness and charm. As long ago as 1930, Colette, in presenting her with a copy of her book *La Chatte* wrote an affectionate inscription on the flyleaf, starting it with "To Cléo de Mérode who defies time." Mlle. de Mérode is still defying time. She is still beautiful, still wears her Madonna hairdo, still lives in her roomy apartment on the rue de Téhéran surrounded by paintings and photographs reminiscent of her highly successful past. She is also still alert and amazingly active. On the several occasions in which I called, she had just been giving a dancing lesson to one of the special pupils she accepts to train for the ballet school. Over tea and delicious cakes she told me of the dazzling Paris she had known, of the celebrities who had been her friends . . . Gounod, Massenet, Proust, Reynaldo Hahn, of her European tours, of the elegant Monday nights at the Opéra when, to maintain the elegance, it was a rule that only men could sit on the parterre — in full dress, of course — while women decorated the boxes in flashing jewels and colorful décolletée gowns from Paquin and Worth. As she talked, her perfect oval cheeks glowed and her limpid eyes shone and she looked as young as when she danced at the Exposition of 1900.

A gentleman to whom I am vastly indebted is Monsieur Géo Sandry. He is a personage in the theatre world and the author of a number of highly entertaining books about the French stage and screen. He himself by no means dates back in years to the

1890's, but he has made an intensive study of that period and written many articles on the subject. He gave me much information about Maxim's, the theatre, the wits of the boulevards, the Parisian antics of the Russian Grand Dukes and the more spectacular duels that were fought by the journalist patrons of the Café Napolitain. I trust that he can realize how much he has my heartfelt thanks.

I am quite well aware that the Paris '90's is a period which has been written about time and again. Yet the more I have studied it, the more I discover there is to find and the more there remains yet to be written about it. Of the aspects I myself have chosen, some were already familiar to me, others quite new. These days of tensions and fears may seem strange ones in which to write a book about a decade of blithe assurance and surface frivolity. And yet it has given me curious pleasure and much satisfaction to turn my thoughts to that last era of gracious living, liberated intellect and vital awareness which once existed on this terror-stricken globe. I can only hope that others may, for a brief time, also enjoy turning their thoughts to Paris during her "beautiful epoch."

# CONTENTS

# ILLUSTRATIONS

---

EMILIENNE D'ALENÇON
*Charmer of men and trainer of rabbits*

LA BELLE OTERO
*The Spanish dancer in her Russian period*

LIANE DE POUGY
*Undisputed star in the top trio of grand horizontals*

# ELEGANT WITS AND
# GRAND HORIZONTALS

# I

## THE FLÂNEUR'S PARIS

**T**HERE IS no English equivalent for the French word *flâneur*. Cassell's dictionary defines *flâneur* as a *stroller, saunterer, drifter* but none of these seems quite accurate. There is no English equivalent for the term, just as there is no Anglo-Saxon counterpart of that essentially Gallic individual, the deliberately aimless pedestrian, unencumbered by any obligation or sense of urgency, who, being French and therefore frugal, wastes nothing, including his time which he spends with the leisurely discrimination of a gourmet, savoring the multiple flavors of his city.

Sixty and seventy years ago there was much to savor during an aimless stroll about Paris. The *flâneur* might have started out on the Grand Boulevards where every stray pedestrian — even the foreigner — feels at home, for it's been said, and all too truthfully, that any hospitality in France is to be found only on the streets of Paris. And he might have braced himself for his morning stroll with an apéritif at a pavement café where white-aproned waiters had just taken down the chairs that had been stacked on tables as though put to sleep for the night and were cleaning the marble tops with a few casual flips of a serving napkin or sprinkling down the *terrasse* with water splashed from a carafe to show what they thought of water. Out on the big thoroughfare, the day's bedlam of noise would have begun . . . a cacophony of hoofbeats, whirling wheels, rattling pushcarts, cries of hawkers and the occasional neigh of an impatient horse. At regulated intervals would sound the clattering thunder of the Impériale, the double-decked omnibus drawn by three giant Percherons, its swaying interior jammed with hatpin-ducking passengers, its open top decorous with elderly gentlemen reading the *Figaro* or the *Gaulois*.

His apéritif finished the *flâneur* would have started sauntering down that long boulevard which is chiefly known in the plural because it keeps changing its name . . . the Saint Denis turning into the Bonnes Nouvelles, the Poissonière into the Boulevard Montmartre, the Italiens suddenly taking holy orders to become the Capucines which suddenly dashes itself against the Madeleine. And at that Roman temple to God and Napoleon, he'd automatically turn down the rue Royale, pass Maxim's, cut an angle across the Place de la Concorde and on up the shaded alleyways of the Champs Elysées. Here loomed the mansions of the wealthy, the luxurious *hôtels privés*, each backed by a formal garden and fronted by a cobbled entrance court with two wrought-iron gates for incoming and outgoing carriages.

Under the Rond Point chestnuts whose restless leaves produced the broken colors and dancing sun flecks of the Impressionists, the *flâneur* might have hired a three-*sou* chair in a spot where he could observe the children gathering in squealing anticipation on tiny benches before the weatherbeaten proscenium and curtain of the Guignol show, or riding wonder-eyed on the carrousel's small painted horses as though in time to Verlaine's "Tournez, tournez, bons chevaux de bois."

But the *flâneur's* chief diversion would undoubtedly have been observing the flow of vehicles out on the creosoted wooden blocks of the Avenue itself. Landaus, victorias, buggies, fiacres, coupés, they rolled along in a ceaseless stream which de Maupassant likened to a river of turning wheels with the coachmen's whips sticking up like the rods of fishermen caught midstream in the current. The sun gleamed on polished harness, on the shiny rumps of hackney ponies, on the glazed hats of *cochers* with florid faces and tiers of capes, on the white piqué stocks of diminutive "tigers" perching with swankly folded arms on the jump seats of phaetons. There might have dashed by the brake of a sportsman on his way to the Jockey Club or the tandem of a man-about-town bound for the Agricole. At funereal pace might pass the black brougham of some ancient duchess, its gloom relieved only by a tiny crest on the door and the white cockade of the Orléanists on the horses' bridles and on the coachman's hat. A society lady late for a fitting at Paquin might come along at a smart clip in her new coupé imported from London while her eldest son, an officer of hussars, would outpace her in his gig.

It was a good show the *flâneur* sat watching . . . "the new verdure all in bloom . . . the spectacle of useless but delightful human beings, handsome horses and pretty gowns that puts the soul in an exhilarated mood." A high spot of the show would have been the sudden clear blast of a hunting horn blown by either a standing footman or an outriding *piqueur* clearing the way for the dramatic passage of the tally-ho stagecoach, driven by some gentleman owner and bearing on its swaying top a load of smart clubmen and fashionable ladies — the latter, in adorable terror, clutching the armrest with one hand and with the other trying to anchor the soaring brims of their immense hats. Elisabeth de Gramont, recalling her girlhood on the Champs Elysées, writes that "when the trumpet-call of the mailcoach rang out, I used to rush to the window to admire the equipage of Charles de la Rochefoucault or of Gordon Bennett. That horn, singing amid the flowering chestnut trees, beneath a blue sky, was truly the fanfare of the joy of living." The coaching party would have been on its way to the Bois, that enchanted region which Mme. de Gramont goes on to call a "typically French woods,

which isn't a woods at all, but a garden of women." Here the
party might have paused for an ice or a Porto at Pré Catelan or
Armenonville and the *flâneur,* had he been in the vicinity, would
have stared with appreciation as the ladies descended the little
detachable ladder at the back of the coach, in hopes of catching a
glimpse of that titillating portion of female anatomy, the ankle.

The Bois was the domain of the elegant. The less elegant
strolled on the damp gravel walks or sat on shaded benches to
watch the parade on the roads and bridlepaths. The painter
Boldini, pencil in hand, stationed himself at the entrance to the
Acacias to catch the swirling motion of wheels, cloaks and
parasols in traps and landaus and the caricaturist Sem made
satirical sketches of gentlemen riding as *escorts d'honneur* beside
the self-driven phaetons of little Parisiennes, while some fifty
meters behind followed the grooms, quite out of calling distance
were their help needed.

On the circus-ring roadways entwining the two lakes would be
moving at a clip the cavalcade of showy vehicles and fine saddle
horses which, thanks to the brush of Lautrec and the crayon of
Degas, will never be quite lost . . . tilburys, cabriolets, dogcarts.
With luck, one might catch the beguiling sight of the actress
Réjane in her victoria hitched to a pair of perfectly matched
white mules, a gift from the King of Serbia. Monsieur Chauchar,
owner of the Grands Magasins du Louvre, would sail by in his
brougham the color of a Havana cigar on his way to a luncheon of
thirty covers at the Cascades. The eminent surgeon Dr. Péan
might roll past like royalty in an open landau, his horses' bridle
chains of sterling silver, his driver and footman in gold-embroi-
dered liveries . . . a warning that the fashionable operation of an
appendix removal by Dr. Péan was an extravagant indulgence.
(Dr. Péan operated in a black frock coat, his immense hands
encased in white kid gloves, fifty students and internists watching

him. At the finish of an operation there would not be a single drop of blood on him or his immaculate attire. Dr. Péan was eventually murdered by one of his patients.) There might have galloped by a detachment of officers of the Chasseurs à Cheval, the ultra-aristocratic cavalry troupe. Their uniforms were jackets of light blue with silver braid and tight scarlet trousers and their mounts were gray half-bred Arabs with long manes and flowing tails.

Occasionally the observer might enjoy the flashy glimpse of a debonair phaeton drawn by a pair of high-steppers with pink carnations in their bridles and, driving them, a deliciously wicked creature in matching shades of pink, from her buckled shoes to her feather boa and frankly made-up face. This would have been one of the queens of the demimonde . . . an "eight-spring luxury model" . . . out to get the air and to make the respectable world shockingly aware of her existence. But for the most part, the passing parade would have been made up of the upper crust which the French first put into culinary terminology when they began calling it *le gratin*. Many of these elegant persons knew one another and a pretty part of the spectacle was the leisurely saluting from carriage to carriage, the women bowing beneath their parasols, their huge hats reaching a perilous angle like flower baskets about to spill, the men lifting their gleaming silk toppers with one yellow-gloved hand and adjusting their monocles with the other.

The daily equestrians would be cantering along the bridlepaths of the Allée des Poteaux and the *flâneur* might have warmed to the prolific sight of Ferdinand de Lesseps sedately trotting past, accompanied by his eleven children, ranged according to size. Five of his brood were the fruit of a first marriage but the remaining six were by his second wife whom he married when he was well in his sixties . . . a feat hailed in France as even greater than his building of the Suez Canal. On the footpaths, squashy from a gentle night rain, bordered by the mossy trunks of ancient trees, would be found the walkers out for *le footing* . . . men in sports clothes, women in tailored suits and small hats made fast by chenille-dotted veils . . . Proust's "masterpieces of female elegance."

The bicycle craze was at its height. On their two-wheelers of the latest make, The Little Queen or The Steel Fairy, the well-known enthusiasts would whirr and occasionally wobble by . . . the writers Jules Lemaître, Octave Mirbeau and Henri Bataille. Fierce old General Gallifet in full dress uniform, plumed hat and complete set of medals would pedal at top speed, his sword banging loudly against the rear wheel. Following him might come that most witty of the Royalists, the Prince de Sagan, in white gloves, top hat, flowered waistcoat and high velvet collar of the *Incroyables,* a ribboned monocle in his eye, a white carnation in his buttonhole. The prince was an ardent cyclist and gave a few amusing tips to a reporter from the *Gaulois,* a royalist news-paper. He is quoted as saying that if one *must* run down a pedestrian, it should never be a man from the same club and that if one *had* to fall, it should always be to the Right, never to the Left. When Monsieur Hervé, another ardent Royalist and mem-ber of the French Academy, took his first bicycling lesson and the instructor told him to lean more to the left, he refused to obey. The machine began to slant at an angle. "You'll fall unless you lean to the left, monsieur!" shouted the instructor. "Jamais de la vie!" Hervé shouted back. The bicycle went into a few convul-sive gyrations and as it crashed, Hervé cried out "Vive le Roi!"

There was much satirical newspaper commentary about the new sport. The *Annales* of May 1891 says: "Everyone knows that a bicycle is composed of two wheels . . . the front one of which is designed to run between the legs of absent-minded pedestrians and knock them down. An experienced cyclist can run down from twenty to thirty people a day. After each collision, the rules are that the cyclist must sound his horn . . . a raucous noise to summon the ambulance. There is one good thing about all this. It may help solve our problem of overpopulation."

Once in a great while, the graceful rhythm of turning wheels and hoofbeats would be shattered by the chugging tuff-tuff of some daring automobilist. For the day of the Panhard, the Dion and the Mercedes was rapidly coming on when, to quote Jules Chastenet, "the harsh smell of gasoline obliterates the noble smell of horse manure." There were those who welcomed the automobile, such as Sir Francis Jeune who wrote in the Paris edition of the London *Times,* "The motor car may become a land yacht with more variety of scenery than its marine prototype and an absence of the frequently disconcerting motion peculiar to the sea." But there were many more who resented its intrusion. A writer named Hugues le Roux sent an incensed letter to the Prefect of Police declaring that henceforth he intended to go about armed with a revolver and if any automobile threatened to run down his wife or child, he'd fire on the driver.

It was, of course, a section of the *beau monde* which the *flâneur* had been viewing. There was plenty far less *beau* to be viewed in the hovels of the fortifications and outer boulevards, in the filthy slums of the Saint Antoine district, in the apache-haunted rabbit warrens of Montmartre. The reverse of this picture of sunny opulence could all too readily have been found in the wretched hideouts under the bridge spans where homeless *clochards* huddled over trash-can fires or in the low-class eating houses near the Halles where, after midnight, for a few sous beggars and vagabonds, both men and women, could sleep for four hours sitting at crude wooden tables, their heads buried on their arms. Or again in unheated attic rooms where tubercular needlewomen with frozen fingers embroidered dress trimmings for the big houses at five pennies an hour.

But the average *flâneur* of those days would never have sought out the sordid aspects of his city. He was untroubled by social consciousness. An easygoing man, he preferred the civilized setting and was content with all he saw. For this was La Belle Epoque, the 1890's in a Paris which found the contemporary scene completely satisfying and seemingly permanent.

It was a decade of assurance. France was secure in her industry, her trade, her army and her navy and the gold franc could see eye to eye with the pound sterling. International affairs were in an agreeable state of serenity and national ones were in the still more agreeable state of chronic confusion sufficient to satisfy the most exacting afficionado of that major French sport, internal politics.* Living was easy. Champagne cost four francs a bottle, *vin ordinaire* three sous the liter. A competent maid-of-all work could be hired for three hundred and sixty francs a year with no vacation and seldom a day off, a fiacre driver was happy with a tip of five sous, a good dinner could be had at Duval's for one franc fifty with an additional twenty centimes for asparagus, and a Latin Quarter student could rent a room with a little balcony for thirty francs a month, spacious enough to accommodate himself and his *petite amie*.

The cost of living was low but the value of life was high. The

---

* Evidently during the '90's France's political parties were as complicated as they are today. The *Annales Politiques et Litteraires* of April 27, 1890, tells of a forthcoming municipal election and predicts, somewhat tongue in cheek, the parties that will be represented:

Liberal republicans, municipal republicans, opportunist republicans, radical republicans.
Autonomous radicals, socialist radicals, revolutionary radicals, anti-Semitic radicals.
Blanquist socialists, possibilist socialists, socialists of the Workers' party, anarchist socialists, anti-Semitic socialists.
Blanquist boulangists, invested boulangists, independent boulangists.
Anti-Semitic conservatives, imperialist conservatists, royalist conservatists.
Plus a certain number of do-nothingists invariable to any election!

century was drawing to a close and among some of the super-aesthetic intelligentsia there was a *fin de siècle* pose of boredom and an affected neurasthenia called *le spleen*. But the prevailing spirit was one of interest in the century to come and a zestful awareness of the present. Jules Renard the playwright, who kept a voluminous journal that is almost as informative as that of the Goncourts, writes in one entry: "I'd be very stupid not to extract from life what it gives us on the instant" and he goes on to say that whenever he meets a friend on the boulevard, he never asks him his news, about which he doesn't give a damn anyway, but quotes some poem he's just read, or announces some new idea he's just been told, "thus making of what would have been an exchange of banalities, a discussion which enriches the day. I have opened a window and breathed the air." To open windows and breathe the air was characteristic of the era.

This was a decade of elegance and perception, of high intellect and of frivolous vivacity, in a country which has always cultivated enjoyment, a cultivation so civilized, that enjoyment itself becomes an art. The great business at hand was pleasure, conducted by a people who knew the seriousness of that business. When Count Boni de Castellane arranged an elaborate fête in the Bois that was to cost a king's ransom . . . and kings still came high in those days . . . the smart set, agog over the expense, asked: "Is it for a charity benefit? . . . Is it for the reception of the Tsar of Russia? . . . Is it to get yourself an embassy?" and Boni replied, "No, my friends, it is for pleasure." But it was pleasure kept within the bounds of good taste and stamped with the distinction of in-dividuality. This was an era of grace which solemnized its elegances and understood what Voltaire meant when he spoke of "le superflu, chose si nécessaire."

It was a decade which gave free rein to adventures of the mind. A person could pursue his own ideas and air his opinions on every topic from Darwinism to the Immaculate Conception, in private discussion, public debate or in the printed pages of an open press. Certain sections of the public might be outraged by the opinions aired, but there was no more thought of censoring opinions than of censoring the air which blew through those opened windows. Darwinism was anathema to the Church and the Church, in turn, was anathema to the anticlericals who were periodically loud in their criticism and, because that holy institution is the most sophisticatedly practical of any Catholic country, nobody seriously objected. Criticism of the Church of France went as unnoticed as the chirping of sparrows in Tuileries Gardens.

The Republic was young but established. The law of 1886 had exiled in perpetuity all pretenders to the throne and yet the Orléanist, the Legitimist and the Bonapartist could campaign for the cause of his party with complete freedom as indeed could the Socialist. Even the Anarchist could speak his mind, as long as his speech was not punctuated with bombs. On January 21, 1893, the centenary of the execution of Louis XVI, a fervid speech was voiced in the Chamber by Lissagaray, a former member of the Commune, extolling the "good and fertile principles of the Glorious Revolution," while along the rue de Rivoli, members of the royalist party sold facsimiles of the 1793 *Gazette de France* with the reproduction of an engraving showing the unfortunate monarch on the scaffold and giving a rather heartrending account of the beheading. The same day, through orders from the exiled Comte de Paris, a solemn Requiem Mass was celebrated in St. François Xavier in commemoration of the victims of the Terror. It was attended by moist-eyed Royalists and any number of dedicated Republicans who joined the rest in weeping softly.

For all its professed republicanism, much of Paris was royalty minded. A Restoration of the House of France struck neither the aristocracy nor the fashionable *monde* as a fantastic anachronism.

Nor did the vision of a possible crowning of young Philippe of Orléans in the cathedral at Reims seem like a scene out of costume melodrama. There were many Parisians to whom the image of the Throne offered more security than an abstraction known as the Republic. The *Liberté-Egalité-Fraternité* system had yet to be proved and often a loudly self-proclaimed Republican, at election time, would instinctively cast his ballot for a royalist or an imperialist candidate. In the proud, musty houses of the Faubourg Saint-Germain, there remained any number of titled old relics whose grandparents had barely escaped the guillotine. Other Parisians recalled the comfortable days under Louis Philippe who, if he did pose as a citizen, was at all events a king and while the Bonapartes may have originated as Corsican upstarts, the recent and freshly remembered court of the third Napoleon and his frivolous Eugénie, exuded a certain tinsel splendor. As the half-hearted Republicans would say with a nostalgic sigh, "How charming the Republic was . . . under the Empire!"

To the *ancien régime,* the Republic itself was an upstart. Even to certain liberal thinkers it seemed a noble but rash experiment. The national figure of Marianne, the flowing-haired peasant girl in sabots, Phrygian bonnet and revolutionary cockade was an offense to those who sorrowed when the tri-color replaced the fleur-de-lis. No one stood at attention during the playing of the "Marseillaise" until well after 1870 and the Glorious Fourteenth was declared a holiday as recently as 1880. The people as a whole, while loyal in theory to the Republic, went easily aflutter over counts, dukes and baronesses. This was an enthusiasm which was not confined exclusively to the "aristo" class. When the Comte de Chambrun, a dashing cavalry officer who looked like a Meissonier hero of Austerlitz about to lead a charge, put himself up for election to the Chamber running on the royalist ticket, he received hundreds of votes from the rough workmen of the Villette district, a bastion of radical socialism. A volunteer bodyguard of slaughterhouse *forts** insisted upon following him about on his campaigning and speechmaking tours of the low quarters as a protection far more formidable than any escort from the gendarmerie. He was wined and dined in the cheap bistros of the Halles by burly butchers and raucous fishwives, toasts were drunk and "Vive le Roi!" was shouted from throats more accustomed to the "Carmognole" or the "Internationale."

This was all a manifestation of the French people's love of drama. They also loved a shifting scene. It was Arsène Houssaye, man of letters and onetime director of the Comédie Française, who said that "France's fondness for good theatre makes her change spectacles frequently; she does not like an old repertory; the comedy her kings offered her now no longer makes money." Houssaye made that perceptive comment not long after 1870. By the '90's some felt the need for another change of repertory. The bourgeois drama of republicanism could lag at the national box office. If not time for a change, it was time at least for the dramatic *beau geste.*

The decade itself opened with just such a *beau geste,* a well-timed bit of drama staged by the young Duc d'Orléans, eldest son of the pretender the Comte de Paris who, with his family, was leading a life of fashionable exile in Lausanne. When on the 7th of January the duke came of age, he put on a false beard, gave the slip to his tutors and, escorted by a fellow student the Comte de Luynes, made it across the French border and onto a Paris-bound train. Upon arrival in the city, he went straight to a recruiting station in the rue Saint-Dominique with the laudable purpose of enlisting as a common soldier to start his stretch of compulsory military service for his country. When the recruiting sergeant asked him his name, the young man replied: "Just put down His Royal Highness Monseigneur Louis Philippe Robert, Duc d'Or-

---

* Strong men used for hauling and slaughtering in the abattoirs.

léans," a reply which all but bowled over the recruiting sergeant. Stunned by the problem of enrolling in the Army of the Republic an heir to the banished throne, he passed him along to the Minister of War. The Minister of War, fairly bowled over too and equally stunned, handed him on to the Prefect of Police. This custodian of the law, though acutely aware of the awkwardness of the situation, was not so stunned as to neglect his constabulary duty. With profuse apologies he informed Monseigneur le Duc that it was his regrettable obligation to arrest and imprison him. At this pronouncement, the royal patriot uttered the sort of declamation that moves Frenchmen to blow their noses loudly and shake hands effusively with whoever is nearby. In a clear and vibrant voice the youth cried out, "Prison will be less cruel than exile, for this prison will be on the soil of France!" The gesture caught the public fancy. So did the royal boy. He was lithe, handsome, fair-haired, with the clear blue eye of the Orléans and the beginnings of a blond beard he was trying manfully to grow. They called him the "Prince Gamelle," *gamelle* being French for "soldier's mess." For a time, the popular prisoner enjoyed incarceration in the Concièrgerie where, from his outer window he could observe an ever growing crowd of admirers on the Quai de l'Horloge that had gathered to doff their hats, wave, cheer and blow kisses. The crowd was made up mainly of Royalists but there were many Republicans among them as well as a fair number of socialist workmen. There were even a few Communists who, when questioned by reporters as to why they would come to salute the Royal Presence, replied "Because of an act so essentially French!" In due course of time, President Carnot had the young man discreetly removed to a less conspicuous house of detention at Clairvaux and after the national fervor had switched to other fields, he was courteously but firmly taken back across the Swiss border.

The times were not lacking in other fields if not for fervor, certainly for excitement and agitation. One short-lived agitation and excitement was the anarchist scare when bombs started exploding all over Paris to such an alarming degree, tourists either fled the city or canceled bookings to go there and many members of the *gratin* remained in their distant manor houses or châteaux "preferring death by boredom in the country to death by bombs in Paris." The Anarchists seem to have used neither sense nor system in their bombings, which occurred in the most unexpected and improbable sections of the city. Public apprehension grew to such a degree that anyone could start a panic with a box that contained a ticking alarm clock. Whoever saw an unidentifiable package that had been dropped on a street corner summoned the police to remove it, a summons that didn't particularly delight the police. A few bombs did go off in strategic locales, one in the Chambre des Députés on December 9, 1893. When it exploded, the guards outside thought it was the sort of fireworks demonstration that was set off after a particularly stirring speech by a member inside the Palais Bourbon. The members inside knew it to be no fireworks. The bomb was a crude affair constructed by the anarchist Auguste Vaillant. Intending not to kill, merely to wound, Vaillant had filled it with nails instead of bullets. The nails flew every which way, wounding many. One ricocheted off the desk of General Mercier, who handed it to his neighbor Joseph Reinach remarking calmly, "Yours, I believe, monsieur." (The episode reminds one of the time the historian Michelet was lecturing to his class at the Ecole Normale on July 27, 1830, when cannon firing started outside in the streets and Michelet, unperturbed, said to his class, "Gentlemen they are making history, we shall write it.")

Vaillant's ensuing trial in the Palais de Justice created considerable panic, one *crise* arising over a fire-extinguisher at sight of which a spectator cried out "We must save ourselves! I see the fuse!" Vaillant was a simple peasant worker of high ideals and little education who had led a tragic life of poverty. When he was guillotined on February 5, 1894, he became a popular martyr. Sympathizers, sobbing and swearing vengeance, thronged La Roquette, the square where public beheadings took gruesome place. For a time, anarchism proved to be a many-headed hydra. Intellectuals became pseudo anarchists in very much the same way a lot of misguided enthusiasts became "parlor pinks" in this country during the 1930's. The Soup Kitchen Meetings which offered free meals to thousands who would gather to hear about the beauties of anarchism caught the imagination of many of the intelligentsia and the artistic world. Anatole France subscribed to the Soup Kitchen Meetings, so did the playwright Octave Mirbeau, and so, of all people, did Sarah Bernhardt. Again it reminds one of our own guileless and overemotional theatre people who have been taken in by fellow travelers. The affectation of anarchist-sympathizing stopped when bombs became plentiful. Except for the explosion in the Chambre des Députés and the blow that killed the unfortunate President Carnot the following year,* this demented revenge of the so-called proletariat against capitalism found only innocent nonpartisans as its victims. One bomb went off in a small hotel on the rue Saint-Jacques, killing nobody but an ancient woman concièrge. Another burst with fearful detonation in Foyot's smart restaurant, scaring diners and personnel out of their wits. The only person who was seriously wounded was Laurent Tailhade, a poet and, ironically, an anarchist sympathizer. He happened to be lunching in a private booth with a lady friend named Mlle. Violette that day. After the bomb went off, Tailhade, a mass of bleeding wounds, was rushed to a hospital. Mlle. Violette, quite unharmed, lay on the floor for half an hour either

---

* This was the blow of a dagger, not a bomb, but the assassin was a member of the Anarchist Movement.

playing dead or believing that she was. The incident did anything but hurt business at Foyot's. Within a fortnight, repairs were made, the banquettes re-covered, new windows installed and the restaurant was more popular than ever. Every day there came masses of customers asking to sit in the area where the explosion took place and demanding to be served by Thomazot, a waiter who had also been hit at the same time as Tailhade, but not so severely. Thomazot walked on a temporary cloud of glory and cracked little jokes at any loud pop of a champagne cork. Two months later, Tailhade, recovered except for the loss of one eye, returned to the same table at Foyot's to finish his interrupted meal. Whether or not Mademoiselle Violette came with him has not gone down in history.

A crisis less menacing to life and limb than the anarchist scare, but far more disrupting in its implications was the agitation caused by the Dreyfus case . . . that crisis which arose over a false accusation of treason against Captain Alfred Dreyfus (who happened to be a Jew), his court-martial and sentencing to life imprisonment, the subsequent disclosure that the incriminating papers had been forged, the army's reluctance to admit having made an infamous error and the eventual exoneration of Dreyfus. . . . The Affair split the nation into two feuding camps, breaking up lifelong friendships and causing bitter family rifts that were hardly healed before the outbreak of the First World War. With the speed of a raging brushfire, the issue flared beyond the mere question of establishing the guilt or innocence of a convicted man. This had become a matter of doubting the integrity of the Glorious Army of France or of blindly maintaining it regardless of overwhelming evidence to the contrary. Only a courageous minority dared stand up for the innocence of one Jew as against the perfidy of a number of Christians. These courageous few were the liberal writers such as Anatole France, the farseeing politicians like Clemenceau and Jean Jaurès, and one or two daring salon leaders such as Mme. Straus and Mme. de Caillavet. The anti-Dreyfusards were the "aristos," most of smart Tout Paris, the Church (who laid the blame to the machinations of the Free-masons!) and, sad to relate, a majority of the Academy. The Antis gained prestige by calling themselves Nationalists and their stirring battle cry was "Vive l'Armée!" It loudly drowned out the sober "Vive la République!" of the Pros. The army was still replete with veterans from the Franco-Prussian débâcle and they branded anyone who defended Dreyfus as a spy in the pay of Prussia. The highly intelligent periodical *La Revue Blanche* boldly took the side of justice and was boycotted as being pro-German. People began turning on the Jews as being traitors be-cause many of them had originally come from German stock, even generations back. Many Jews were among the country's finest and most loyal citizens but that didn't count with the fanatics.

This time of bigotry seems as inconceivable to associate with the French character as the fanatic puritanism of the Cromwell period does with the British. France, unlike Germany, even unlike Eng-land, has never had an overweening sense of race. She has, how-ever, always had an overweening sense of La Patrie. The Patrie had suffered some severe and humiliating setbacks since the even worse defeat of 1870. Chauvinistic Frenchmen had to blame someone so they turned on the Jews. The fact of Dreyfus being a Jew opened the floodgates to a torrent of anti-Semitism that had been welling up ever since the publication in 1886 of Edouard Drumont's *La France Juive,* a two-volume diatribe which blamed the Jews for all the ills that beset the country . . . the postwar de-pression, the Panama scandals and the collapse of the Union Gén-érale, an organization which, with the blessing of the Pope, aimed to take over the government, oust all Jews and seize all Protestant control of federal money. Drumont's *La France Juive* was a clever, shocking book. It went into a hundred editions. The Anti-Semitic League with Jules Guérin as its president added witch-burning fuel to the fire with a publication called *l'Anti-Juif* and the gifted artist Forain, along with the only slightly less gifted cartoonist Caran d'Ache, brought out and illustrated a vicious little Jew-baiting sheet called *P-s-s-t!* Even the reputable *Gil Blas,* which among its contributors listed such liberals as Clemenceau and Zola, frequently appeared with cover drawings by Steinlen, repetitive of the same ugly theme . . . the innocent Aryan virgin in the clutches of the evil Hebrew. A shy country girl awkwardly disrobing before a hook-nosed lecher, an impoverished errand girl intercepted by a Semitic brothel madam, an oily diamond-ringed impressario selecting his prey from a lineup of little ballet novices. The collection is not pretty.

Nor were the jibes of the boulevard wits which were repeated all over town. Forain, tireless in his venom, upon encountering a wealthy Jewess who had recently become a Catholic convert turned aside and said well within her hearing, "She's known the Blessed Mother for only a month and already she's calling her Mary!" And to the playwright Henri Bernstein, who during a heated argument protested, "But your Jesus Christ was a Jew!" Forain retorted, "Yes. To show his humility." When the elderly Baroness de Rothschild was waiting somewhat impatiently for her carriage on the steps of the Opéra, a clubman named Franz de Vauloge said to her, "When someone like you, madame, has been hoping for your Messiah for two thousand years, you certainly can wait five minutes for your carriage." Edmond de Goncourt wrote in his journal and no doubt told it to his friends, for Goncourt was no more lenient than the rest, about Jean Lorrain the column writer screaming out in a nightmare: "Maman, help! I've got Jews in my bed!" as though they were bedbugs. As intelligent a woman as the Comtesse de Martel who wrote bright novels under the name of Gyp, when summoned in a high court case as a witness and asked her profession, promptly answered "Anti-Semite."

Incidents occurred comparable in ugliness to those in Nazi Germany. When the writer Ernest La Jeunesse, a member of the boulevard coterie who happened to be a Jew, was sitting at his customary table in the Napolitain Café, a total stranger came over to him, called him "un sale youpin,"* slapped him in the face and walked away after leaving his card. A few days later another unknown poured a carafe of water over his head saying, "I baptize you in the name of the Father, the Son and the Holy Ghost" . . . a vulgar prank which scared La Jeunesse so, he hurried off to a priest to find out if that sort of baptism counted.

The subject, needless to say, was dynamite in social circles. Hostesses lived in terror of its being brought up at their tables, with the inevitable warring results. They tried to manage their dinners like meals during an army bivouac, the guests resting their arms in the foyer. Guests and hosts heaved sighs of relief at the finish of any evening when the subject was adroitly by-passed. Forain with his brilliant pencil presented the situation in a drawing which shows a couple leaving a house in a furious huff, their outraged host and hostess about to slam the door on their backs and the caption "Somebody mentioned *IT!*"

Meanwhile, far from this discord, broiled by the relentless sun of Devil's Island by day and chained to a prison cot at night, a colorless, completely uninteresting military captain brooded, not at all over the vast issues at stake, but only over his personal exoneration and eventual reinstatement in an army that had so senselessly persecuted him. The story of that exoneration is as familiar as the story of the persecution. André Maurois writes

* A dirty kike.

of *l'Affaire:* "It has been said that in no other country would such an injustice as the Dreyfus case have been possible, but that in no other country would that injustice, once committed, have been fought with so much courage or redressed with so much generosity."

If anti-Semitism gradually died down, hatred of Prussia persisted. The Cock of Gaul was still licking the wounds inflicted at Sedan. The religion of the flag ran high, the statues of Metz and Strasbourg in the Place de la Concorde were still draped in black (and would remain so until 1918) and in the maps of schoolbooks Alsace and Lorraine were printed in the deep purple of mourning. A militant group, the League of Patriots, dedicated to Revenge against Germany, was formed under the fiery leadership of Paul Déroulède. Déroulède was a politician, a hero of the Franco-Prussian War and a writer of a book of rather appalling patriotic lyrics called *Songs of a Soldier.* He was given to splendid utterances, his most quoted being "Monarchist, Bonapartist, Republican . . . these are only first names. Our family name is LA FRANCE!" The motto of the League of Patriots was *La France quand même* and under it the dates 1870–18? — leaving blank the year for the recovery, by force, of the lost provinces. To the League, anything German was as a red rag to a bull. Their membership included a number of Left Bank students who when a performance of *Lohengrin* was given at the Opera, formed a marching delegation that forced its way onto the stage and pelted the audience with balls of asafetida, while outside police on horseback charged a bunch of screaming rioters. Paul Déroulède shouted from the rooftops that while he lived, no German music would be heard in France's capital. Whenever the Lamoureux Orchestra took the risk of giving an all-Wagner program, Déroulède would station his Leaguers about the hall with orders to boo, hiss and whistle from the opening bar to the last notes of the finale. Music lovers rash enough to enjoy Wagner — "melo-manics" they were called — were equally noisy with cheers, stand-ing applause and cries of "Bis!" Members of the police were eventually placed on guard and leaflets were inserted in the programs saying: "Le public est prié de ne siffler ni bisser les auditions Wagnériennes!"*

For all the political battles, all the strides in science and the arts, all the intellectual sophistication, there still lingered in this aging century much of the romanticism of its youth and middle years. The influence of Offenbach and Musset had not gone out with the hoop skirt and bustle. To the bourgeoisie the ideal of man was still the dashing cavalry officer with waxed mustache and corseted uniform. To the fashionable world, it was the irresistible seducer, the conqueror of the dimly lit boudoir smell-ing of French cologne, Russian leather and English pipe. He was the suave clubman, the sportsman of honor who could, when righteously provoked, handle sword and pistol with equal skill, and French chivalry still survived in the Gentleman's Duel, most of them, happily, quite bloodless.

The ideal of woman was the exquisite, perfectly dressed Parisienne, the gracefully agitated beauty of the canvas by Boldini, that "Paganini of the teagowns," whose swirling brush made fairly audible the rustle of taffetas and the whisper of satins. She was the heroine of the popular novel by Paul Bourget, the alluring little married woman whose soul was complicated, whose mind was simple and who was constantly, madly and clandestinely in love. It was usually an involved but superficial love, one which could find fulfillment only in that afternoon rendezvous which was known as the "four-to-five," the hour when she could risk rushing to her lover's apartment for an all too brief encounter.

* The public is requested neither to hiss nor to shout *encore* during the Wagnerian performances!

It was essentially an erotic era. The novels of Bourget and Marcel Prévost, the comedies of Capus and Caillavet de Flers, the farces of Feydeau all deal with "four-to-fives" or marital infidelity. In Paris woman was queen. She was an erotic queen whose very clothes rustled with erotic innuendo. The lifting of her skirt was erotic. The act of pulling up skirt and petticoat together to just the proper height was an art. The movement could be highly seductive or comically awkward. Emile Bergerat, a well-known observer of the passing scene, used to sit out on a café *terrasse* on windy days for the pleasure of watching ladies defend the honor of their legs. And in those times one would have called them *limbs!* Another subtly suggestive gesture was the assistance a lady gently demanded from a gentleman to push the great puffs of her leg-o'-mutton sleeves into the armholes of her coat, giving him a chance to brush her shoulder and underarm with his hand. The froufrou of her taffeta petticoats, the curving outline of her waist and hips all hinted at what lay beneath the delicate outer garments and every man of the period was at heart a "voyeur." Not excepting the days of the sixteenth Louis had feminine fashion been so enchantingly complicated. An elderly roué reminiscing about past explorations amid these bewildering furbelows told a reporter, "Whoever has not undressed a woman of the Eighteen Nineties, has missed one of the better refinements of love-making, from the first tiny pearl button of her rose-point cuffs, to the lacings of that inflexible bastion of honor, the corset."

And inflexible the corset was. The actress Germaine Gallois would never accept a role in which she had to sit down, because her corset went from directly under her breasts to below her knees with two heavy steels all the way down the back and six meters of lacings. How much a "bastion of honor" the corset was is a matter of speculation. An 1894 copy of *Le Rire* comments: "The defense of virtue by the corset seems easily overcome if we are to judge by the number of these garments turned in at the Lost and Found, having been left on benches or on the banquettes of fiacres."

The moral code was realistic. Madeleine Brohan of the Comédie Française expressed its attitude when she wrote in the autograph album of an admiring theatre fan, "I prefer dishonor to death." However, the moral code had its strict rules. In good society, illicit love was permissible as long as it remained clandestine. If one broke the Seventh Commandment, one broke it with style and above all with discretion, for among the *monde,* appearances were of paramount importance. The little Parisienne who kept her "four-to-five" trysts with her lover would have blushed with pretty guilt had she been caught in the act of reading Maupassant's *Bel Ami* or Daudet's *Sapho,* for those two books, both of them masterpieces of fiction, were considered quite wicked and an editorial in the *Figaro* made the stern pronouncement that "a woman who reads a novel is no longer entirely respectable." She would never have been seen at an exhibit of Rodin's sculpture (although she might have sneaked in when nobody she knew would be present) and she would have severed social relations with anyone depraved enough to praise Ibsen's *Ghosts,* a play dealing with a disease no polite person would ever mention, although every now and then one of them was unfortunate enough to acquire it.

Arnold Bennett once called France "the land where dalliance is so passionately understood." But it was dalliance conducted with tasteful prudence. Even its terminologies were prudent. Dalliance itself came under the bowdlerized heading of *galanterie.* A kept woman was a *courtisane,* or to get even more classical, a hetaira. The coarse epithet, even the frankly realistic one was not countenanced at formal gatherings. At one soirée, a lady of fashion who was noted for her easy morals suddenly slapped the playwright Henri Becque in the face and ran sobbing to her husband because Becque, who was slightly in his cups, had used the word "lover" in her presence.

A young man was expected to sow his wild oats, a husband was expected to have a mistress. A wife might even have a lover, as long as she was never found out. What was not countenanced was divorce. For any woman, divorce was a deep disgrace, worse than if she were to become a cocotte. To members of the aristocratic *gratin,* a divorced woman was a social outcast. The Duchesse de Mouchy had a friend who had not only been divorced, but remarried. The duchess still corresponded with this friend but her letters were always delivered by hand in envelopes on which nothing was written, as the duchess refused to accept her friend's new name.

There was even a code for infidelity and a woman felt herself to be truly honorable if, after taking on a lover, she managed somehow to break off marital relations with her husband. To remain faithful to one's lover was considered exceptionally splendid.

Moral niceties were not confined to the upper classes. Even the Latin Quarter had its contradictory rules of conduct. The Board of Governors of that most amoral of institutions, the Beaux Arts, held meeting after meeting to discuss the grave problem of whether or not the models who posed in the life classes in the women's department should wear tights. The Quat'z-Arts Ball . . . *Brawl* is more like it . . . continued to be the Left Bank debauch of the year, with everyone drunk and couples cohabiting in any and every dark corner, yet Sarah Brown, the top model at Julien's, was arraigned before Senator Béranger because in a tableau which preceded the festivities, representing Delacroix's "Death of Sardanapolis," she had appeared as a slave, naked to the waist.

It was all part and parcel of the contradictions of this city of consistent contradictions. The arts had never made such strides. The Symbolists had given poetry new and shimmering dimensions. Anatole France had brought more stature to the novel, Bergson was making psychology available and understandable to a reading public, Antoine and Lugné-Poë had given the theatre the new infusions of Ibsen, Maeterlinck and Shaw. Yet the high intelligentsia would jam the Ambassadeurs, the Alcazar or the Casino to see a series of adolescent little acts called *Les Déshabillées* which were all the rage ... "The bedtime of Yvette," "Josephine takes her bath," "The morning of a Parisienne." They were early strip-tease acts with very little stripping and one can't imagine what teasing. Simple pantomimes with soubrettes taking off or putting on their underclothes or nightdresses in time to musical accompaniments and managing deftly to slip something over any complete or even partial exposure.

This was the high afternoon of Impressionism and French painting was as joyous as April in the forest of Fontainebleau yet the yearly Academy awards were in the same Bouguereau-Cabanel tradition. Official art had never been more awful, with any amount of commemorative statues being unveiled ... those busts on garlanded shafts always accompanied by an unidentifiable and somewhat nude lady. When in 1894 President Carnot was assassinated, Edmond de Goncourt commented tersely in his Journal, "What a lot of bad sculpture this will produce! If Caserio had been an artist, the thought of that would have restrained him."

Discriminating art lovers had discovered Japan. De Goncourt's collection of Japanese prints was the talk of the intellectually discriminating. At the same time "Art Nouveau" was coming into its curious own ... that "Modern Style" of Maxim's and the Métro stations, Guimard's "vermicelli art" which people likened to badly baked meringue or carved Gorgonzola ... swirling lotus leaves, writhing water lilies, stylized cabbages and peacock feathers, umbrella stands of tortured bronze, kidney-shaped mir-rors, lamps in the shape of aquatic plants and shades of Tiffany glass in Loïe Fuller color effects.

It was a decade which, on the surface at least, was one of lightheartedness. When, after a bitter transit strike that had lasted for months, the trams were put back into service, they appeared festooned with ribbon confetti and garlands of flowers. During a strike of cabdrivers in '94, when a few "scabs" appeared on the streets to try to do a little quick business the striking *cochers* purloined the scabs' horses and fiacres, went to the races in them, and at the end of the day returned them to their owners with instructions not to try that game again.

It was a decade of conformity on the one hand and of eccen-tricity on the other. And always France remained true to her tradition of being a nation of individualists. Father Hyacinthe, the preaching monk of Notre Dame, made so many conversions that he felt no compunctions in discarding his cassock and marry-ing a young American widow. A delightful man who called himself the King of Arucaria, a country of his own invention, gave lavish dinners and handed out medals to all visiting celeb-rities. He was quite popular and had no trouble getting people to attend his functions. Another victim of *folies de grandeur* was a distinguished-looking gentleman who called daily at the British Embassy, claiming to be Henri V the only legitimate King of France and handing in his visiting card on which was printed his title, dynasty and a demand for the intervention of England in his behalf. Another pleasant manic was a Monsieur de Saint Crick, a baron of wealth and good family. Every afternoon he'd put in an appearance at Tortoni's where, seated at a pavement table, he'd order two ices — one strawberry, one vanilla. When they came, he'd take off his shoes, dump the vanilla into the right and the strawberry into the left. If he made the occasional error of confusing the flavors, he'd empty out his shoes, repeat the order and correct the procedure. Except for this eccentricity, M. de Saint Crick appeared to be a pleasant conversationalist with a knowledge of old books and nobody would have dreamt of having him locked up. A Marquis de Bièvre who called himself "Titular of the Necrology Code" could go about the city with his "familiar," a pet white rat, on his shoulder and no one minded. And when a Maître Goguillot, who had a consuming hatred for railroads and their complicated regulations in regard to baggage checking, took out his venom by demanding on one journey that his toothpick be checked in the van, the only person who minded was the man in charge of the van.

Above all, this was an epoch of color. Even the peeling walls of dingy streets were enlivened by the posters of Steinlen and Cheret, Bonnard and Toulouse-Lautrec announcing the current *caf'-conce'* attractions of Montmartre, bright with the red muffler of Aristide Bruant, the yellow dress and black gloves of Yvette Guilbert or even the familiar blue apron of the little schoolgirl writing *Chocolat Meunier* on a blackboard. April and the Sunday cyclists returning to town with tons of lilacs filched from the public parks of Viroflay or snatched from over the walls of private gardens in Saint Cloud, their handlebars so laden, the rest of the bicycles are hidden and they each appear to be sailing along on great clumps of lavender bloom. The first of May and the shop-girls and midinettes all wearing *porte-bonheur* sprigs of lily-of-the-valley. Grand Prix night and intoxicated young blades who had backed the winner dancing crazily down the center of the Champs Elysées with lighted candles stuck in the brims of their silk toppers. *Mi-Carême* in the Place de l'Opéra with its confetti battles like snowstorms of multi-colored flakes. The Fair of Neuilly with its flying balloons and wrestlers in pink tights. Two A.M. and the stars sparkling above the earthy star of the Etoile, and on the dark streets the glow of cab lights and the occasional firefly glimmer of the lighted cigar of an elegant clubman on his way home . . . or somewhere. This was all part of what the average *flâneur* might have seen.

Paris had its miseries and injustices, its vices and its cruelties, its poverty and its crime. For some reason the sordid aspect, which heaven knows was there, is not what arises when one sees the phrase "Paris in the '90's." Even the word "crime" evokes only the theatrical picture of the apache *souteneur* and his street-walking *môme,* although we know that far less picturesque and far more vicious crime existed. Seen, and to be sure only partially seen, through the exonerating vista of seventy years, what comes to view are the flavors of the place and its time, its stimulants, its graces and its joys. It was an epoch that can never occur again and perhaps ought never to occur again, but one is grateful that it did and in that city of charm and exasperation, and I think there are those who wish they might, if only for a brief day, be back in Paris during La Belle Epoque.

## ROBERT DE MONTESQUIOU

### *The Magnificent Dandy*

I N A CHARMING book of memoirs Elisabeth de Gramont, the Duchesse de Clermont-Tonnerre, tells of leaning on the railing of her upper balcony one bright spring morning, gazing down onto the Avenue "when," she writes, "I was suddenly struck by the appearance of a tall, elegant personage in mouse-gray, waving a well-gloved hand in my direction as he emerged swiftly from the green shadow of the chestnut trees into the yellow sunlight of the sidewalk." This early caller must have been in an unusually conservative frame of mind that day to have appeared in mouse-gray. He might, likely as not, have turned up in sky-blue, or in his famous almond-green outfit with a white velvet waistcoat or in yet more startling examples of his extraordinarily colored and perfectly tailored wardrobe. He selected his costume to tone in with his moods and his moods were as varied as the iridescent silk which lined some of his jackets. Sir William Rothenstein once met him at an all–von Weber concert wearing a mauve suit with shirt to match and a bunch of pale violets at his throat in place of a necktie "because," he explained, "one should always listen to von Weber in mauve." His scarfpins, when he wore a scarf, were exotic examples of the jeweler's art, ranging in motif from an emerald butterfly to an onyx death's-head. On a smooth tapering forefinger he wore a large seal ring set with a crystal that had been hollowed out to contain one human tear — whose, he never revealed.

This sartorial eccentric was the Comte Robert de Montesquiou-Fezensac, royalist, social snob, literary diletantte and Symbolist poet . . . of sorts. There is little doubt that he served as a partial model for Proust's Baron Charlus although in many ways J. K. Huysmans' fantastic Des Esseintes, the hero of *A Rebours,* comes closer to being a direct portrait and Rostand is said to have created the character of the Peacock in *Chantecler* with him in mind. With ease and contemptuous elegance, he assumed an exalted position in both fashionable and literary circles. Graham Robertson, the English artist who painted appalling portraits but wrote delightful memoirs, said that Montesquiou was "a typical member of that curious little world of amateurs which hangs midway between the worlds of art and society." The categorizing would have outraged the Count, who considered his own literary output anything but that of an amateur. And yet he would never have lowered himself socially to the level of being considered a professional writer. Even his association with certain genuine men of letters was done with somewhat the condescending attitude of the drawing-room liberal who mixes with the working classes.

Slim and graceful as a Siamese cat, he was absurdly handsome, with dark, wavy hair and a silky mustache beneath a proud Roman nose which Jules Renard in his gleefully acid journal likens to the beak of a bird of prey nurtured on vanity. There was something definitely artificial about his skin and Léon Daudet, Alphonse Daudet's clever and snobbish son, describes him as being "ageless, as though varnished for eternity, every line of his brow cleverly ironed out."

The count and his family were direct descendants of the dukes of Gascony and it pleased this exquisite to trace his haughty ancestry back through some early crusaders to the barbaric majesty of the Merovingian kings. Touchily proud, and at the same time sublimely self-assured, he held lyrical sway like a perfectly groomed Apollo over a worshipful band of muses, titled ladies with literary aspirations, poetry-conscious society women and a number of effete young Symbolists. He was invited everywhere, to the houses of the high-born and wealthy, into many of the leading salons, he even had entrée into circles of serious literature. He was often asked by the generous and lovable Alphonse Daudets to their apartment on the rue de Bellechasse for one of their Thursday dinners to which the literary world flocked. Edmond de Goncourt, the exquisite and aristocratic old *maréchal de lettres,* was his good friend. The only genuine symbolist of the whole vaguely irresponsible movement, Stephane Mallarmé, welcomed him in his humble flat up four flights of stairs on the smoky rue de Rome where all the intellectual youth of Paris crowded into a small bourgeois salon that could accommodate fifteen with difficulty for those shimmering and golden Tuesday evenings of the best of philosophical and aesthetic talk and rich discussion. Such evenings might amuse the count but not for long. His native milieu was the world of smart aristocracy to which he felt himself to be of prime importance. When he invited any distinguished men of letters to special ceremonies of his own devising, his engraved invitations, topped with the family crest, invariably wound up with the reassuring information "Ladies of society will be present." These special ceremonies included his flowery funeral oration over the casket of Leconte de Lisle, his speech at the unveiling of a statue he had arranged to be erected to the memory of the neglected poetess Marceline Desbordes-Valmore and he sent out announcements that he would be present at the funeral of Paul Verlaine, that tragic and sumptuous farce when the persons who had spurned Verlaine in life paid him expensive homage in death. The count also sent out engraved invitations to much of smart Tout Paris asking them to be present at the ceremony of the christening of his cat.

Robert de Montesquiou had a constantly shifting set of mannerisms. At the beginning of any conversation, he'd remove one glove and start a series of gesticulations, now raising his hands toward the sky, now lowering them to touch the tip of one perfectly shod toe, now waving them as though conducting an orchestra. His conversation was hardly conversation at all but long monologues filled with exotic anecdotes, mysterious allusions and obscure classical quotations all told with a rich vocabulary "at the end of which," according to Léon Daudet, "the count would burst into the shrill laughter of an hysterical woman, then suddenly, as though seized with remorse, he'd clap his hand over his mouth and rear back until his inexplicable glee was controlled . . . as though he were coming out of laughing gas." Probably the reason for his clapping his hand over his mouth was that for all his arrogant handsomeness, the count's teeth were small and quite black. Many of his hangers-on and admirers . . . for absurd as this man was, he had a definite magnetism and could exude great charm when he wanted to . . . aped his mannerisms of speech and gesture. Proust, who was to be his devoted slave, even went so far as copy his laugh and his gesture of hiding his teeth, although in contrast to the count's, Proust's teeth were even and white. Regarding his conversation, Jules Renard found it "very refined, very precise, very insignificant." Gustave Kahn in an article for the *Revue Blanche* called him "the world's most laborious sayer of nothing" and Sir William Rothenstein said that Montesquiou had the affectation of Oscar Wilde without Wilde's touch of genius and without his geniality and sense of fun. And certainly without that Irishman's capacity for friendship, for the count himself is quoted as saying, "However amusing it may be to speak ill of one's enemies, it is even more delectable to speak ill of one's friends." His talk was mostly on the subject of himself, a subject he treated with respect and elaboration. He once told

Mme. de Clermont-Tonnerre (Elisabeth de Gramont) that he was like a Greek temple with exquisite sculptured friezes that were hidden by climbing vines and that now he was about to unveil himself to the world. Mme. de Gramont found his conversation at times sparkling, at other times funny. Full of strange imagery — a combination of erudition and frivolity. It could be startling too as when he asked her if she hadn't been sprinkling aphrodisiac on her furniture as "the armchairs seem to want to embrace the small chairs, the library is opening out rapturously to receive the piano."

In later years, Robert de Montesquiou was to reside in the rue Franklin in a house which he chose to name "The Pavilion of the Muses." During the '90's, he lived on the top floor of his father's Quai d'Orsay mansion in a remote suite of rooms that were reached by climbing a dark, twisting staircase and passing through a carpeted tunnel lined with tapestry. The quarters into which a visitor emerged were partly Japanese, partly *Arabian Nights* and partly God knows what. Each room, he would explain, was decorated so as to fit a mood and thus he could move from one to the other. The first was painted and hung in tones of red which went from deep crimson to shell pink. The adjoining chamber was a symphony in gray with gray hangings, gray upholstery on gray furniture and four immense gray urns for which he ransacked Paris every week in a desperate search for gray flowers. The search was seldom successful. In a further sitting room, on a spotless polar-bear rug stood a large Russian sleigh while overhead from the beams of a vaulted roof there hung a collection of ancient musical instruments, lutes, rebecs and some objects handed down from an early Montesquiou troubadour which their owner said were mandores and theorbos. Maybe they were. High lancet windows with panes of seventeenth century glass shed a dim and not too religious light by day and at night there were curious electrical effects which went by the title of "Sunlight through tropical water" or "Moonlight on northern snow." At one special soirée, the host, by way of entertainment, plunged the room into almost complete darkness and served his guests a series of liqueurs which supposedly blended with gusts of perfume which by some mysterious means were wafted into the room, while the only illumination came from the jewel-encrusted shell of a live turtle who crawled disconsolately about the Persian-carpeted floor, gleaming with genuine diamonds, sapphires and amethysts. The guests survived the ordeal. The less fortunate turtle turned over onto its Fabergé'd back and expired.

Montesquiou's library was housed in a glass conservatory where the works of his favorite authors, Baudelaire, Swinburne and his friend Goncourt, were displayed on low shelves as a background for a small forest of Japanese dwarfed trees, a rare collection of miniature oaks, century-old pines, and tiny delicate maples . . . all no bigger than cabbages. Goncourt, who had been one of the "discoverers" of things Japanese, said that seeing them, one was tempted to stroke them as if caressing the back of a dog or a cat. The count's bedroom was an Arabian nightmare of heavy curtains, low sofas, satin cushions and hanging brass lamps with colored glass. The bed was fashioned out of a mammoth ebony dragon on which the pillow nestled into a coil of the tail while, serving as a footboard, reared the monster's head with savage ivory teeth and glaring mother-of-pearl eyes.

Edmond de Goncourt was one of the few elect to be allowed a view of this exquisite's bathroom. All gauze curtains of muted blues, green walls painted with vague, dreamlike fish, it must have resembled a Gordon Craig setting for an allegorical play by Maeterlinck. Behind a diaphanous hanging with gold and silver flecks was the tub, an immense Moorish bowl whose water was

heated by a brass boiler of oriental repoussée. The dressing room
was a pretty folly known as the Hortensia Room, partly in tribute
to Louis Napoleon's mother Queen Hortense from whom Montesquiou claimed descent, partly because stylized hortensias along
with water lilies were the current rage in "art moderne." Here,
painted, molded, carved, cast in green bronze, hortensias bloomed,
climbed, writhed and swooned in fashionable convulsions. The
door to the count's clothes cupboard was of clear plate glass
behind which a floodlight could be turned on for the dramatic
exhibition of one hundred neckties "aux nuances les plus tendres,"
their owner's fond description. The ties were hung like banners
on either side of a blown-up photograph of a certain La Rochefoucauld . . . not the seventeenth century duke famous for his
maxims, but an acrobat of the Cirque Molier, famous for his
muscles and the erotic uses to which he could put them. The
photograph, which was hand tinted, showed him in bright pink
tights exhibiting what Goncourt called "his elegant ephebic form."

In every room were elaborate gewgaws . . . Dresden china,
Venetian glass, mounted butterflies, perfumed fans to wave as
one sipped Russian tea and bouquets of peacock feathers . . . "the
influence of my dear friend Whistler," he would say. What
Whistler said about him is to be conjectured. Montesquiou's very
absurdity may have appealed to that acid genius. Among the
treasures he had after he moved into his Pavilion of the Muses
were a number of strange keepsakes . . . the bullet that killed
Pushkin, a cigarette partially smoked by George Sand, a tear
(dried) once shed by Lamartine and the slippers of the last love
of Lord Byron, the Countess Guiccioli. He kept Mme. de
Montespan's pink marble tub in his garden, filled with rambler
roses, and he would show admiring visitors a birdcage that had
once housed Michelet's pet canary, along with a jewel box containing a single hair from the beard of the same historian. On special

occasions he might, with great reverence, exhibit a bedpan used by Napoleon after Waterloo. He had also acquired a plaster cast of the knees of Mme. de Castiglione, the *femme fatale* of the Second Empire Court who, in her rosy time, had had herself photographed one hundred and ninety times. Montesquiou, not to be outdone, had himself photographed one hundred and ninety-nine times.

Here in the home of this exquisite who termed himself a Symbolist poet, one looked vainly for a desk. The inquisitive visitor rash enough to ask him where he did his writing would be given the languorous answer, "My servants bring me the necessary things." (One is reminded of the remark of Villiers de l'Isle Adam's hero Axël: "Live? Our lackeys will do that for us.") The "necessary things" were a small eighteenth century writing table, a pen made of a peacock feather and ink . . . mauve or green according to the poet's mood . . . kept in a jade phial that was half buried in a goblet of rose petals.

This was the period when the Symbolist Movement was at its height with Mallarmé its leader and prophet, Verlaine its incomparable songbird, Maeterlinck its dramatist, while across the Irish sea was Yeats, its English interpreter. Certainly de Montesquiou's verse abided by Mallarmé's tenet that "Symbolism is a mystery to which the reader must find the key." It is doubtful if there were a key to be found to this man's poems which appeared in select privately printed editions under the titles of "Bats," "Peacocks," "Bending Reeds," "The Blue Hortensias" and "The Chief of Subtle Odors" (*Le Chef des Odeurs Suaves*). They were brought out in costly print and with startling bindings. *Le Chef des Odeurs* had a cover of midnight blue satin, embroidered with golden griffon wings, while *Chauves-Souris* was bound in gray moiré decorated with a flight of bats made of jet beads. Their author managed to persuade certain amazingly well-known

artists to do the illustrations. *Chauves-Souris* had illustrations by
Forain, Gandara and Whistler and *Les Hortensias Bleus* was
fancifully enlivened with sketches by the popular painter Helleu.

These exotic publications enjoyed a brief success of curiosity
in the literary world and of snobbery in social circles. Ladies of
fashion flocked to hear the poet read selections from his works,
sighed "How exquisite!" over the darkly turgid passages they
could not remotely have understood and fairly swooned over the
names of classical personages culled from their author's own private mythology . . . Anabaxare and Anacyndaraxe, Parameizes
and Planiandrion.

He took adulation as his due, for his vanity was as prodigious
as his exaggerated sense of importance. He had a habit of saying,
on his way to the table at a dinner party, "The place of honor
is where I find myself." He once made a trip to England telling
all his Paris circle for weeks in advance that he would be traveling
"incognito," a curious precaution since he could hardly have been
of serious interest to the British public, few of whom had so
much as heard of him. When he got to London, he adopted
fantastic aliases, wore strange disguises and stalked like a stage
assassin in the shadows of buildings, occasionally darting furtively
down side alleys. His friend Graham Robertson said of his visit
that "Montesquiou was so wrapped about in thick mystery, no
intelligent acquaintance within the three-mile radius could possibly have failed to notice him."

The same preposterous vanity prompted him to commission
innumerable portraits of himself. Jean Lorrain in his "Pall Mall"
column said that every season the Salon of the Champs de Mars
exhibited, for the delight of an admiring public, a Montesquiou
immortalized by the current artist in vogue. And he added that
the princely subject always invited some five hundred "intimate
friends" from Tout Paris to the unveiling. Jacques Blanche

painted him on a narrow panel in tones of gray, to hang later in his Gray Room amid those elusive gray flowers. He posed for La Gandara in a Chinese robe, clasping his knee with tapering jeweled fingers and Mandarin nails. Whistler obligingly made two studies of him. In one he wore black and carried a fur stole over his arm. For the other study the count selected a pearl-colored coat with an edging which was, he said, "of a shade, a shade which cannot be expressed but which my own eyes epitomize."

There was one portrait which led to a *cause célèbre* of the drawing rooms that became known as "The Affair of the Cane." The artist was the popularly facile Boldini "who painted the way gypsy violinists play czardas." In this canvas, the count was seated in a dashingly insolent pose, holding out before him a turquoise-handled walking stick. This gave the boulevard wags a perfect opening for double-meaning comment. They titled it "l'Homme à la Canne" and Jean Lorrain went further (and in print), saying it should be called "Indecision," or "Where Shall I Put It?" then went on to say, "Monsieur de Montesquiou takes communion before his cane . . . swooning before it as Narcissus might swoon before a mirror," and added the lines:

> Nous avions l'Homme au Gant,
> Nous avions l'Homme à la Canne,
> A quand, Messieurs, l'Homme à l'Encensoir?*

To all such venomous prattle, Montesquiou was superbly in-different. He brushed it off, saying, "It is better to be hated than unknown." But then came the incident during the tragic after-math of the Charity Bazaar Fire a ghastly holocaust which oc-curred in 1897 on the afternoon of May 4. The Charity Bazaar

---

* *We had the Man with the Glove,*
  *We had the Man with the Cane,*
  *When, Gentlemen, shall we have the Man with the Incense Burner?*

was a big annual event sponsored by society and the Church which attracted not only Tout Paris but throngs of ordinary people eager to rub elbows with the high-ranking females whose names appeared daily in the social columns. For this worthy cause, fashionable hostesses and Faubourg Saint-Germain duchesses came down from their pedestals to serve as saleswomen and waitresses at the various booths and counters. That year the bazaar was held near the Place des Vosges in the rue Jean Goujon and set up in a temporary structure of canvas and plywood with floors of Norwegian pine. The overall décor represented a section of medieval Paris with little twisting lanes lined by house façades of painted scenery. On either side of the narrow passageways were some twenty-two booths and counters gay with banners, bright-colored bunting and paper festoons. The most popular attraction was a primitive motion-picture exhibit. It was a great novelty at the time and every session was jammed. The projection machine was a crude affair which, for some obscure reason, required occasional doses of ether, an open bottle of which was beside the mechanic. A spark from the sputtering mechanism fell into the ether bottle, which exploded and shot a geyser of flame through the flimsy wall. It caught the ribbons and draped laces of an adjoining booth, ran like lightning up the paper streamers to the roof and in seconds the entire place was a roaring inferno. Blazing pieces of wood and smoldering tatters of canvas fell onto the crowd of some two thousand below, igniting women's tulle ruffs and feather boas, setting fire to straw hats and taffeta capes. Smoke and roaring flames made it impossible to see and indescribable panic ensued. People crowded toward the single exit in desperate attempts to escape, most of them ending up in an ever increasing pile of humanity. The screams were frightful and most horrible of all, according to one witness, "every now and then the sound of a loud report . . . a skull cracking from the hideous heat." Amid the frenzy there were scenes of heroism and heartbreaking pathos. The Duchesse d'Alençon, sister of the Empress of Austria, refused the help of a worker who wanted to carry her out on his shoulders. "Because of my title I had to be the first to enter here. I shall be the last to go out," she said and sat quietly behind her booth awaiting an unspeakable death. And there was the Sister of Charity in charge of a group of blind orphans who held to her smoldering skirts their pitiful whimpering heads while she intoned the prayers for the dying.

The real heroes of this dreadful day were, as always, men of the French laboring class. Some workmen on a nearby scaffolding and the cooks, waiters and porters from the Hôtel du Palais rushed time and again into the raging furnace, their own clothes and hair on fire and dragged out whomever they could reach, saving over a hundred and fifty. Many of the coachmen and *valets-de-pied* from the private carriages of the bazaar patrons waiting outside in the street made their way through the holocaust to save their employers. A cabdriver named Eugène Geordès grabbed General Munier as he ran down the street his clothes ablaze and flung him into the watering trough of the Rothschild stables at 26 rue Jean Goujon. Levelheaded rescue work was done by an intrepid butcher the back of whose shop was adjacent to one of the burning walls. With his cleaver he bashed out the bars of a window, formed his men into a lifeline and saved two hundred people. Other heroes included a plumber named Piquet, a street sweeper named Gustave Dhuy and a roof tiler named Léon Déjardins. The disaster was over in half an hour during which time it literally carbonized one hundred and twenty-seven human beings. Only five of these were men. Amid the heroism of the rescuers and the fortitude of some of the victims, the cowardly behavior of the dandies and young clubmen who had come to patronize the fair was a shocking disgrace. When the fire broke out, they ran like rats to save their well-tailored hides, beat their hysterical way to the exit, using their canes as cudgels, stepping on the bodies of the wretched women and children they had knocked down. This became an immediate public scandal and roused violent resentment among the *peuple* who said, "If it had happened in Montmartre, we would have saved our women."

The rumor got about that Robert de Montesquiou was among the cowards who had fought their way to freedom. This was not true, for at the time of the conflagration he was nowhere near the rue Jean Goujon. The next day, however, he did turn up at the Palais de l'Industrie where the bodies had been laid out for identification. It was a gruesome spectacle, for most were charred beyond recognition. A desperate husband identified his young wife by bits of her new red corset, a dowager was recognized by the pearl dog collar about her blackened neck and pretty Mme. de Luppé's gold wedding ring was found thrust into her heart as though at the last moment she had held her hand over it and the intense heat had annealed the gesture.

Montesquiou, under the pretext of looking for possible friends but doubtless attracted by the macabre, minced along with the line of frantic relatives and agonized mourners. Before each laid-out corpse, he paused and lifted the covering sheet with the tip of his elegant cane. A gendarme on guard duty watched him as long as he could stand it, then cried out in anguish, "One does not touch the dead with the end of a cane, Mr. Clubman! If it disgusts you, I can do the unveiling!"

Jean Lorrain got wind of the incident and lost no time in publishing an account of it in his column "Pall Mall" and the Montesquiou cane became again the subject of the gibes of the drawing rooms and boulevard cafés. This gave rise to the count's one affair of honor, not with Lorrain, but with the courteous and aristocratic writer Henri de Régnier, a charming and tactful person "and such a gentleman," it was said, "one would never take him for a poet." Régnier on one occasion had set tact aside long enough to announce at a soirée of the Baronne Alphonse de Rothschild that instead of a cane, Montesquiou would do better to carry a muff. The remark was repeated to the count, who lost no time in challenging the poet to a settlement with swords. This was a dauntless step to prove his courage after the Charity Bazaar libel and also because he had the assurance that his adversary was as inexperienced a duelist as he.

They met at an early hour in a deserted park at Neuilly. The park didn't remain deserted for very long, however, for the count had sent out invitations to all his friends and acquaintances and they arrived on the premises in varying states of sincere concern or of wild amusement. One palpitating titled lady had brought along her family chaplain to administer a possible last sacrament. Some hundred or more, they flocked to the scene as though to an outdoor pageant. The pageant must have been well worth the ten-kilometer trip. Neither contestant had the remotest idea of how to handle a sword. After the signal to start, Montesquiou leaped to and fro posturing like an amateur d'Artagnan, Régnier stood stiff and pallid, his monocle shaking visibly. Eventually Régnier managed to snip Montesquiou in the thumb, an indulgent surgeon pronounced the slight incision to be a wound, the onlookers applauded and the count retired to a hero's couch (that carved dragon affair) from which he received a steady stream of worshipful visitors. He himself announced that it was the best party he had ever given. The next day, cool, collected and perfectly groomed in faun color, he gave a conference on d'Annunzio.

Most people found Robert de Montesquiou fantastically absurd. Yet many toadied to him for he had entrée everywhere . . . through the doors of the most exclusive clubs and restaurants, into the drawing rooms of the Plaine Monceau, past the crumbling posterns of the old aristocratic houses of the Faubourg Saint-Germain. He was a welcome guest in the salon of that beautiful and unchallenged sovereign of sophisticated Paris, the Comtesse de Greffulhe as well as in that leading intellectual cénâcle on the Avenue Hoche which Mme. de Caillavet maintained for the pleasure of Anatole France. He went occasionally to Mallarmé's Tuesday evenings but couldn't have enjoyed them much because Mallarmé and not he was the respected deity of these occasions. Edmond de Goncourt was as close a friend as ever Montesquiou could have had and was often his champion, yet he seldom patronized that author's literary Sundays in his famous *grenier,* finding them "trop vulgaire."

That he should make such a comment about the Goncourt gatherings was a typical Montesquiou affectation. Edmond de Goncourt was a polished "aristo" from the tips of his fine fingers to the points of his white mustache and his *grenier* was anything but *vulgaire.* It wasn't an attic at all, but a perfectly appointed salon of his elegant flat in Auteuil. This "grenier" was in the best of what then was considered intellectual good taste. It was filled with original drawings and crayons by Chardin, Boucher and Gavarni, Japanese bronzes, delicate porcelains and, above all, carefully preserved records and testimonials of whatever pertained to his dead brother Jules. This sentiment for the person with whom he wrote the first nineteen years of the famous Journal and with whose sensitive collaboration such excellent novels were produced, was probably the only great love of Edmond de Goncourt's life. Twenty-odd years after the death of Jules, Edmond seemed constantly to be turning to his younger brother for the joint observations and opinions they had shared for so long. They had always given the impression of being one single entity even to the point when if one of them started referring to himself in the first person singular, he'd instinctively and almost immediately go into the first person plural . . . "I saw such-and-such and we thought," etc. Whereas in their stupendous Journal, the two merge into one in a continuous first person singular . . . "I saw" . . . "he wrote me," etc. It was a strange relationship, almost like Siamese twins of the mind and spirit. At one period, they even shared the same mistress and felt no compunction in admitting it. Emile Bergerat once wrote:

> Did you ever watch Edmond de Goncourt going down a street? He isn't going straight ahead, he's following someone. It's a habit he acquired years ago with Jules during their *observation promenades*. The younger man alive, petulant, nervously darting on everything the fire of his black eyes, always ten paces ahead. The elder brother, more absorbed, less tender, more docile toward the overall and more apt to coordinate, kept his distance. They never exchanged a word during this ambulatory work. Only when something extraordinary struck Jules, he'd half turn to consult Edmond with a mere look; the latter had caught whatever it was at the identical second and had it classified. It was "in the basket"! Jules took the clippers and Edmond the basket . . . one was the poet, the other the philosopher. Today, the elder man has kept the habit of this four-legged march. The genius of Jules still drifts ten paces ahead, and even sometimes turns back; the accord takes place, the annotations made and entered in the workroom at the double desk. Edmond writes with both hands and does double work.

Goncourt's *grenier* meetings lacked the warmth of the good and simple gatherings at the hospitable hearth of his close friend Alphonse Daudet. They also lacked the intellectual stimulus of Stephane Mallarmé's Tuesday evenings in his bourgeois little apartment on the rue de Rome where the schoolteacher poet conducted a brilliant cénacle of advanced young intellectuals who sat in worship at his feet. The leader of the Symbolists and author of *l'Après-Midi d'un Faune* held forth with the appealing simplicity of an Athenian philosopher. William Rothenstein, who never missed a Mallarmé Tuesday, said of this profound aesthete that "while his poetry was obscure and rather difficult, his conversation was crystal-clear." The atmosphere of Goncourt's *grenier* was more conventional, more formal. His assemblage included, in addition to Alphonse Daudet, Joris-Karl Huysmans, François Coppée, Clemenceau, occasionally Ernest Renan and sometimes Mallarmé himself, in addition to any amount of young writers who shook with terror when the master of the house entrusted their awkward hands with a fragile and precious bibelot to admire. With a white scarf wound about his aristocratic neck, Edmond de Goncourt received them all with a manner both cold and courteous. During the 1890's he was a beautiful old man with silver hair, an aristocrat in bearing and intellect . . . anything but a liberal, a passionate collector of art especially of the smaller art objects. Whatever his shortcomings, he has bequeathed to his country the Prix Goncourt which, even if he did bequeath it in a certain spirit of spite against the Academy to which he was never admitted, stands for one of the country's most coveted rewards for literary merit. And to the world in general he — and Jules too for the time he was alive to collaborate — have left the fine novels and the incomparable Journal. The Journal begun by the two brothers in 1851 was originally intended not to be published until after their death. After Alphonse Daudet persuaded Edmond into letting some of it appear in the *Figaro Illustré* in '85, Renan protested that such publicizing was indiscreet (and anyone who has dabbled in the Journal can vouch that in many entries it is not only indiscreet but downright salacious). To this Goncourt replied, "Ever since the world has existed, any interesting memoirs have been written by the Indiscreet. My only crime is that I am still alive."

In the estimation of certain people, mainly himself, Robert de Montesquiou passed for a wit. He undoubtedly had wit of a rather satanic sort. Certainly he had the talent for making amusing and rather lacerating remarks, and was, to quote his own words, "Addicted to the aristocratic pleasure of offending." A frivolous little society woman of questionable morals was the mother of five small children and he called her house "La rue des Cinq Pères." He couldn't abide bores and when one fatuous old dowager blocked his way into an art exhibit with an exuberant "Ah, mon cher comte, comment allez-vous?" the "cher comte" answered, "Très vite, madame!" and beat a hasty retreat. He had an obsessive loathing for all social climbers. When one parvenue hostess tried to wheedle him into procuring her an entrée into a particular salon because, she said, it was so exclusive, de Montesquiou snorted, "Impossible, madame! For the moment you appear there, it will cease to be exclusive!"

Living in Paris was a Mrs. Kate Moore, an American millionairess, kindly, generous, socially ambitious and not a little absurd. Like other American international hostesses even down to our present day, she was an easy target for the fashionable wags. She entertained lavishly and those same fashionable wags accepted her invitations with alacrity. For the series of the Italian operas held yearly at the Châtelet, she bought a subscription that included thirty grand tier boxes all of which she filled nightly with the people who formed the trellis for her constant climbing. At one of her dinners, Mrs. Moore suddenly burst into floods of tears saying that she had swallowed a tooth, an announcement which convulsed her guests whose muffled laughter deeply offended her. The maître d'hôtel got control of the situation by announcing in calm and all too clear tones: "Rest assured, madame. Madame has not swallowed her tooth, she only forgot it and left it on the dressing table. La voilà!" and he handed her the porcelain incisor on a gold platter. Mrs. Moore was determinedly out for titles. The more dukes, duchesses and princes she could snare for her parties, the happier she was. The great triumph of her life was when she finally managed, after machiavellian maneuvering, to get Edward VII for dinner in her Biarritz palace which she called her "Folly." The King was amused by her good-natured vulgarity and her blatant social ambition. "You should have lived in the days of Louis XIV, madame," he said. "In those days there were kings everywhere." Kate Moore was not above making munificent gifts of money or negotiable art objects to certain people who could get her into soirées in the upper circles, and those certain people were not in the least bit above accepting the gifts. When she died, the kind silly woman in a number of legacies remembered generously those who had managed to hoist her up a rung or two of the society ladder. Montesquiou's comment was: "Mrs. Moore has departed from life as she would from the Ritz, handing out tips."

When another American, the Princesse de Polignac, formerly a Miss Winarella Singer and heiress to the Singer Sewing Machine fortune, sent the count an invitation to a buffet supper which was then called "supper at little tables" he accepted, saying "It will, I know, be charming, your supper at little sewing machines." Needless to say, Robert de Montesquiou was anti-Semitic along with most of the social snobs, and during the Dreyfus commotion he proudly flaunted his prejudice. He did stoop low enough in his own estimation to ask a Jewish banker he knew — a man generally admitted in social circles — to lend him some jewels to wear for a costume ball in which he wanted to appear as a Persian prince. The banker politely excused himself on the grounds that the pieces Montesquiou wanted were family jewels, to which the count coldly commented, "I knew you had jewels. I didn't know you had a family."

It gave him infinite delight to entertain with huge receptions and outdoor fêtes. Not the least of the delights was the making up of two lists of people: one, the "inviteds," the other the "excluded," the latter affording him endless glee. Though never a person of great means, he spared no expense for these fabulous galas. Debts meant nothing to him and he was quoted as saying "It is bad enough to have no money. It would be worse if one had to deny one's self anything." During one season he rented a seventeenth century house at Versailles where at an elaborate housewarming, with the grand manner of Louis XIV distributing favors, he received an array of titled *gratin,* men of letters, actresses and sycophants. In his torchlit garden was a small marble amphitheatre where Sarah Bernhardt and Julia Bartet recited poems. The poems were written by the host, of course, and one can imagine the tongue-in-cheek languor of the divine Sarah as she intoned:

> *J'aime le jade,*
> *Couleur des yeaux d'Hérodiade,*
>     *Et l'améthyste,*
> *Couleur du sang de Jean-Baptiste.**

Montesquiou adored Bernhardt and she was curiously fond of him. He was even reported to have had a twenty-four-hour love affair with this incandescent and unpredictable woman, followed, alas, by a week of vomiting. But despite this unfortunate interlude, if indeed it was true, theirs was a warm friendship until some years later when Sarah opened in *L'Aiglon.* The actress's appearance as a young man in white skin-tight trousers offended the count's aesthetic sensibilities and he felt that, regretfully, he must never speak to her again.

It was around 1898 that Robert de Montesquiou found Marcel Proust . . . or rather that Proust found him. They met in the

---

* *I love jade,*
  *Color of the eyes of Herodias,*
    *And amethyst,*
  *Color of the blood of John the Baptist.*

salon of Madeleine Lemaître, a popular woman artist who had, according to the young writer, "created more roses than anybody after God." She painted pretty pictures which sold well, illustrated a number of books with equally pretty sketches and watercolors and she ran a pseudo-intellectual salon where one met the better-born of the literary set and ate delicious little cakes. Madeleine Lemaître was said to be less famous for her paintings than for her *petits fours*.

Montesquiou proved to be one of the most rewarding finds for that insatiably observant chronicler of times past. The count, with magnificent condescension, allowed himself to be a patron of the pale, delicate author with his oriental features, his hacking asthma and his religious passion for the upper crust. It was a passion not so much that of the social climber as of the watchful student constantly gathering material and endless minutiae of customs, dress and décor for his meticulously detailed writings. The fashionable world was Proust's field of study. Léon Daudet said perceptively that "the *monde* mattered to him as flowers matter to a botanist, not as they count to the man who buys the bouquet." Montesquiou was the passkey to that hitherto off-limits zone of the genuine remaining aristocracy living in their elegant *hôtels privés* of the fashionable Right Bank or desiccating with austere formality behind the peeling walls of the Faubourg Saint-Germain . . . fabulous personages to the dream-struck novelist, behind whose ancient titles he beheld all the pageantry of the great families of France. They were the prototypes for his Guermantes, his Villeparisis, his Swann. And yet, Proust's characters are none of them direct portraits . . . he took the type of one person, gave it the character of a second, added the mannerisms of a third and gradually made up the entire person. Swann was probably partly the Prince de Polignac and a greater part Charles Haas, that popular man-about-town whose charm alone gave him entrée everywhere for he had neither fortune nor family; moreover he was a Jew, the only one in the Jockey Club or the Cercle Royale except the Rothschilds. He was a close friend of the Prince of Wales and the Comte de Paris, a steady member of the Comtesse de Greffulhe's coterie as well as the salon of the Princesse Mathilde and when he journeyed to England he always went out to Twickenham to pay his respects to the Empress Eugénie.

Proust's Duchesse de Guermantes was also a composite, the main components being the two most enchanting hostesses in Paris — the Comtesse de Chevigné and the Comtesse de Greffulhe — and added to them the occasional flashes of wit of Mme. Straus. Laure de Sade, the Comtesse de Chevigné, was a noblewoman whose family dated back to twelfth century Avignon and her ancestress that other Laura, the inspiration of Petrarch. She was spirited and satirical, courageous and gracious. She dressed with simplicity and style and continued to dress in the same style which, even when it was no longer in vogue suited her royally as Queen Mary's manner of dressing suited her. Mme. de Chevigné, lithe, energetic, took a brisk two-hour walk every day of her life, wearing a smart tailored suit from Creed's and a tiny hat with a veil. Young Proust waiting in the shadow of a building to see her daily emergence into the rue d'Anjou, as later the narrator of *Guermantes' Way* would wait for the sight of his unattainable duchess, said that she made of her morning walk "an entire poem of elegance." When she was well over seventy some housepainters on a scaffolding watched her slim, graceful back and her free stride of a girl of eighteen, and one of them called out in admiration, "Ah, la belle gonzesse!" to which the countess cheerfully called back in her husky voice, "Attends un peu, mon petit. Tu n'as pas vu le devant!"* She had a way of

---

* "Ah, the beautiful babe!" and the countess replied. "Wait, little one, you haven't seen the front view!"

addressing people, even those she didn't know, in the intimate second person singular. For all her noble bearing, there was a lot of the *gamine* in her and something completely beguiling about her cracked voice of the heavy smoker that she was. When Proust met her, she was no longer young. Before their introduction, he had written her a note saying, "Madame, you live a few houses from me but far more, whether you will or no, you live in me in the light of an eternal summer." And when at last they did meet and he saw at close hand the clarity of her wise blue eyes and the shimmer of her softly piled hair, golden red like that of Petrarch's Laura, he felt that this ageless lady had drunk less at the Fountain of Eternal Youth than at the Fountain of Eternal Loveliness and paid her the graceful compliment: "You were as lovely years ago as you are today."

Laure de Chevigné was homeloving and liked to receive her friends informally in her own drawing room. Her husband Adheaume de Chevigné, an elderly Royalist who was in the active service of the Comte de Chambord and a tireless worker for the King-in-exile, returned every day for lunch, departed immediately afterward for his club, and at two on the dot, the countess's faithful coterie would arrive . . . elderly adorers who came daily to perch on uncomfortable little chairs in a small, dark drawing room for two hours, partly through blind devotion to their lively and lovely friend, partly through blind jealousy of each other. They were for the most part some of the more intellectual "aristos" and politicians. They were so used to this daily ritual that they hardly greeted each other or even their hostess. The talk would be relaxed and witty. No refreshments were ever served. Laure de Chevigné would chain-smoke Caporal cigarettes in an amber holder and occasionally one of her elderly beaux would help himself to a Vichy pastille from a candy box kept open for the use of the dyspeptic. Sometimes distinguished visiting Europeans would drop in, the Grand Duchess Wladimir, a British viscount or a titled Italian. Mme. de Chevigné had friends all over Europe. She started the Cercle Interallié and was its president until it began to have too many members. Sometimes young Jean Cocteau would put in an appearance and Proust came as often as she'd allow him to. Her interests were varied and never precious. She liked to hear about new trends in the arts, but didn't go overboard about them. There was something distinctly earthy about this exquisite noblewoman who would undoubtedly have far preferred the Bouffes Parisiennes to the Russian Ballet.

The sponsor of the Russian Ballet who was first responsible for bringing Diaghilev to Paris was the other ingredient of Proust's duchess. She was the beautiful Comtesse de Greffulhe, leader of the smart intelligentsia and unchallenged queen of the upper *monde*. Besides the ballet, she had brought Chaliapin out of Russia, she had been the backer of Moussorgsky and Stravinsky, an early devotee of Richard Strauss and the discoverer of Caruso. Earlier she encouraged Debussy by heading the subscription committee which made possible the first performance of *Pelléas et Mélisande*. Her interests were countless. She organized exhibits for impecunious but always worthy artists, including an "Apotheosis Showing" of the works of Alfred Stevens at the Georges Petit gallery where she herself pushed the old painter around in a wheelchair. She made greyhound racing popular and she arranged, through President Poincaré, for the physicist Edouard Branly to receive the Osiris Prize at the Pasteur Institute for his invention of the radio-conducting tube, a first step toward the wireless.

Mme. Greffulhe carried out most of these activities at a distance, for she seldom went beyond the elegant confines of her mansion and gardens on the rue d'Astorg. She and the guests who flocked

regularly to her salon were known as the "d'Astorg Set." They
were very pro-British and very smart. Elisabeth de Gramont in
describing Mme. Greffulhe's life, which was anything but a constant social whirl, says: "One cannot be frivolously pleasure-seek-
ing and be the most beautiful woman in France." She was that
indeed, she couldn't help but know it and she went only to
functions where she would be the chief attraction. Her entrance
into her box at opera or theatre was like that of royalty and when
she passed through a drawing room, it was with the swiftness
and grace of a doe. Her litheness was almost legendary. A Diana
by Houdon which stood by her mantelpiece was her double.
Her daughter, who later married the Duc de Guiches, wrote
poems at the age of six to her lovely mother. One of them goes:

> *Maman walks like a flower.*
> *I would like to plant her in my garden.*
> *But I would never pluck her*
> *For to break the stem would break my heart.*
> *Her feet and hands are leaves.*
> *How beautiful, beautiful she is!*

The count, her husband, was a fine sportsman and an art connoisseur who every morning would make the rounds of the
galleries and antique dealers to keep his eye trained . . . as he'd
explain: "One must correct one's aim and keep firing tirelessly."
The count was also a gay blade and another of his daily rounds
was a series of calls on those charmers his wife called "the little
women who enjoy performing on mattresses." His calls were
done with such regularity that his horses would stop of their own
accord before the door of each of his houris.

Mme. de Greffulhe was a cousin of Robert de Montesquiou,
who took Proust to one of her outdoor fêtes. The writer was immediately struck by that incomparable loveliness which made

Boldini, László and all the portraitists of Europe want to paint her. "All the mystery of her beauty," he wrote, "is in the enigmatic light of her eyes. I have never seen a woman as beautiful." He loved her bell-like laugh, which he likened to the carillon of Bruges. The countess didn't especially take to young Proust, and didn't ask him to her house, but in one quick encounter he was able to make a mental sketch to help construct his final portrait of Oriane de Guermantes.

Robert de Montesquiou initiated Proust into what he termed the "poetry of snobbery." He himself, in all unconsciousness, posed for much of the unforgettable portrait of Baron Charlus. The "sittings" cost the artist much patience and incessant blows to his self-respect for Montesquiou treated him with insolence and sometimes with cruel mockery. But the indefatigable disciple put up with it for the sake of study of his model and the further models this patron made available. Moreover, according to André Maurois, Proust "understood the thirst for admiration with which Montesquiou burned and quenched it generously." Polite, self-effacing, ingratiating, he trotted meekly in the wake of the ambivalent eccentric, lavishing those extravagant compliments which made people who received them call him "the hysterical flatterer." His letters to Montesquiou are embarrassingly fervent. "Your mind is a garden filled with rare blooms," he says in one, signing it "Your humble, ardent and wholly fascinated Marcel Proust." In another, referring to the count's rented villa at Versailles, Proust effuses: "When will you return to that Versailles of which you are the pensive Marie Antoinette and the conscious Louis XVI? I salute your Grace and Majesty." The pensive Marie Antoinette and conscious Louis XVI took such flowery adulation in his mincing stride and Proust kept following his guide "through the inferno or paradise of aristocratic society" and storing up reams of notes. As Elisabeth de Gramont points out, "Proust flattered him like the fox in the fable. Montesquiou opened his large beak and out fell the prize."

Marcel even went so far as to write a short eulogy entitled "The Simplicity of the Count de Montesquiou." Be it a testimonial to the integrity of the Paris press that no newspaper would ever publish it.

# 3

## "LE GRATIN"

**T**o be an accepted member of the pure *gratin* which so intrigued Marcel Proust, one must, according to the critic Francisque Sarcey, "have an up-to-date jacket and a fairly old title." It was certainly true concerning the title; if not a title, at least a good birth certificate. For despite all the principles behind the Revolution, and its subsequent political upheavals, birth still counted in France and even so modern a thinker as Paul Valéry likens the existence of birth in a republic to the existence of poetry in literature.

The upper social strata had its own stratifications. It would be easy to divide it roughly into the old aristocracy and the smart Tout Paris, but each of these divisions had still further stratifications. There was the royalist nobility and that too was subdivided into the Legitimists and the Orléanists, and to understand that situation one would have to go back to Henry IV — if not Louis IX — and it's still confusing. It would seem that even amid her monarchists, France had politically to have any number of parties. Then there were the Bonapartists and the Empire nobility descended from the twenty-four families to whom Napoleon gave titles, and the select Catholic aristocracy as well as the Good Protestant Society, known as the "B.P.S." On slightly lower rungs, but still well established on the social ladder, were the better-bred members of the Bourse and the world of high finance, the wealthy provincials who came to Paris each season, silk barons from

Lyons, Bordeaux wine kings and shipbuilders from Le Havre. Finally there were the few "armorial Jews" who were accepted and were what some wag called "coated-of-arms."

The purest *gratin* lived in that proud and musty bastion of high nobility, the Faubourg Saint-Germain, a district bordered on the north by the Seine, on the south by the Quartier Saint François Xavier, on the east by the rue des Saint-Pères, and on the west by the Avenue de la Bourdonnais. Sainte Clothilde, the leading church of aristocratic piety, is in the center of the Faubourg and it is reassuring to know that a wall of the Académie Française flanks one corner. Elisabeth de Gramont called it "a fortified region to which few have access . . . having cut its moorings, the ship of state of the Faubourg Saint-Germain flops along on the river of time." The titled women of the Faubourg were the magnificent old dowdies who, like certain venerable English countesses and a few Boston matriarchs, dressed like charwomen and gazed down on the rest of the world . . . if, indeed, they ever came in contact with the world, for most of them kept their shutters closed against the noises of the oncoming century. Theirs was a philosophy of pride, resignation and the stern belief that one is not on this planet for fun. "The frivolity of the women of the eighteenth century was ransomed by the austerity of their nineteenth century descendants," says Mme. de Gramont. She recalls that they were anything but hospitable. "I know certain families who, although well-to-do, have never so much as offered a glass of orangeade to a caller." Shadowy dowagers of Merovingian age, they were constantly garbed in black as though in perpetual mourning for the *ancien régime*. Such very possibly may have been their sentiments since they were practically all Royalists, descendants of *émigrés* or of what few noble families escaped the Terror. These were the historical anomalies. One felt that they kept track of an imaginary court calendar as they waited patiently, majestically for their king to return and claim rightful possession of Versailles. Comtesse Jean de Pange, recalling her childhood upbringing in a devoutly royalist family, says that her grandmother who was considered to be dangerously liberal once announced during lunch that she didn't believe the Dauphin died in the Temple prison. Her father, blue with rage, threw down his napkin, rose from the table, shouted, "You say that to excuse the Republic from having committed a crime!" and strode out of the dining room.

The larger and looser division of the *gratin* was the antithesis of these grand old bores. This was the fashionable Tout Paris which wasn't *tout* at all but an exclusive elite of the smart, the wealthy and the well-born . . . including a clever few who were not so well-born. They were the people whose names appeared daily in the social pages and every now and then in the gossip columns, and that was a hazardous distinction, for in those times gossip writers were far more blatantly outspoken than any of ours would dare be today.

Paul Bourget, who knew whereof he spoke — for not only did he write with keen observation about this section of the *monde,* he was welcomed in all their houses — writes of the younger men of this hierarchy: "At the top of the social scale is the genuine gentleman of leisure, the one who actually owns the 150,000 francs per annum that his way of life demands. His name is good. His position in society is unquestioned. If he has adventures, it will be with the more frivolous women of his own set or the best-class demimondaines. Anyway, there's a good chance that he'll ruin himself in the usual way but when he's about forty, he'll get back from the feminine sex all the money it has wrung from him by marrying a woman with a sizable dowry."

Bourget was describing the typical dandy, one of "les clubmen" (the use of English words was chic) who were, according to the leading cocottes, the best lovers in Paris. They were also the best dressed. Because of the popularity of the Prince of Wales they aped English fashions ... trousers with the new crease down the front instead of at the sides, waistcoats with the lower button unfastened (a style started by an oversight on the part of the prince who, late for an appointment, had forgotten to button his), high stiff collars and starched shirtfronts, and the true glass of fashion and mold of form shipped his linen weekly to London for proper laundering. Hair was worn parted in the middle and plastered down flat with brilliantine. By the end of the century, most men had shaved off that badge of masculinity, the beard, but every self-respecting gentleman clung tenaciously to his mustache, which "lends itself to gracious gesture, gives authority to the timid and a martial air to the most peaceful of office-workers. Also it softens, say ladies who know, the harshness of the kiss." A story is told of a young lieutenant of Hussars who had a beautiful blond mustache which one day got so badly burned while he was lighting his pipe that he was forced to shave it off. As an officer could not possibly be clean-shaven, he resigned from his battalion and later died of chagrin. Accessories such as canes were a sartorial requisite. A cane was both elegant and useful, it could be used for applause or, on occasion, for balancing a lady's hat. The monocle was important too, if not always an optical necessity. Some monocles were of plain glass but that was neither here nor there because the monocle was a symbol of status. To screw it into place was to become actively present, to remove it was to retire. When the well-known maître d'hôtel of a famous restaurant walked in the Bois wearing his monocle, he quietly removed it if he encountered any particularly illustrious clients, by way of a gesture of respectful recognition which demanded no return salutation.

Certainly the most important sartorial concern of the well-dressed man was his silk hat, that eight-reflection *haut-de-forme* whose proper brushing and polishing was a serious business. Octave Mirbeau gave the account of a swank English coachman named William who was in charge of the stables of a wealthy baron. William's personal wardrobe was one of the wonders of the French capital and his topper was the most dazzlingly polished to be seen on the Continent. William was a racetrack celebrity as well as a familiar figure in the café-concerts of Montmartre. His name appeared in sporting journals and now and then in society columns. The baron's acquisition of this paragon was regarded as a signal victory for France over Perfidious Albion. William's salary was augmented by a mysterious income and a talent for fixing races . . . a further distinction in the eyes of some. A young marquis, coming across William on the paddock at Longchamps and admiring the shine on his *haut-de-forme,* asked how it was done. "It's very simple," William replied. "Every morning I require my valet to run for half an hour. He sweats, and sweat contains oil. Then, with a fine foulard handkerchief, I take the sweat off his brow and polish my hat with it. Of course, one must have a clean, healthy fellow . . . as blond as possible, as all sweats won't do. I gave the recipe to the Prince of Wales."

The clubs of these elegants were the Jockey, the Agricole, the Travellers' and, most exclusive, the Cercle de la rue Royale, known simply as the Royale. The Jockey and the Royale were the sporting clubs. They ran the Sunday races at Longchamps and Chantilly. The Jockey had baccarat tables and expected its members to gamble or else resign. The Paris clubs had none of the hushed and slightly mortuary atmosphere of the London ones. They were always social and often gay. They put on art exhibits and concerts which women could attend and sometimes balls were held. The clubman was regular to his Monday subscription night at the Opéra and his regular Thursday at the

Comédie Française. Of the two, he undoubtedly preferred Mondays . . . not because of the music through most of which he snored gently, but because between acts he could leave his wife in their box nibbling Boissier bonbons, held by silver tongs so as not to soil her white gloves, while he slipped back to the Foyer de Danse to pay his compliments to the ballerinas . . . and often it was to one ballerina in particular. To be one of the *abonnés* received in the Foyer de Danse was as chic as to be invited to the better embassies. These enchanting dancers were frightful little snobs and would admit no man to their Green Room who was not a member of the Jockey, the Royale or the Agricole. Entr'acte receptions were for the cream of masculine society. Here one encountered the royalist dukes . . . Brissac, Gramont, Rohan, Uzès, Mouchy and Luynes, and the Bonapartist princes Murat, Essling and Wagram. It must have been a pretty sight, like a Gavarni drawing . . . the slender pink legs and airy white tutus of the dancers contrasting with their visitors' red-lined opera cloaks, immaculate shirtfronts and those gleaming black toppers which even indoors seem never to have been removed from their heads. The subscriber to the Thursday evenings at the Comédie Française was usually less enthusiastic. He'd leave his club around seven saying he had to get dressed for the Française. At nine, he'd be back for a game of baccarat. About eleven-thirty he'd say: "I must put in an appearance at the theatre. It's my subscription night," and arrive in time to be seen and to have missed five acts of Racine.

The clubman's wife, or his feminine counterpart, might have been either the highly cultivated hostess or the frivolous *petite femme* that Paul Bourget and Marcel Prévost wrote about. Whichever she was, her day was a busy one. Actually it was every bit as hectic as that of any present-day New Yorker. Seen from afar, what gives it an air of leisureliness is the fact that she had to make her demanding rounds in a carriage. Starting at ten in the morning she'd put in an appearance in the Bois, driving, riding horseback or taking a brisk walk along that footpath which bears the charmingly respectable name of "The pathway of chastity." She'd be back home by eleven-thirty in time to change for a luncheon in town or a wedding at Saint-Philippe-du-Roule or maybe a baptism at Sainte Clothilde. In the afternoon, she'd put on more dressy clothes for a charity bazaar or a vernissage in some art gallery. If it was spring and the weather were fine she might even feel obliged to go to a garden party. Garden parties were the latest importation from England and most Parisians were bored stiff at them, but the stylish supposition was that they were charming, especially when held in some outlying forest with women in white frocks and wide-brimmed straw hats. If the average Parisienne were able to get home from all her activities in time to change into a lacy teagown, she'd try to fit in five o'clock tea . . . called "le fif'-o'-clock." This was another British importation which Frenchmen deplored, just as they deplored tea, which up to 1890 they considered merely a medicinal. A husband when proffered a cup of tea would protest that he didn't need it, he wasn't sick. He might have been if he'd had to consume all the small sandwiches, cream puffs, madeleines and marrons glacés the lady served with her "fif'-o'-clock." Twice a week, every hostess maintained an "at home," which meant being accessible to callers from three-thirty till seven. During the season there was a formal dinner nearly every night and often as not, a late ball.

There were plenty of other obligatory engagements for the lady of society, including the tiresome round of duty calls which she had to pay on other hostesses in return for dinner parties . . . they were known as "digestion calls" and were quite excruciating for both caller and callee. From December through Easter, a woman in the social swim would make as many as ten calls an afternoon. In the blessed event that the hostesses she stopped to see were out, she still had to leave cards. In addition to this, there were the hours-long fittings at dressmaker, milliner and corsetière. Some women of fashion were not so obsessed with fashion as to neglect their intellects and they did their utmost to avail themselves of the many opportunities there were for the pursuit of culture. With a busy froufrou of tafetta petticoats, they rushed at various hours of the day from public lectures to art exhibits, from art theatres to the Pasdeloup or the Lamoureux concerts, preferring the latter because of the amorous implications in the name. They bought subscription tickets for conference series, took notes with tiny gold pencils in tiny ivory notebooks as Jules Lemaître discussed Jean-Jacques Rousseau and they wrinkled their blameless brows in the Collège de France in valiant attempts to understand the lectures of Bergson. They slipped cautiously into small, avant-garde theatres in noble attempts to dig out the hidden meaning in the plays of that shocking new playwright from Norway; but they seldom admitted having been at a performance, for Ibsen was a name not mentioned in polite circles.

If, on the other and less serious-minded hand, the lady were the *petite femme* type of amorous flibbertigibbet, she had, above all, to manage her "four to five." A successful "four to five" required intricate scheming on the lady's part. There was first the problem of giving the slip to her ever vigilant coachman, ordering him to wait outside some shop or tearoom while she escaped through a back door and scurried down a side street to her lover's flat. Once arrived in this bower of bliss, there arose the further and serious problem of her clothes . . . taking them off and getting them back on again without the assistance of her personal maid. After returning to her own house, there was the risk of facing that same maid whose all-seeing eye might note a button unfastened or a hook caught in the wrong eyelet. There would follow the lady's stammered explanation that she'd been for a fitting at the dressmaker's and had had to take off her frock . . . which did not explain, as sometimes happened, why she had brought back her corset concealed in her muff. In "Minutes Parisiennes," Georges Montorgueil reprints the actual letter of a *petite femme* written to a friend in whom she is confiding the problems of her projected "four to five." She says that she has stipulated that her lover must have on hand a lady's maid, expert and, of course, discreet, because she simply could not undress, then dress again all by herself.

> Figure out, chérie [she writes], how many times a day I am obliged to change. I get out of my negligée to take my bath . . . that's one. I take off my street suit for my fittings at the couturière, that's two. I change my afternoon calling frock, which is three, for my dinner gown, number four, and every other night there's a late ball which makes a fifth change . . . and my nightgown makes an exhausting sixth. And so I told my handsome friend "If you want me to undress a seventh time, I must have a maid to help me. *And that's not all!* I warn you that I don't know how to do up my own hair so I must have a coiffeur, preferably from Lenthéric, to arrange it." At which the charming wretch assured me that he wouldn't dream of disarranging a single strand, to which I countered, wasn't that as much up to me as it was to him and wasn't he taking for granted my immobility?

Most of fashionable Tout Paris lived in their own *hôtels privés* in the better Right Bank districts, the Champs Elysées, the Avenue du Bois or the Plaine Monceau. Each of these mansions was backed by a formal garden and had enough terrain for its private stables. Every well-to-do family owned a variety of carriages and a string of fine horses. There were large horses for the calèche and d'Orsay, smaller ones for landau and victoria and nervous little high-steppers for the sporting vehicles. There was also a "night horse" to take the family to concerts or the theatre and later to drive Monsieur to his club or to some other address which the discreet coachman never divulged. Private coachmen took great pride in their horses and equipment and took equal pride in the families for whom they drove. They had a habit of addressing one another by the names of their employers. In the carriage yard of the Opéra where they lined up after a performance, one would often hear them calling out, "You're blocking my way, Rochefoucault!" "Hey, Rothschild, look where you're going!" or "Move the hell over, Wagram!"

A vast amount of entertaining went on in the great houses . . . receptions, musicales and banquet-sized dinner parties. Elisabeth de Gramont, Mme. de Clermont-Tonnerre, wrote that during her girlhood in their two houses, the first on the Champs Elysées, the second on the rue de Chaillot, her mother who was a famous hostess received over forty-five thousand people while her father, the Duc de Gramont who lived on after the duchess's death, kept accurate count that he had received ninety thousand.

The giving of a dinner party was a full-scale production for even the most skillful of hostesses. In addition to planning the meal, the wines and the floral arrangements, she was faced with the problem of protocol and she often did her seating with the Almanach de Gotha in hand, making a careful study of titles and their registration dates. She knew she might make herself into a social outcast if she were to seat anyone below his or her rank and that the moment her guests entered the dining room, each would look quickly to be assured that people were in their proper places. In the face of overwhelming difficulties of protocol, two tables would be set up. The top or the bottom of the table was of great importance. Whenever the Comte Aiméry de la Rochefoucault was informed of an impending wedding, he'd start counting on his fingers. "I'm calculating their future place at table," he'd explain. And when Robert de Montesquiou heard that a cousin of his was about to marry beneath her rank, he snorted, "One month of happiness and forty years at the end of the table!" A duchess who learned through her maid, who in turn had learned it from a footman, that at a forthcoming dinner she was to be wrongly seated, dispatched a telegram to her hostess which said "Impossible to dine with you tonight. Too concerned over the fate of Europe." And the artist Forain summed up the attitude in his sketch of an elderly *grand seigneur* studying his table which is set for a banquet and saying, "How am I going to arrange to place myself on my own right?"

Those dinners with from thirty to fifty guests must have been small pageants with the soft blaze of hundreds of candles in ancestral candelabra, gold place plates, baroque centerpieces and successive services in Sèvres, Saxon, Japanese and Dresden. The food was Lucullan and one reads that even the delicate little Proustian duchesses fell to with the relish of peasant women at a wedding feast. There was always a choice of two of every course. Paul Morand in his book *1900* reproduces the somewhat terrifying menu that would be at each person's place:

*Potage Brunois aux perles*
*Velouté aux nids d'hirondelles*
*Cassolettes morilles*
*Rissoles Conti*
*Truites saumonées sauce Toricelli*
*Filet de boeuf aux truffes*
*Poularde de Bresse Rosière*
*Jambon de Bayonne Provençale*
*Pain de bécasses en bellevue*
*Spoom au porto doré*
*Canetons Duclair rôtis roumaine*
*Poulardes de Granville à la russe*
*Asperges en branche sauce mousseline*
*Glaces Nelusko*
*Condés grillés*

This light snack would be accompanied with seven or eight wines. Certain abstemious ladies placed their white kid gloves in their *flute,* the long narrow champagne glass, to indicate that they drank only water.

After dinner, gentlemen remained to enjoy their one smoke of the evening, for smoking was not countenanced in the presence of ladies, then joined them for general talk which was often brilliant, for there were quite a few wits among the fashionable *gratin.* Sometimes dinner would be followed by musicales when lesser guests were asked to drop in to hear a string quartet play Mozart or a baritone sing "Ich Grolle Nicht" while the gentlemen lurked disconsolately in the background and dismal young daughters sat rigidly on gilt chairs beside their *mamans.* The French *jeune fille* has always been one of the most unalluring beings on the continent of Europe. How these gawky, pasty creatures managed ever to emerge from their dreary chrysalises and develop into the dazzling butterflies of their later married years is one of the mysteries of natural and social science. Pallid, polite and pimply, they had seldom known any exercise more vigorous than five-finger ones at the piano. When eventually one of these forlorn young things was married off to an eligible *parti,* chosen by her parents in exchange for a sizable *dot,* small wonder the groom's mistress frequently trailed them on their bleak honeymoon. Grim little dances for well-born juniors were periodically held. They were called *bals blancs* and were about as appetizing as junket. At these the gawky fillies were more or less paraded before the young stallions of the blood, who had the chance to look them over and weigh their possible dowries against their depressing appearances. Looking them over was about all it amounted to, for if a girl danced more than twice with a young man it was either a scandal or a sign that they were engaged. Elisabeth de Gramont, recalling her own *jeune-fille*-dom and the tortures of a *bal blanc,* writes of overhearing one arrogant youth say to another, "It stinks of armpits here. Let's get the hell to Maxim's."

The year-round social schedule never varied. The "little season" was from December to Easter. During the ten days after Easter, people might make a short stay in the country or venture abroad (daring for the French!) to visit friends or noble relatives. The "Grande Saison" started immediately after that. This was the apotheosis of activity for the social set whose members seemed insensible to fatigue. The day after the Grand Prix in mid-June, everybody left for their summer *vacances,* at shore or mountains. Any family unfortunate enough to be obliged to remain in town did so behind closed shutters, in order to give a definite impression of being away. Besides the regular vacationers who went to the beaches or the French Alps, there were a number of determined music lovers who never missed the Bayreuth Festival. Many of them didn't care for Wagner and a few of them didn't know a note of music, but the Bayreuth Festival was the smart thing. The Parisians who went there bought hideous little Parsifal Holy Grails in Bohemian glass and sighed in dutiful ecstasy at the finale of each night's curtain.

At Trouville, the more intrepid souls bathed in the icy waters of the Channel, which the French for some reason prefer to call the Sleeve. Ladies with their maids in a somewhat reluctant attendance, went prawn fishing in billowing skirts, black cotton stockings and oilcloth boaters fastened beneath the chin with veils of Chantilly lace. The *grande saison* at Deauville was rapidly eclipsing the jaded round at Trouville. Everybody at Deauville, with the negligible exception of children and governesses (the latter British, so they didn't count) turned their backs on the sea and their attention on the Casino recently opened by Cornuché, the justly famous proprietor of Maxim's.

After August 12, the sporting-minded might go to Scotland for grouse-shooting. That was all very chic, but for those who loved their ancestral native land, September and October were the enchanted months in which to stay in the great châteaux ... golden months in those fairy-tale castles beside broad and gentle rivers which seem deliberately to pause in their flow to reflect willows, ancient turrets and bridge spans. Or perhaps they were those balladlike fortresses, set in dark forests "where the startled deer, the scampering hare and the majestic pheasant were the descendants of those chased by Louis XV."

As domiciles for country houseparties, some of these heraldic manors, with their towers, their portcullises, and especially their moats which were God knows picturesque and God knows stagnant, could be damp and drafty. However, everyone, imbued with the spirit of tradition, put up with the discomforts and talked cheerfully of "leading the life of a Valois for a fortnight." There was a special excitement in going for a stay at one of the grand old castles, not the least of which was the initial arrival. Elisabeth de Gramont wrote of her family château at Montelontaine in the Oise. Her parents left their fine horses back in Paris and in their country domain used chiefly sixteen large grays with knotted tails, wearing huge collars with bells, most of them ridden by postilions. The station omnibus which met the guests was pulled by five horses in front and two *en flèche* at either side. "In autumn the woods turned the tawny color of pheasants and wild duck flew over the lake ... deer came down softly to graze and the air resounded with shots."

People who didn't own a château usually knew people who did. Houseparties lasted for as much as a month at a time and life was healthy and strenuous. The preoccupation was hunting and shooting, interspersed with gargantuan lunches, dinners and the addition of a hearty *goûter* after the hunt, an elaborately indigestible *fif'-o'-clock,* sandwiches and orangeade before retiring and beside each bed, silver biscuit boxes filled with further provender. Some owners ran their châteaux with the splendor of an early eighteenth century royal shooting lodge. Lackeys wore the traditional family livery and in one proud old manor house each manservant was required to keep his hair tightly crimped and dyed bright yellow. Sportsmen and sportswomen shed their outdoor attire the moment they returned from the hunt and put on smart but formal dress. The illustrated magazines of the times show scenes of flower-covered terraces where ladies reclined on rattan settees wearing large hats and tulle scarves and holding open parasols while gentlemen sat solicitously beside them, wearing bowlers and carrying gloves and cane. Every night dinner was a ceremonial affair, the women in décolletage and jewels, the men in full dress and medals, if they had them. After dinner they might dance to a small orchestra imported from Paris. Sometimes a dancing master would be brought in to teach guests the new steps, such as "the Consuelo," the latest import from America. Or else, as being more in keeping with château tradition, they might be taught some ancient dances, Napoleonic quadrilles, Versailles minuets, Henri IV pavanes while some risked possible heart attacks attempting the wildly active *brawl* of the Vendée. Sometimes there were elaborate charades and quite often truly ambitious private theatricals with costumes ordered from Paris and a professional actor brought in to direct. This last could be a bit of a bore for those who had neither talent nor interest in acting, spending as they had to tiresome hours rehearsing and even more tiresome ones trying to memorize lines. Sometimes there'd be two performances, one for the aristocracy living in the surrounding countryside who had to drive miles to attend and would have to be put up overnight along with their personal servants. The other would be for the local people . . . the doctor of the nearby village, the small town banker and his family, the provincial lawyer, etc. To elderly members of the *gratin* there was something reminiscent of the Court about these affairs. As one of them remarked "There is hope for a society which has to go to so many pains for its pleasure."

Dances and private theatricals were not the only nocturnal pastimes of château life for gallantry still flourished within those ancient walls as it must have for two or three centuries. Every houseparty had its complement of affairs and intrigues, for love was a prime occupation of this nonworking class. There was much surreptitious note-passing, much planning where to meet, how to get rid of lady's maid or valet, how to change one's room to be further away from wife or husband. Love was largely a game of waiting and anticipation which added to its piquancy. A woman often stayed on through the autumn after her husband had gone back to town. She was free from the vigilant eye of her coachman, her maid was conveniently installed in a distant wing or tower and if one of the guests happened to be her lover, who was the wiser? A story is told of a pastoral romance between a lady's maid living in a château and a handsome young farmer from the nearby village. Every night the rustic suitor managed to make his way over the outer gates, across the garden and former moat, up the vines of a stone wall and in through a window kept open for him. The seigneur of the château found out about these nightly gambols and asked his watchman if he knew what had been going on and why the hell hadn't he reported it. "I knew about it, Monsieur le Comte," the watchman said, "but I didn't report it because I thought the young man was going in to visit Madame la Comtesse."

For lady guests who weren't interested in stag hunting or bird shooting, there were all sorts of daily entertainments. They might gallop off on what was called "rallye papers," or paper chases on horseback, popular with horsewomen who liked the excitement of the hunt but were squeamish about the final kill. Some followed the hunt in dogcarts or surreys, and at pigeon shoots those who didn't take part stood at a safe distance behind the guns, their fingers in their ears. At one duck shoot on a lake in the Midi in honor of the Duc de Chartres, the flower of Orléanist femininity followed the royal craft in rowboats. The duke had inadvertently placed a loaded gun on a seat of a rowboat and as one handsome young woman sat down, she received a discharge of shot in the plumpest portion of her anatomy. Needless to say there was much consternation, a surgeon was summoned, the shots removed and the men of the party vied with one another to get them for shirt buttons. Goncourt, who gives the account, calls it "very eighteenth century." In the "Notes Mondaines" of the *Annales,* Baronne Staffe wrote that the latest thing in smart country living was the "cold dip" at those châteaux that were favorably situated on rivers. The châtelaine would send out sea-green invitation cards decorated with wavelets and mermaids and the words: "Mme. X invites you to a *bain froid* which she is giving in the river of her park under the willows."

Her guests would turn up in lace-trimmed bathing costumes, black for the blondes, red for brunettes. They'd all jump into the river at once, emit little screams, swim for half an hour or so, then retire to a large, green and white striped tent that was divided into dressing rooms, one for every guest, equipped each with a mirror, a dressing table, a crystal bottle of rose water and a personal maid in attendance to dry her off and get her into her handkerchief linen underwear, each garment, if she were a noblewoman, embroidered with a tiny fleur-de-lis or, in the case of Empire nobility, a small golden bee.

There was a fad of holding morning courses for the ladies. In certain châteaux there were courses in cooking, in others, courses in heraldry. In many, gymnastics were given under the super-vision of an American exercise teacher, the ladies, still in their nightgowns and peignoirs, stretching their arms and touching their toes while their men were away assassinating rabbits. The Comtesse de Greffulhe augmented these laudable practices with courses in beauty and dress, as well she could for the Comtesse de Greffulhe was the best dressed and most beautiful woman of her set. The Vicomtesse de Trédau held singing courses. The Marquise l'Hervey de Saint-Denis hired artists to instruct her guests in oil painting and watercolor. And the madly energetic little Duchesse d'Uzès gave lessons in riding and hunting.

The Duchesse d'Uzès was the best sportswoman on the Con-tinent. A tiny lady, she could outlast any man on the saddle of either horse or bicycle. She and her husband had been among the first cycle enthusiasts, the duke having been the initial president of the original cycling club of Europe known as the "Omnium." In those early days, they rode on those lofty and frightening con-traptions which had one high wheel in front and a small one at the back. Every year the duchess showed her own horses riding them herself at the Concours Hippique, coming away always with bouquets of blue ribbons and, not content to drive a four-in-hand, she dashed about the countryside controlling the reins of a six-in-hand. She was an early automobilist and was probably the first woman to be arrested for speeding . . . she was racing through the Bois de Boulogne at twenty kilometers an hour! At the age of eighty-three, she was president of the Women's Automobile Club of France.

She was an extraordinary little woman, an ardent Royalist and, even more exacting, a Legitimist who once turned down a dinner invitation from the Duc d'Aumale (son of Louis Philippe, and an Orléanist) but later thought better of it, accepted and became a good friend of the duke. Yet with all such traditional nonsensicality, she kept herself keenly up to date with a lively interest in literature and the arts. For years she was the president of the Union of Women Painters and Sculptors. She was both modern and feudal, a feminist with an ancient coat of arms. Her great-grandmother had been Madame Cliquot who, widowed at twenty-five, had launched the Veuve Cliquot champagne business. The duchess herself was widowed at thirty-one and left with four children, an *hôtel privé* in Paris and the Château of Bonnelles near Rambouillet. In Paris, she ran a spirited and not overintel-lectual salon, nationalist in character, which at one time backed General Boulanger, that comic-opera hero who, for some wild reason, she thought was going to restore the Throne to France. Her chief joy, however, was to set forth from town with a group of sporting friends for a day's hunt at Bonnelles or Rambouillet. Their manner of setting forth was in a *wagon-restaurant* loaned to her by the Compagnie Générale des Wagons-Lits which she fixed up with a long buffet table and bar. At the finish of the day, the car would be attached to the first train back to Paris. The duchess was the master of the Rambouillet hunt. Rambouil-let belonged to the estate and was then, as it is now, the country residence of the President of France, but the President wasn't there too often. Especially during Sadi Carnot's tenure of office. Poor Monsieur Carnot was a modest, hard-working and shy man who was anything but a sportsman. However, he felt that hunt-ing at Rambouillet was part of his presidential duty. With many misgivings he purchased a gun and went reluctantly forth after rabbit in the Rambouillet forest. The huntsman called out, "Rab-bit on your right, sir!" and Carnot in his nervousness shot to the left and hit the chief of the presidential guard, General Brugère, in the rear. The incident was spoken of as "the first time one of our military chiefs has been wounded since 1870." After that, Carnot contented himself with no further arms than the cane with which he wandered peaceably about the Elysée Palace, and left the Rambouillet forest to Mme. d'Uzès. Hers must have been a pretty hunt, the women, sidesaddle of course, in red, gold-trimmed jackets, sky-blue skirts and little Louis XV tricorne hats with black ostrich feathers. In 1927, white-haired and intrepid, the Duchesse d'Uzès was still galloping in pursuit of the stag at the age of eighty.

A great house of ancient tradition and Old World formality was Dampierre. Originally built by Louis XIII and given to his favorite, d'Albert, whom he created Duc de Luynes, it had remained in that family ever since. Its chatelaine, during the latter nineties, was the exquisitely regal Duchesse de Luynes. Yolande de Luynes was a lady of the *ancien régime* and of the highest of Catholic aristocracy. Her father was the Duc de Dondeauville, who had so many grandchildren he could never keep their identity straight, and when one time a gleeful yokel from an adjacent village sent into the château to greet him the brat of the local whore, the old gentleman kissed the child tenderly. Mme. de Luynes, as a young wife with two children, had lost her husband in 1870 in the battle of Loigny. Hours after the conflict when hostilities had stopped for the night, she went out alone onto the field, lantern in hand, to find his body and drag it back to shelter. She lived on in her Paris house and her château at Dampierre, bringing up her children in strict royalist tradition (it was her son the young Duc de Luynes who had been the companion of the Duc d'Orléans on his enlistment escapade) and ruling like a gracious but distant queen over the select and devoted court that formed itself around her. At any of her soirées and receptions, the guests with whom she wanted to talk were brought up to sit beside her, one at a time, then dismissed after they'd been there long enough.

Elisabeth de Gramont, who was the duchess's niece, wrote of

her aunt that "she was her own admirable stage director. Sarah
Bernhardt in her plays didn't study her effects to the finest detail
as did the duchesse." She knew how to pose charmingly with
her two children. She would make an exit of royalty after High
Mass at Sainte Clothilde, bowing right and left, shaking hands
with a special few. Then she'd spring with grace into her open
calèche, place the children on the seat facing her, open a tiny
sunshade, smile and wave at the little gathering of onlookers
outside the church and disappear in a clatter of hoofbeats. She
was a lovely-looking person, a Queen Alexandra type of beauty,
and all her life she wore semi-mourning . . . soft grays, white and
shades of mauve, all of which were vastly becoming. Like many
of the old *gratin,* she had her own private priest. Every morning
in the family chapel at Dampierre, he'd wait Mass pending her
arrival. She'd appear never less than five, never more than ten
minutes late, coming in through a side door near the altar, pale
and grave, a white lace mantilla accentuating her pallor. She'd
kneel on her red velvet *prie-dieu,* her head in her hands, remaining motionless during the entire service, her small daughter beside her on a cushion, her long eyelashes sweeping her prayer-
book, her son serving as altar boy. Mme. de Gramont says that
"when Yolande de Luynes knelt, she did so for God and for the
King."

There were immense houseparties in the château at Dampierre.
All the dethroned Bourbons visited there, along with monarchs
who still had thrones, Carlos of Portugal, Peter of Greece and
Princess May of Teck who as Queen Mary had yet to come to
hers. With all her formality and deep religiosity, it is rather heart-
warming to find out that Mme. de Luynes had humor. A certain remark retrieves her from being a complete ivory saint.
When one of her guests, a count who was a religious fanatic, announced that the Virgin Mary visited him nightly, the duchess

ROBERT DE MONTESQUIOU
*Aristocratic Apollo and literary gadfly*

Photo Otto, Bibliothèque Nationale, Estampes, Paris

CLÉO DE MÉRODE
*"Gloria in excelsis Cléo"*

Photo Reutlinger, Collection Yvan Christ, Paris

MALLARMÉ
*Leader and prophet of Symbolist school of poetry*

Collection A. Jakovsky, Paris

DUCHESSE D'UZÈS
*Incomparable sportswoman and ardent feminist with an ancient coat of arms*

Photo Otto, Bibliothèque Nationale, Estampes, Paris

Aurélien Scholl
*Writer, journalist and occasional duelist*

Photo Reutlinger, Collection Yvan Christ, Paris

BONI DE CASTELLANE
*Turn-of-the-century Sun King*

Musée Carnavalet, Paris

"LA FÊTE DU TIR AUX PIGEONS"
*Print commemorating the extravagant party Boni gave in
the Bois de Boulogne for his wife, the former Anna Gould
of New York, on her twenty-first birthday*

whispered to a woman friend, "He is luckier than Joseph was."

Surely the ultimate reward for the socially ambitious would have been an invitation from the Duc d'Aumale to spend a weekend at Chantilly. Whoever has seen that story-book castle with its gardens and lakes, its racetrack and royal stables, its parks and deep woods, can imagine it in its final days as a residence under the ownership of the magnificent Duc d'Aumale, son of Louis Philippe, uncle of the pretender and last of the Grands Seigneurs as he rode his thoroughbred about his vast domain, reining in to talk to the country people, the peasant in the field, the milk girl taking home her pails, the old woman gathering fagots, with even an indulgent wink for the poacher. Known as the Hero of Sedan for his gallantry in that gory débâcle, he was also hailed as the Conqueror of Algeria having led the "Glorious Zouaves" who conquered that country for France, whether or not France is grateful for the conquest. As inheritor of Chantilly, he had not lived extensively on his estate, but had been obliged to spend a good many years in exile, owing to the fact of his being in a direct line to the throne. After Louis Napoleon came into power, Aumale was banned from his country for the twenty-two years' duration of the Second Empire. In September of 1870, with the overthrow of the Bonapartes, and the Prussians storming across the border, he was summoned to command the Army of the Republic. He did his best but by then his services came too late. After the defeat of '71 he said, "France is broken, but the pieces are still good." It was part of Aumale's dashing character to utter the grand phrase. When he presided at the trial of Maréchale Bazaine, who had deserted the Army at Metz and was trying to explain his cowardly actions stammering, "There was no government, no order, there was nothing!" Aumale said in his clear, ringing voice, "There was still France!" In spite of his royal birth, the duke was first and foremost a soldier. At the age of fifteen when he had received his commission as a sublieutenant of infantry, he said, "My only ambition is to be the forty-third Bourbon killed on the field of battle." He must, eventually, have been awfully glad that this extravagant ambition was never realized, because the old boy had a wonderfully good life.

He was head of the Army for a time, then inspector general, and he did a turn in politics serving in the Chambre as deputy for Oise. He did have to spend another three years of exile after the 1886 law banished in perpetuity all possible pretenders to the throne, but his former services to his country, plus the information that he intended to will Chantilly to the Institut de France, made the authorities relent and he was welcomed back as the Republic's most popular Royalist. The duke was far more than a soldier and a prince of the realm, he was a historian, a man of letters who wrote a number of books including a seven-volume work on the lives of the Princes of Condé. He was an art and book connoisseur, and his knowledge of those subjects is attested to by the great collection still on view at Chantilly. He was a charmer of wit and erudition and a welcome addition to the Dîners Bixio, informal bimonthly dinners of the literary set, like the Magny dinners. Ernest Renan, who was a regular of the Bixio gatherings, said of the duke, "We talk, but he converses."

The prince once had a wife, but she had piously expired in the early years and there was no end to the number of women eager to console him for her loss. His most famous mistress was Léonide Leblanc, an actress noted less for her dramatic powers than for her flawless beauty. She had been in her heyday during the late '60's and early '70's. Abel Hermant in a book of souvenirs, writes of coming across Léonide Leblanc one afternoon in 1894, quietly dressed, her figure a trifle replete, but her face still lovely and her smile as dazzling as ever. They chatted briefly, then she said, "I'm home every afternoon between five and six-thirty. Ah, but don't come on Thursday as my old friend pays me a visit on his way back from the Academy." Hermant knew that the "old friend" was the aging Duc d'Aumale, as devoted as ever. During the duke's exile, which he spent in Belgium, Léonide used to go periodically to visit him. Her subtle way of giving out the information of a forthcoming trip would be to enquire of any friends, "Have you some commission I could do for you in Brussels?" No one ever had, but everyone looked impressed and Abel Hermant added, "We honored the Royal Exile as today we honor the Unknown Soldier, with a moment of reverent silence." Mademoiselle Leblanc divided what is politely termed her "favors" between the Duc d'Aumale and the somewhat radical statesman, Charles Floquet, president of the Chamber of Deputies. However, she did not publicize this second alliance. The duke was kudos, the president of the Chamber a utility. The French in their resolute dedication to the Republic preferred to ignore their president's little lapse of morality. But the glamour of royalty still hung in the air and the liaison of a well-known courtisane with a duke of the realm was in the grand tradition.

The duke was frequently in residence at Chantilly, a short train ride from Paris and a convenient distance for the visits of Léonide. Traveling there one weekend, she shared a first-class compartment with some society matrons whose country estates were in the vicinity of the château. Each was showing off how well she knew its master. "I'm lunching with the duke tomorrow," announced one. "We're having tea with him Saturday," chimed the next, while a third kept up the round with "We are invited to dine there on Sunday." At this moment the train pulled into the Chantilly station. Léonide rose and said with her sweetest smile, "And I, ladies, am sleeping with His Highness tonight."

When Aumale was in Paris, he and Leblanc often dined at

Voisin's. The authorities took the precaution of stationing a
soldier on guard in the building across the way. He stood behind
a lattice in a window on the second floor overlooking Voisin's
intimate *salles privées* and he stood there every day because no
one knew for certain when the duke would come. It is rather
endearing to think that a determined Republic should take such
care of its remaining highnesses. In 1898, a year after the duke's
death and four years after Léonide's, it was discovered that the
soldier was still on guard . . . an interesting example of military
red tape although, no doubt, the view from the window being
what it was, the soldier enjoyed his duty.

In his old age, the Duc d'Aumale still had plenty of what the
French call *panache* — an untranslatable word meaning *dash,*
only more so. He held two or three stag hunts a week at Chantilly, outriding any of his huntsmen, went in for bird shooting,
greyhound racing and would occasionally join the Duc de Join-
ville in a nearby forest following a pack of one hundred and fifty
hounds in pursuit of the wolf. After he'd given the legacy of
Chantilly to the French Academy, he invited its other thirty-nine
members to come out for the day to lunch with him and look
over their property. The old boys, sedentary, distinguished and
bent, got off the train blinking in the unaccustomed sun as the
duke, on his Irish charger, rode up to greet them, his back straight
as ever, his waist still wasplike, a brass band played appropriate
selections and, according to one spectator, "the air was full of
glory." The lady friend of the duke's final years was a Mme. de
Clinchamp who lived with him in a highly dignified somewhat
Mme. de Maintenon fashion. The river which ran past her windows was the Nonette and gossips referred to her as "La Main-
tenonette." It may well have been a purely platonic situation, for
the duke, by then a gouty old man, once remarked to some
friends, "As a young buck, I always had four supple members

and one stiff one . . . now I have four stiff and one supple!" He was loved by every member of the courts of Europe, all the young people affectionately calling him "Oncle Aumale." One of his nephews was the highly unpopular Ferdinand who became the unwelcome King of Bulgaria. When Ferdinand came to visit him at Chantilly, the duke came into the room without noticing him and upon being told of his presence exclaimed, "Tiens, Ferdinand! I was being like the rest of Europe. I didn't recognize you!"

He loved his château and its great collection. It gave him delight to turn the pages of the Duc de Berry's *Book of Hours* for special guests and to take them through the picture galleries. He had a little sightseeing patter like that of a regular guide. Stopping before Raphael's "Three Graces," the allegorical nude figures of Summer, Autumn and Winter, he'd point out, "The master has painted Winter from the viewpoint of where women age the least."

One of his favorite nieces was the Duchesse d'Alençon. The news of her terrible death in the Charity Bazaar fire was too much for his heart and he died a few months later. A solemn Mass was held and the Republic gave full military honors to this son of its banished Royal House.

One of the rewarding sights in the daily carriage parade of the Bois was that of a swank *calèche à la Daumont,* in eighteenth century style, four horses in single file, with two of them ridden by postilions, who wore raspberry-colored livery and powdered wigs. Two footmen in similar uniform perched with folded arms on tiger seats behind. Sitting back on the white upholstered cushions was the owner, a man beautiful as a blond Adonis, in a perfectly tailored morning-coat of pure white, white topper, a carnation in his buttonhole, a well-gloved hand gracefully resting on the golden top of an ivory cane. Seated beside him might have been a glum little woman whose appearance even in her Paquin frock and her hat the latest creation of Reboux could never have been anything other than dreary. The man was the Comte Boniface de Castellane and the glum little woman was his countess, the former Anna Gould of New York, doubtless wishing to God she'd never left that city. Count Boni, a turn-of-the-century *roi soleil,* was out to enjoy his morning drive and to dazzle the common people. He would already have held his morning levée, which was not unlike those the Sun King held at Versailles. At this morning ceremonial, he'd be called by his number one valet, helped into his robe by a second, the maître d'hôtel with footman in attendance would bring in his coffee and brioche after which his barber would arrive, then his masseur, then a Chinese pedicurist who painted his toenails a shade of shell pink. Awaiting his orders in an adjoining salon, like an assemblage of courtiers and petitioners, would be his shirtmaker, his tailor, his bootmaker and an assemblage of the art dealers and antiquarians for whom he was easy prey. Sometimes his political associates would drop in to pay their respects, for the count dabbled in politics after a dilettante fashion and had once planned, along with the artist Forain, to start a right-wing Catholic party.

Boni de Castellane had an assiduously cultivated taste for the princely past . . . his own in particular. That he should bestow the glory of his family name on a lowly American heiress was in his estimation an honor for which she should repay him with adoration and a lifelong gratitude, over and above the $15,000,000 dowry with which she was already repaying him. The count was one of the first Europeans to open up that aspect of international trade, a New World heritage for an Old World title. It became such a practice for a time that whenever an eligible American millionairess appeared on the Paris scene, unmarried young noblemen murmured, "Merci, Christophe Colombe!"

Ever since coming of age, Boni de Castellane had been the matrimonial catch of the aristocracy. He had also been a highly successful Don Juan of the boudoirs. When in 1894 he married Anna Gould, there was many a *petite femme* who sighed sadly, but once she'd set eyes on Anna she sighed no longer, feeling confident that her Boni would come back to her. The new countess was hopelessly plain and sallow, with heavy eyebrows that almost met over her nose. Her scrawny arms were covered with hairs in a dark fuzz that went clear up to her shoulders. A malicious English marquis, himself on the lookout for an American heiress, after being introduced to Anna in Newport remarked, "That girl will never be fool enough to marry anyone who'd be fool enough to marry her."

After a honeymoon spent in the Jay Gould mansion in Irvington-on-Hudson, the happy couple settled in Paris. By way of celebrating Anna's twenty-first birthday, Boni gave the first of his resplendently lavish parties. He cheerfully admitted his extravagance. "Before sending out invitations to any of my fêtes," he said, "I start by opening the windows and throwing out all the money I have" . . . all the money he had being Anna's. For this initial fête, he hired the Tir aux Pigeons in the Bois, an extensive area on which he ordered the construction of a stage large enough to accommodate eighty dancers. Here he presented the complete corps de ballet of the Opéra accompanied by an orchestra of two hundred musicians. The grounds were covered with fifteen kilometers of red velvet carpeting and the whole place was lighted by eighty thousand Venetian lanterns. A further effect was created by six hundred flaming torches, each held by a lackey in scarlet livery. A *dîner intime* of two hundred and fifty friends preceded the main gala, which was attended by some three thousand guests who watched a ballet in which the dancers were reflected charmingly in the lake, marveled at a display of fireworks and, as a grand finale, fairly swooned at the moment when two hundred white swans were let loose. The great birds swooped up and down and flapped in bewilderment at the lights and the noise, then made a series of graceful landings on the lake.

Boni de Castellane, last of the preposterous dandies, was a man out of an eighteenth century court. Maurice Donnay said that he "smelled of Versailles" and in his memoirs Boni himself wrote: "Faced with an uncomprehending middle-class society, I put myself back in the past, and there I composed for myself an existence of curious pageantry, beautiful women and rare spectacles. I was an exile, not from my country but from my age, and so I have consoled myself by the past as much out of an urgent craving for beauty as out of distaste for the world which surrounded me." At a costume ball given by the Duchesse de Rohan in honor of Queen Isabella of Spain, Boni arrived in white doublet with gold frogging, boots trimmed with real gems, purple cloak bordered with sable, powdered wig and plumed hat. "I seemed dressed as I always should have been," he wrote. And yet, Boni was not primarily a brainless exquisite. He was a person of polish and culture who could talk politics, poetry, fashions and gardens, diplomacy, bibelots, finance and love. His crime was to have been born in the wrong century.

The better to make the pretense of living in his proper one, Boni ordered the building of his famous Palais Rose on the Avenue du Bois. The architect was Samson who not only used the Grand Trianon for inspiration, he imported pink marble cut from the same quarries as those which furnished the material for the Sun King's folly. The Palais Rose was more pretentious than the Grand Trianon and its furnishings far more lavish. When people speculated the cost, there were others to remind them, "But Boni has more money than Louis XIV." The palace throughout was lit only by candles, its owner claiming that electricity was for servants. "The difference between an electric light bulb and a candle," he said, "is the difference between a glass eye and a real one." The entrance foyer and grand stairway were on the scale of that of the opera house, there was an immense ballroom, a theatre which could seat five hundred, salons and libraries filled with Gobelin tapestries, rare paintings and furniture many pieces of which have subsequently found their way into leading museums. Upstairs, the count had his own private suite of rooms and his wife had hers. There was a joint bedroom which contained a large, canopied double bed. Boni in later years was inclined to refer to this room as "La Chapelle Expiatoire." Altogether, the Rose Palace was the most magnificent, many-splendored private residence created in the latter half of the nineteenth century. Boni's aunt, the somewhat outrageous old Comtesse de Beaulincourt, after inspecting it for the first time, commented tersely, "My nephew and his wife march up their grand stairway with peacock feathers stuck in their rears."

The opening of the Palais Rose was in the Castellane manner. First came the ceremony of the blessing of the house by the Curé of Saint Honoré d'Eylau with two assistant priests and thirty choristers. Then there was a luncheon to which were invited everyone who had had a hand in the construction, from the leading architects to the last carpenter, mason and plumber. The gala housewarming was an immense affair with the carriage lineup stretching well beyond the Arc de Triomphe. The house was lighted with thousands of candles in crystal chandeliers. On each of the many steps of the Grand Stairway, holding a gold candlestick with lighted taper, stood a lackey so rigidly immovable some wag stuck a pin into the calf of one of them to find out whether or not he were real. Guests were announced one at a time by Clément, the impressive Swiss. Clément stood over six feet tall, never made a mistake, knew how many times to bang his staff according to the rank of the arrivals, and understood the proper pause between "Monsieur X." and "Madame Z.," who might have come together but whose tie was solely one of clandestine love. The host and hostess received at the top of the stairs while an orchestra of fifty pieces accompanied by voices gave forth with "Long Live Henry the Fourth!" The Castellanes were Bourbon Royalists and "Vive Henri Quatre" was the only national anthem Boni would acknowledge. The "Marseillaise" would have been the equivalent of "Marching through Georgia" to a Southerner.

Anna presented her husband with two sons. After the first was born, she suggested naming him after her father. Boni was outraged, and declared that he'd never allow his heir to be named after a thief. "And yet," Anna wanly observed, "you don't mind taking the money of a thief." With that same tainted money, Boni, after the birth of the second son, bought the beautiful old château of Marais in Seine-et-Oise. It meant country air for the children and for himself, royally prodigal houseparties costing some $40,000 apiece and offering a variety of entertainment from stag hunting and hawking to ballet and operetta. The guest of honor one week-end was King Carlos of Portugal. For this state occassion, Boni hired extra lackeys which together with his own household ones, made up an assemblage of six hundred. He had them all dressed in purple livery adorned with the Castellane coat of arms, then, at the last moment, deciding that purple clashed with the color of his walls and hangings, ordered six hundred new liveries of white, pale blue and gold and requested his guests to dress in colors that would tone in with the general décor. It seemed a pretty idea until King Carlos came down the first evening wearing a dinner jacket of bright purple.

Not content with one château, the count purchased Mme. de Sévigné's former manor house at Grignan. Also, for two or three weeks every season he rented a large and luxurious villa at Deauville. Here at the beach, when Boni condescended to honor the sea with his presence, he paraded forth across the sands in a red robe, preceded by his valet whose duty it was to test the temperature of the water while a footman followed with his mastiff Bouboule on a leash.

Needless to say, each of Boni's habitats was superbly replete with the best and most expensive of art objects and bibelots. He once stated that his idea of heaven on earth was to live in a palace whose furnishings and décor would be in a continual state of change and replacement, while outside in formal gardens would be rare fountains and ancient statues, also being constantly moved about. This restless paradise would of necessity be located near a town exclusively peopled by Duveens, Seligmans, members of French and Company and further art dealers of similar excellence.

Large and palatial yachts were in fashion and Boni quite naturally had to have one, a 1600-ton three-master with auxiliary engines, eighty officers, a crew of one hundred and the name of *Walhalla.* Yachting was in the leisurely pace of the times. The Baronne Staffe, that indefatigable chronicler of the social scene for the *Annales,* describes a typical day.

> Life on board is very restful. One dresses, has a cup of tea and goes up onto the bridge to admire the ocean and the fishes. Then lunch and a game of cards. Then back on deck to watch the sunset. Then, dreamy and thoughtful, one goes down again to dress for dinner, and afterwards, wrapped in a soft, white wool cloak, one goes up again to admire the stars and breathe the night winds. At midnight everyone is in bed.

In whose, the baronne doesn't say. Boni might have been in one of many. It hadn't taken him long to reassemble his stable of *petites femmes* and Anna suspected as much. She hired a private detective from New York, a clever and personable young man whom she passed off as a wealthy F. F. V. . . . not that First Family of Virginia would have meant anything to Boni. The fellow knew how to play the gentleman, and in no time the spoiled darling of the Castellanes was taking him about town, confiding in him tales of his love adventures and even showing him a few charmingly incriminating letters. Anna sued for divorce. She must have sensed from the start that she'd eventually have to, because at the time of her marriage she had refused to become a Catholic, giving as an excuse the fact that if she did, she'd always have to keep him as her husband. She cut off his money, threw him out of all his houses, sent his clothes, his only remaining fortune, after him in several large bundles in care of his parents, and shortly thereafter married Boni's cousin, Hélie de Sagan de Périgord, Duc de Talleyrand. Years later, when some friend was treating Boni to dinner at Maxim's, Hélie de Sagan walked in and neither he nor Boni spoke to the other. "Don't you know the duke?" the friend asked. "Certainly," Boni replied. "We've both served in the same corps." Boni de Castellane ended his days making a meager living through commissions from dealers for overselling antiques and paintings to rich Argentinians, gullible Americans and a number of softhearted friends.

The shining soul of the *beau monde* was the well-known and universally beloved Abbé Mugnier. He was in some ways the prototype of the eighteenth century drawing-room priest, confidant of the high-born and wealthy who went the rounds of the great houses for purposes of confession, absolution, extreme unction and entertainment. In larger ways he was a scholar and a man of God. He was invited everywhere and knew the best people. He also knew the worst people and took on their problems and sorrows with equal compassion for underneath his worldly poise and his delicious wit, he was a deeply spiritual divine, dedicated to his faith. Edith Wharton said of him, "His quick sense of fun and irony is so lined with tender, human sympathy that the good priest is always visible behind the shrewd social observer," and Elisabeth de Gramont said that the naïve Christian faith and the antique serenity of the philosopher had fashioned his soul.

Father Mugnier had been canon of Notre Dame at one time, then vicar of the aristocratic church of Sainte Clothilde. However, he preferred his final post as almoner of a small convent back of Montparnasse where he worked tirelessly, administering to the sick, helping the poor, praying, studying and meditating. Toward the end of his life, he was almost blind but his spirit was a glowing light, his wisdom infinite and his humor irresistible. When one woman asked him if he believed in hell, he answered, "I must, madame, because it is a dogma." Then he added with a smile, "But I don't believe there's anyone in it." A doctor, speaking about women, said, "We medical men, not you, are their true confessors." "No doubt," answered Mugnier, "but the doctor cannot give them absolution."

His charm and lively conversation made him much in demand at smart dinners and the feminine guests begged to be placed next to him. At one gathering, some gay blade seeing him seated beside an unusually pretty female asked if he'd dare to kiss her. The abbé replied "Certainly not! She's not a relic yet!" And when an actress coyly asked him if it was a sin to look at herself naked in a mirror, he gave a quick glance at her overfulsome figure and solemnly replied, "No, madame, it's an error."

He had the nature of a true Franciscan, loving animals, flowers and trees. He told Edith Wharton about a time when he was administering supreme sacrament to a parishioner and the dying man's pet canary, escaping from its cage, flew down and started nibbling the Host. "What did you do?" asked Mrs. Wharton. "I blessed the canary," he said.

It was the Abbé Mugnier who converted J. K. Huysmans. He also converted Paul Bourget, who after his conversion, became such a zealously devout Catholic, he was at times a crashing bore, even to the good father with whom he insisted upon discussing no subject other than theology and the Church. One day when Bourget was being particularly tiresome in his devoutness, the abbé cut him off, saying, "I have two cassocks, Monsieur Bourget, would you like one?"

The father knew and loved literature and had for his favorite authors a veneration which was akin to his veneration for the saints. He'd make little solitary pilgrimages to their homes and the places they wrote about . . . Victor Hugo and Lamartine. And he would occasionally journey to Weimar to burn temporal incense at the shrine of Goethe's birthplace, although he kept quiet about that, the Franco-Prussian War being still so fresh in national memory. His best beloved writer was Chateaubriand. He read his works over and over, wrote little monographs about him and paid quiet visits to his country haunts in the outskirts of Paris. After the abbé died, his faithful old maidservant, dissolved in tears, exclaimed to one of the mourners, "Ah how pleased he must be, talking with Monsieur Chateaubriand in heaven!" No doubt the pleasure was mutual.

With all its nonsense, all its extravagances, all its painstaking frivolity, the *gratin* of the Belle Epoque stood for a certain bloom of French culture . . . a hothouse bloom, if you like, and certainly not representative of the complete flowering, but still a handsome blossoming. These people gave a hallmark stamp to their decade. Theirs was the noble folly of elegance . . . elegance of manners, elegance of living and, in many instances, elegance of mind.

# 4

## THE BOULEVARD
## AND SOME BOULEVARDIERS

HE BOULEVARD is not to be confused with the Grand Boulevards, even though *it* is situated on *them*. The Boulevard comprised merely the section between the rue Caumartin and the rue Taitbout or, as someone of the period put it, the Paris of the Parisians began at the Madeleine and ended at Tortoni's. Any further stretches to the east or west were the provinces. At least they were to the habitués of this particular district, for here were the celebrated cafés patronized by the men-of-the-world, of politics, of journalism, of sport, and of the theatre. This was the daily and nightly haunt of that essentially Parisian individual, the *boulevardier,* in no other city could he have developed. London may have had her eighteenth century coffee house wits, even some New Yorkers may look back with a certain nostalgia to the 1920's and that caustically clever group which sat about the Algonquin Round Table, but these are not comparable. The *boulevardier* was Parisian, his wit was Parisian, his outlook was bounded by the Boulevard itself . . . its cafés, its theatres, its easy access to the rest of the city, but no further than the Bois. He was the man of bright sophistication, the man who knew the serious value of gaiety, the man sharply aware of the present scene. Neither an intellectual nor an aesthete, he could have told you about every play then running, with special emphasis on the shape of the leading lady, but he'd never have bothered about Antoine and the Théâtre Libre. He might have condescended to see something by Maeterlinck, but Ibsen would have been beyond the pale. Certain of the *boulevardiers* had an eye for good art and a few even collected Japanese prints, while one or two went so far as to collect the Impressionists, but most of them, if they gave painting a thought, remained true to Bouguereau, Cabanel and the other painters who dipped their brushes in soft soap. They read, of course, current literature, periodicals like the *Revue Blanche* and the *Revue des Deux Mondes, Gil Blas* and their fellow writers' newspaper articles and columns some of which were of true excellence, but serious writing like that of Bergson was not for them. Except for Catulle Mendès and Henri de Régnier, two poets who were steady members of the Boulevard coterie, poetry and the Symbolist movement was for the long-haireds. What made the *boulevardier* unique was his wit, his talent for coming out at the right moment with the right word, the *mot juste*. He was a celebrity less for his literary or journalistic output than for his *mots** and was often spoken of as a *diseur-de-mots*. A *mot* uttered one afternoon would be all over town by the next day.

Boulevard wit had a style of its own, sometimes epigrammatic, sometimes satirical, always spontaneous as when the playwright Alfred Capus remarked, "How many happily married couples are estranged only by the ceremony," or when Tristan Bernard after someone had been raving about the city of Venice agreed that it had its points, then added, "Paris wouldn't be too bad either if the Municipal Council would only open up the sewers." Or Maurice Donnay's observation: "How many women, the first morning after their marriage are widows of the husband they've imagined!" Again, there was the night at Maxim's when the farce writer Georges Feydeau was served a lobster which was

---

* One might say, though somewhat hesitantly, that a *mot* was the equivalent of the American wisecrack.

minus one claw and, after complaining to the waiter, was informed that lobsters are combative beasts and sometimes fight each other in the tank. "Ah?" said Feydeau, "then take this away and bring me the victor." A cruel *diseur de mots* was the artist Forain. When a silly woman who dressed far too youthfully for her years declared that the moment she started to show signs of age she'd shoot herself, Forain tersely said, "Fire!" There was the time when a well-known *boulevardier* — and again it was Tristan Bernard — was about to start off in a fiacre and the horse either took fright or had some sort of insane seizure. It reared, kicked, pawed the air with its front hoofs, then fell onto its knees and eventually flopped supine on the ground, and Bernard getting out of the fiacre quietly asked the coachman, "Is that all the tricks he knows?" Another of the wits was Alphonse Allais. He was a playwright of bright, somewhat offbeat comedies. He was once asked by a culture-seeking group to address them on the subject of the theatre and playwriting. He opened his address with "Ladies and Gentlemen, I have been asked to talk to you about the theatre, but I am afraid the subject will make you sad. Shakespeare is dead, Molière is dead, Racine is dead, Beaumarchais is dead, Marivaux is dead . . . and I'm not feeling too well myself."

Boulevard life had come into being during the Second Empire when the smart and literary gathered at a café called Tortoni's . . . the leading spirits being Alfred de Musset, Alexandre Dumas and the Duc de Morny. Tortoni's reigned supreme for some thirty years (which is not so old in a city where Maxim's is still going strong at seventy-five). During the '90's the Napolitain started attracting the boulevard set and Tortoni's had to close. But by then boulevard life had taken hold and there were other cafés which men began to regard more or less as their own private clubs. As Georges Courteline remarked, "A man will change his religion sooner than change his café." What patrons did in their favorite cafés was mainly talk. Some played checkers or dominoes, some wrote letters, but the chief attraction was seeing one's friends — enemies too could be diverting — picking up ideas, catching the latest gossip . . . and talking. They drank too, of course, mostly beer or cassis with soda, a few went in for absinthe but few were addicts and drinking was merely an accompaniment for talking. Jean Moréas the poet, recalling the height of the boulevard enthusiasm, wrote, "You arrived at your café at 1 P.M. and stayed until seven. You went out for dinner. You came back at nine and stayed till 2 A.M." Wives, even mistresses were temporarily forgotten in the cheerful ease of one's favorite café. Antoine Albalat, an essayist and literary commentator, on the day of his wedding turned up as usual at his café saying, "Friends, here I am, and I'm married, but it's agreed between my wife and myself that nothing will change my way of life. I shall continue to come here after lunch, before dinner and after dinner." François Coppée gives an account of one wife who, in a desperate attempt to keep her husband at home, fixed up a room to look like a café with small tables, rows of bottles, zinc counter, even a door marked W.C. But her husband soon started going out again because the beer wasn't on tap.

An early and almost legendary *boulevardier* was the writer and journalist Aurélien Scholl, a survivor from Second Empire days and the personification of what was considered to be the *esprit du boulevard*. He was brilliant, often vicious, sometimes shamelessly Rabelaisian, impeccably dressed and never without a monocle through which a malevolent eye pierced any opponent like a gimlet. The Boulevard was his only life and it was a cliché to say: "Aurélien Scholl goes to the Boulevard as the rivers go to the sea." He cared for nothing but city life and the only time he ever saw a cow was at Pré Catelan where at five in the morning he might join the all-night joymakers in a somewhat nauseating glass of warm milk fresh from the udder. Scholl was anything but a pleasant man, although he could be ingratiatingly charming when he cared to take the trouble, which was seldom. He'd destroy a reputation for the sheer hell of it and he'd often cut close acquaintances dead as they came into Tortoni's. His arrogance was highly irritating to certain people, one of them Catulle Mendès. Mendès was a novelist, playwright, and a poet of the Parnassian school, married for a time to Judith Gautier the daughter of Théophile Gautier. He came from Bordeaux and his name wasn't Catulle Mendès at all but he'd invented that appellation, concocting it from Catullus, the Roman poet of libidinous verse, and Mendès an Egyptian god with an ox's head. During his younger days, Mendès had been superbly handsome, almost too much so, with a shock of wavy blond hair, a silky reddish beard and the face of a pretty Christ from a religious art shop. In later life he grew heavy, gross and baggy, a sort of obese Silenus, and was a natural target for the caricaturists. One sees him in Sem's and Capiello's cartoons of Maxim's and the other haunts of Tout Paris. Mendès, as a result, hated all caricaturists and if he saw any one of them nearby, he'd start beating him with his umbrella. He was a fiery man with a violent temper and a talent for taking offense and was frequently fighting duels over the most asinine of provocations. One of his combats was over the question of whether Hamlet was dark or blond and another was provoked by a discussion about the skeletal thinness of Sarah Bernhardt.

Scholl had cut Mendès, whom he knew perfectly well, once or twice and Mendès in fine outrage was determined that Scholl should acknowledge his greeting. Seeing him at his regular place in Tortoni's one afternoon, Mendès strode over to his table, planted himself directly before him, pointed an accusing index finger all but in his face and in the voice of a declaiming tragedian shouted "BONJOUR!" Scholl adjusted his monocle, studied the menacing finger for a moment or two, looked up at its owner and asked politely "Where would you like me to put it, monsieur?"

It is surprising that this incident did not lead to a duel. As this was a period when duels flourished, particularly among journalists and men-of-letters, they all felt it some point of honor to have at least one encounter to their credit, and the physically inactive Edmond de Goncourt in his Journal regrets that at the beginning of his career as a writer he didn't find an excuse to fight. Goncourt's exact words are: "I believe it necessary, useful, self-preserving for a man of letters, on his entrance into literature, to have fought." There was some sort of affinity with the Heidelberg student in this attitude, except that the average Frenchman would never have welcomed a permanent scar on his cheek. With the duel as an inevitable eventuality, most newspapermen took some sort of training and the fencing studio and pistol gallery became as necessary a part of their existence as the editorial room. Mendès was the exception as far as training went. He fought with zeal, fury and no knowledge whatsoever and was always being hacked up. When asked why he didn't take a few fencing lessons, he replied, "Because I'd find out how dangerous it is and I wouldn't fight so well." Actually Mendès won most of his duels by scaring his opponents half to death. He went at one with the expression of a maniac and such ferocity, the poor man turned and started to run. Mendès called out, "Are you leaving us, monsieur?" which convulsed the seconds, the duel was called off and the antagonists went away arm-in-arm to the corner bistro.

Quite a number of duels ended in this amicable fashion. Fortunately, little blood was shed and the mortalities were almost nil. These comic-opera affairs of honor arose over trifles until the Dreyfus Affair, which automatically forced people into bitter enmities. The proprietress of the little café across from the dueling grounds at Villebon, where together with the island of the Grande Jatte most encounters took place, clapped her hands joyously and said to one group, "Ah, gentlemen, we'll be back in the good old days of Boulangism when we'd have as many as three duels a morning!"

There was pretty much of a farcical character to many of these combats. Jules Bois, an essayist specializing in the cult of satanism, and the Marquis Stanislas de Guaita, a spiritist, felt obliged for some occult reason to engage in a duel, though neither of them knew the first thing about the arts of self-defense. They both consulted the same professor, albeit at different appointments, who after trying in vain to give them a few pointers, advised each man to hold his sword horizontally and well out from his body. "If your adversary recoils," he said, "advance. If he advances, you recoil." They met on the grounds, the seconds took their stands and the referee called out, "Allez, messieurs!" For several minutes the two men stood motionless, rigidly holding their swords at arm's length. They appeared to be in some sort of hypnotic trance. Then one of them lost his balance and, in spite of himself, stumbled forward, at which the other retreated. This inspired the first one to continue his advance, which he did for some three hundred yards. Then the other took the initiative and the process was reversed for the same distance. The first one then started again and this curious stalking act continued for two solid hours. Eventually the witnesses, finding the novelty wearing thin, called the duel, as such, off, the opponents shook hands, in fact they embraced, and they all went across to the café for the traditional libation of peace.

There were any number of other ludicrous encounters. There was the duel some years earlier when Sainte-Beuve had been challenged and being the aggrieved party had chosen pistols. He met his adversary and they were about to start shooting when it began to rain. Sainte-Beuve called for time out, walked to his carriage, got out a large umbrella, opened it and returning to the field of honor, resumed his position, the pistol in his right hand, the umbrella handle in his left. His opponent cried out that this was absurd, to which the great scholar answered that he didn't mind getting killed, but he did mind getting wet. One farcical fray was between two young reporters who were so ill with fright that when the command came to start, they both threw up in unison. After a mortifying cleanup, they started afresh. It was a wild encounter, with only surface wounds but much gore. The reason for their ineptitude was that each was so humiliated over his childish mishap, he couldn't bring himself to face the other and they fought ashamedly, looking the other way. Then there was the time when an expert swordsman named Doncière suddenly realized that his adversary had gotten a cramp in his arm and, with a gesture of handsome gallantry, decided to plunge his own weapon into the ground, only instead of the ground he plunged it into his own foot. The doctor declared this to be a wound and the duel was canceled.

It would be wrong to give an impression that all duelists were ineptly amateurish. There were some artists among them whose skill was a joy to witness. Such an expert was Jean-Joseph Renaud. He'd change his dandy's monocle for a professorial pair of spectacles, take his time before starting, like a maestro pausing before conducting an orchestra, then lunge into action with a grace which was a combination of Tybalt and Cyrano de Bergerac. As one admirer observed, the whipping of his blade through the air was "pure geometry." He could open up a midriff or snip off the fraction of an inch from a mustache with the accuracy of a surgeon.

The most endearing handling of a duel challenge was done by the much-loved comic author Georges Courteline. Some cocky would-be writer, wishing to get himself some free publicity, wrote Courteline an insulting letter demanding satisfaction for some trumped-up slight. The letter was badly written and the spelling execrable. Courteline, who could be a caustic grumbler but beneath whose gruff exterior was a sweetly human man, took his quaint pen in hand and replied:

> My dear young sir. As I am the offended party, the choice of weapons is mine. We shall fight with orthography. You are already dead!

Unlike the grousingly amiable Courteline, Aurélien Scholl never flinched from any challenge and was a fairly skillful swordsman as well as a good shot. According to Goncourt, who was never generous about people, Scholl was always apprehensive about any encounter. He'd go about for several days beforehand, bearing a regular arsenal of swords, revolvers and American knuckle-dusters, and the day of the duel he'd set out for the grounds, his pockets bulging with bandages, lint and medicaments.

One challenger of Scholl's was a banker of a rather shady reputation who, on certain occasions, had carried out a number of deals which had all but landed him in prison. Angered by some insinuating remarks Scholl had written about him in his newspaper, the banker burst into Tortoni's and challenged Scholl to a duel. Scholl, as always adjusting his monocle, stared coolly up at the man and asked, "You really want to fight?"

"Oui, monsieur!" roared the banker.

Scholl shrugged. *"Bon,"* he said, "I daresay that when we arrive on the grounds they'll remove your handcuffs."

Scholl's *mots,* which were much quoted, were quick and seldom kind. One afternoon when he and some friends were discussing an attractive married woman they all knew and one of them asked, "Do you think she really loves her husband?" Scholl answered vehemently, "Does she love him! She loves him so much, she takes on the husbands of other women in order not to wear out her own!" And when he was introduced to a well-known politician whose appearance was somewhat arresting owing to the fact that he had both very black hair and an almost white beard, Scholl's comment was, "It's obvious that he spends more time eating than he does thinking."

There had been a number of gruesome murders in one district of Paris, the victim in each case having been shot through the stomach. A timorous and somewhat effeminate man who lived in the *arrondissement* where the murders had occurred was telling Scholl about the ghastly fright he'd had the previous night when he woke to hear the sound of someone cautiously trying to open his outer door. He was terrified that it might be the assassin come for him this time, but as the sound persisted, curiosity got the better of him and he felt that he must find out who it was. By way of protection, he stuffed a pillow under his nightshirt and cautiously opened the door, his huge stomach protruding before him. "And what do you suppose was there!" he asked. "A midwife," replied Scholl. (It turned out to be a large tomcat.)

Aurélien Scholl had a way with women. The list of his mistresses is impressive. Among the first was the lovely actress Mme. Doche who was the original Marguerite Gautier in *La Dame aux Camélias*. When that tear-jerker was first produced in 1852, Mme. Doche was the toast of the capital. An entry in Goncourt's Journal of 1892 tells of his sitting at the theatre in front of two tatty old women whom he wanted to kill. One was deaf and her companion kept trying to hiss in her ear the gist of the lines. In high irritation, Goncourt turned to silence them. The old deaf woman looked familiar. It was Mme. Doche. Another of Aurélian Scholl's lady loves was the beautiful

Léonide Leblanc who also enjoyed the amorous attentions of the Duc d'Aumale. There was a soubrette from the Bouffes Parisiennes and a girl who seems to have had no other name than Céleste. But Céleste must have had further qualifications to make up for her lack of a second name, for Jules de Goncourt cast an eye on her and she walked away from Aurélian, who was a tyrannical lover, and into the more peaceful arms of Jules.

The Goncourts had both befriended Scholl. They had helped get him started in the newspaper business when he was young and shy. He didn't stay shy very long. In a later Journal entry they write: "To see Scholl, as I saw him, a youth nervously twisting his gloves on a bench in the waiting room of the *Paris,* and to see him today, arrogant and insupportable, I think how many petty souls stand up badly under good luck and how success makes them ridiculous." They found him absurd but amusing and were indulgent of his arrogance and his tantrums. The Céleste-Jules episode almost ended the friendship. Scholl was jealous of his women to a hysterical degree. If any one of them was the first to break off an affair, he'd become wild with rage, sink into weeks of sulky despondency, then cure himself only by taking on a new affair. He eventually married the daughter of a rich London brewer, a far from felicitous marriage which in no way interfered with his successful pursuit of other women. His witty approach had an individuality of its own. When one little married woman, wanting to give way yet struggling with her conscience, pleaded piteously, "Let me be for a time, my friend! Let me retire into myself," Scholl replied with gallant ardor: "Allow me, madame, to accompany you."

During the late '80's, Aurélien Scholl took his patronage over to the Café Napolitain. His hangers-on followed, and in 1893 Tortoni's closed for good. Some of the faithful Tortoni-ites were bitter and Jean Lorrain, who hated Scholl, wrote petulantly in

"Pall Mall," "Why didn't they wall him up in the ruins of Tortoni's which he abandoned!"

In the final decade of the century, the Napolitain, known affectionately as the "Napo," was the café *par excellence* of the leading *boulevardiers*. It stood opposite the Vaudeville Theatre and it doesn't do to look at the site today, for what it now faces is the lurid façade of the Paramount Cinema. The Napo became virtually the leading boulevard club, the qualifications for membership being a certain position in journalism or the theatrical world, a quick intelligence, an up-to-date pace with the times and the power to amuse. Smart dandies came here to catch up on news of the theatre and ballet ... Politicians finished off their correspondence on its marble-topped tables. Dramatic critics corrected the pages of their reviews ... Henry Bauer of the *Echo de Paris* was a steady patron, as was Francisque Sarcey of *Le Temps,* the soundest and best-known critic in France and more dreaded in his day by actors and playwrights than Alexander Woollcott or George Jean Nathan a quarter of a century later. The big shots from the newspaper world hardly missed a daily stop at the Napolitain ... Arthur Meyer of the *Gaulois* and Léon Blum of *Le Matin,* unaware that some day he'd be the Premier of France. There were the popular novelists, Paul Bourget, Henri Bataille and Paul Hervieu. Guy de Maupassant used to drop by until even the pleasant atmosphere of the Napo could no longer distract him from his demons. And there would occasionally come in, brought by her overbearing husband, a shy, wide-eyed girl who also wrote books, but nobody knew it then because the books were all signed by the name of her overbearing husband. Eventually she was to sign her own name to those enchanting works and the name she signed was Colette. Playwrights were the main steadies of the Napolitain ... Henri Lavedan, Maurice Donnay, Georges de Porto-Riche and the rest of those facile craftsmen who were able to turn out elegantly groomed plays all dealing with the same subject . . . the "eternal triangle" as viewed from every angle of the solid geometry of "l'Amour." Their plays no longer bear rereading. Even in the days of their easy success, discerning playgoers must have realized they were fashionable and not very profound. Goncourt, who was often in a grouch, dismissed most of them as "the apotheosis of the literature found in *La Vie Parisienne.*" And he was right. But the public as a whole considered them fine drama and there is no doubt that the dramatists went along with popular opinion.

The one playwright who didn't take himself too seriously was Georges Feydeau. He never made a pretense of being anything but a writer of slapstick farce, and yet certain authorities place him as France's second great comedy writer . . . Doubtless Feydeau himself would have been glad to have conceded first place to Molière. Feydeau's high position is due not only to his glorious comic sense, but because of his skill as an architect, one might better say a cabinetmaker, for these plays, idiotic as they may appear to be, are of a meticulously perfect construction found in few, if any serious dramas of the period and certainly in no other farces. These glorious romps are still to be seen at the Palais Royale, that entrancing theatre which Richelieu may not have planned for anything quite so slapstick . . . but how does one know? *Occupe-toi d'Amélie, La Dame de Chez Maxim,* they are joyously zany pieces with insanely complicated yet perfectly worked out plots and, of course, all the time-honored, gleeful devices such as husbands turning up unexpectedly, lovers escaping through second-floor windows minus their trousers, wives screaming, ingenues fainting, doors closing in people's faces, paperhangers turning up at inopportune moments and elderly prelates drifting into rooms no prelate should know about. No Feydeau farce, no matter what its gaily libidinous situations, could ever be shocking. The pace is too swift and the acting in exactly the right mood and tempo. Feydeau directed most of his greatest successes himself, and directed them with a serious eye to detail as though he were directing not a farce, but *Oedipe Roi*. Besides his Palais Royale plays, there were Feydeau's vaudeville one-acters, those little ribald gems which bear such titles as "Don't Walk about Naked," "Léonie Is Ahead of Time" (meaning in regard to Léonie's pregnancy) and "Baby Is Being Purged!" The plays and the one-acters still have their audiences rocking in the aisles as they did fifty and sixty years ago. Sarcey's review of *Champignol Malgré Lui* could still hold true in regard to most of Feydeau's plays today. On the opening night, he wrote, "the public was worn out, exhausted with laughter, they could hardly stand it. At the end of the play, the hysterics that took hold of the entire audience was so loud, nobody could hear what the actors were saying. The act was done in pantomime."

Georges Feydeau, born in 1862, was the son of a Second Empire writer who himself was not without wit. The elder Feydeau had produced a fairly shocking book called *Fanny* which in time induced the disapproval of the Church. The book had had almost no sale until the Archbishop of Paris denounced it from the pulpit, after which it leapt into popularity and a second edition came out with a dedication from the author saying: "To the Archbishop of Paris, in grateful homage." Feydeau's mother, a beautiful Pole, had her own streak of humor. She was known for being a bit promiscuous and the rumor went about that Georges was the result of an interlude with Napoleon III. When someone told her of the rumor, she cried out indignantly, "How could anyone think that a child as intelligent as Georges could be the son of such an idiotic emperor!" Georges was indeed an intelligent child and even as a boy began writing plays and short skits.

Success did not come easily for him. He started out on a newspaper as assistant to the theatre editor, his job being to handle the amusement releases brought in and get them ready for printing. Being unfamiliar with such work, he asked a fellow employee for some pointers and was told, "It's merely a question of scissors and paste. You take the stuff given you by the press agents, paste each one on a strip of paper underneath the ad for the play, then hand it in at the copy desk." Feydeau followed the instructions mechanically for a week or so, then it occurred to him to read some of the blurbs. Boosting a show which Feydeau knew to be doing appallingly bad business, its press agent had written, "At yesterday's matinee, they turned away 300 people." Feydeau couldn't resist adding, "And they were wrong to do so." That ended his newspaper career. He then turned his energies to writing his farces, which he managed to get produced, but they attracted little attention. One was even booed on the opening night because the character of a priest was treated with ridicule. Feydeau, who was standing at the back of the house, going through an author's opening night tortures, at the first sounds of the booings and whistlings rushed down an aisle, took a stand beside one of the demonstrators and began making more noise than the rest. A friend ran down after him and asked if he'd taken leave of his senses. "This way I can't hear them," Feydeau explained. "And it doesn't hurt so much." After this, his plays began to take on and by 1892 they had reached a pinnacle of popularity from which they never came down until well after his death in 1921. He died in a mental institution, hopelessly insane.

This great comic writer had always been a melancholy man, with the moody temperament of some of the world's great clowns. He was aloof and cordial in a cool way. Marcel Achard says that when he shook hands, he did so as if he regretted it. He was an exquisite of sorts, handsome, with princely bearing. He dressed well, owned a collection of one hundred and fifty stickpins which he changed twice a day, and he drank nothing but mineral water. He lived for many years in a small room in the railroad hotel of the Gare Saint-Lazare, having fled there one night after a quarrel with his wife, intending to return home the following day. He never did. Gradually he fixed up his quarters with an assemblage of porcelain jars, two hundred perfume bottles, stacks of books, any amount of fine etchings and some excellent canvases by the contemporaries from the first Impressionists to Utrillo. He loved his pictures and would get up in the night to turn on the light and look at them.

Actually he wasn't often in his room most nights, for he hated to go to bed. After closing every café, every *boîte de nuit,* he'd take a stray fiacre back to his hostelry and rather than turn in, would hold long conversations with the policeman on the beat or the woman who sold newspapers at the all-night kiosk. Noctam-bulatory as a Montmartre cat, he'd return to his railroad hotel sometimes as late as eight in the morning and he'd always call out a cheery "Goodnight!" to the woman at the desk who in astonishment would protest, "But it's broad daylight, Monsieur Feydeau!" at which he'd whisper in her ear, "Don't believe every-thing you're told!" Every situation he encountered, every chance remark, was grist to his mill. One 4 A.M., on emerging from Maxim's and seeing a strange red streak in the sky, he turned to a streetsweeper and said, "Is that the dawn?" The man came back with the answer, "I don't know, monsieur. I'm not from this district." Feydeau used it in one of his plays.

In spite of his all-night wanderings, Feydeau was physically one of the laziest men in Paris. Once settled in a chair at a restaurant or cabaret, he hated to stir. Louis Verneuil wrote of the time he and Feydeau were in a café when a pretty female entered. Verneuil exclaimed, "Ooh! The beautiful babe!" Feydeau, who liked lovely women, asked, "Where?" Verneuil indicated, "Back there." Feydeau turned his head as far as it would go, then realizing he'd have to turn his body too, settled back in his seat and said, "Tell me about her." If a doorman started to help him on with his overcoat, he'd stop him, saying, "Don't, my boy. It's my one form of exercise."

Georges Feydeau's nightly trips about the city were all in the serious line of work, observing, taking notes, studying types, talking with offbeat characters, gathering material that was all to come out in those plays which on the surface appear to be mere giddy nonsense, but are based on a realism as carefully studied as Zola's. He'd seek out every possible and impossible sort of cabaret, disreputable dives, opium joints, and the haunts of homosexuals which he called "Babels of love, on account of the confusion of sexes." There was a fair amount of lesbianism during the '90's. One sees the strange type in the drawings of Lautrec and some of the illustrations of Steinlen . . . the harshly handsome female in severely tailored suit, man's collar and tie, and fedora hat. Feydeau, visiting a lesbian hangout one night, started to tell a luridly off-color joke, hesitated, then continued, saying, "Why not? We're all men together."

His wit could have its edge, especially when he was faced by a bore. One tiresome ass, who was serenely unaware that his wife was continually having affairs with other men, boasted fatuously about his small son and his devotion to his mother. "My little boy," he said, "is so loving. He's always under his mother's skirts." And Feydeau muttered, "He'll meet some relations there." Like a number of other *boulevardiers,* Feydeau was prone to playful pranks, and not always kindly ones. There was an actress, popular in revues at that time . . . pretty, talented but incredibly sloppy about her person. As a matter of truth, she was just plain dirty and was said to take a bath only twice a month. Meeting Feydeau on the Boulevard one afternoon, she announced coyly that the next day was her birthday and the farce writer, with a courtly bow, promised to send her a present. What he sent her was a box containing three tiny cakes of soap and his card on which was written "For life!"

This was typical of the *boulevardier* prank, which bore a certain similarity of childishness comparable to some of the goings on of the Algonquin set . . . the same exuberance, the same assurance of the man of intellect deliberately playing the fool. There are endless instances. Tristan Bernard, one day noticing a hearse waiting outside a church, walked over to its driver and said, "Cocher, are you free?" There were two playful brothers named Ravaut who did mad things such as hiring a bus which they passed off as a genuine one in transit service and driving its occupants on a wild jaunt with the explanation that it was the birthday of the director of the company who was treating them to a banquet, explaining that they couldn't stop to let anyone off because the Eiffel Tower was being moved to the Bois de Vincennes and if it were to fall, the third platform would hit about where they were. Shouting further nonsense, the Ravaut brothers drove their panic-stricken passengers at a gallop to the top of Montmartre and left them in front of Sacré Coeur. One practical joker was Alain Sapek who would occasionally dress himself up in work clothes, go out with some surveying equipment, stop a passerby at one corner of a street, then another at the opposite corner, explaining to each that he was Chief Surveyor of the City of Paris, his assistants had mistaken the place to meet him and would each kindly hold an end of the surveying cord while he went to find them. The two would obey, holding up both the cord and the traffic, and Sapek would retire to watch from behind the trellis of a nearby bistro. Sapek owned a monkey who used to run loose over the rooftops, sometimes leaping through the open windows of other apartments which he'd occasionally rifle. One day the monkey stole a diamond ring from the woman who lived next door. The glittering bauble seemed to delight the beastie, who carried it about clenched on its thumb. The monkey's reputation in the *quartier* being suspect and somebody having seen it wearing the ring, its owner was called up before the local *commissaire* who asked him, "You own a monkey?"

"Oui, monsieur" Sapek replied.

"Did you know it stole this lady's ring?"

"Why no, monsieur."

"Haven't you noticed the creature wearing it?"

"Why yes," said Sapek, "but I thought it was his."

Alphonse Allais was another childish wag who, to amuse himself and his friends, went in for quaint Rube Goldberg-esque inventions . . . ventilated shoes, a lady's fan that worked by a pedal, a smoker's pipe with a whistle that went off when the light was about to die, a gadget to remove mustard from the sides of pots.

Playwrights were dominant at the Napo. There was Jules Renard who wrote *Poil de Carotte,* a touching little comedy in which, under the title of *Carrots,* Ethel Barrymore played early in her career. And there was Alfred Capus. Myopic, smartly grotesque, Capus was the image of the caricature Sem drew of him with black, satanic goatee, squinting eyes emphasized by a black-ribboned monocle and thick red lips through which bubbled his laughing epigrams . . . "It is not enough to say that a man has arrived . . . one must know in what condition" or "Women keep a special corner of their memories for sins they have never committed."

Like many true Parisians, Alfred Capus was not born in Paris. He came from Provence and all his life spoke with a slight accent

of Marseilles, a city he loved, "where one eats fish and sunshine."
His nature itself was full of the meridional sun. He was slyly
humorous, gaily disillusioned and amazingly successful as the
creator of frothy comedies of charm and sophistication. He
had begun his literary career during the '80's with a solemn and
weighty treatise on Darwin which it is safe to conjecture that
practically nobody read. Then he switched from evolution to
matters more frivolous, writing a cheery, bantering daily column
called "Chroniques Parisiennes" for the *Gaulois*. The *Gaulois*
was the paper read by the aristocratic smart set and it was definitely pro-royalist. After a time, he changed over to the *Figaro*.
Gaston Calmette was its editor and his reign came to an end when
a feminine reader, outraged over a scandal item involving her
husband, walked into Calmette's office and shot him dead. (A
gallant, all-male jury, regarding her act in the light of marital
honor, handed in a verdict of Not Guilty.) After this editorial
tragedy, Capus became the *Figaro's* political director and the
direction in which he steered was strongly to the right. It is not
for his politics, however, that Capus is to be remembered, but for
his bright, inconsequential comedies, abounding in *joie de vivre*
and easy morals . . . the two go so happily together. Louis
Verneuil said it was "a smiling theatre." Every season there'd be
a smash hit by Capus at the Variétés and often two or more
running at other playhouses. His royalties brought him a fortune
which he'd spend the moment it came in. He was continually
broke and would say, with a sigh, that he made money only in
order to pay his debts. He was an incurable gambler and once
after winning several thousand francs at baccarat he said to
Etienne Grosclaude, a fellow journalist and gambler who was
also constantly in debt, that he was tired of this life of senseless
chance and frivolity. He was going to pay off his debts and never
again look at another card. A few days later there appeared in

*Gil Blas,* Grosclaude's periodical, an announcement inviting creditors of Monsieur Alfred Capus to present themselves at 44 rue des
Martyrs from five to seven to settle their affairs. Capus was wild
with rage. He was then on the *Echo de Paris* and, in the space
reserved for official government announcements, he inserted the
further announcement that the creditors of M. Etienne Grosclaude
could present themselves after 9 A.M. at 2 rue LaFitte. If no room
on the stairway or in the courtyard were available, they could line
up on the even-numbered side of the Boulevard des Italiens, then
on that of the Capucines and after that on the Boulevard de La
Madeleine . . . after which they could get information from a
special police service set up to handle the situation.

In addition to his comedies, Capus wrote essays and other
works of a caliber to get him into the Academy. But he never took
writing seriously. He was an easygoing sensualist and he once
told Robert de Flers that he would willingly compose a five-act
tragedy in heroic couplets in order to sleep with an actress. His
wit ran true to *boulevardier* form. At the dress rehearsal of a
play, not one of his own, he was horrified by the bad performance
of a young ingenue playing the lead and asked the director why
on earth anyone so amateurish had been given such an important
role. The director, in apologetic *sotto voce* explained that the
producer of the show was "interested" in her. *"Bon!"* said Capus,
"but it's not brought out enough in the first act."

The domestic life of Alfred Capus is a bit indefinite. When a
dinner partner asked him if he had a family he replied, "Yes, I
have a wife . . . if my memory is correct." Then he added, "A
ménage is in a parlous state when one of the partners loves and
the other doesn't. If only neither loved, they could live quite
happily together." Like so many humorists, Capus had his dark
side. There were times when he seemed afraid of his own
laughter . . . when he murmured gloomily, "Those who are too

happy are like professional thieves, they're always caught in the end." And he cast a brief pall over one apéritif hour at the Napo by remarking, apropos of nothing in particular, "It's not worthwhile repeating to oneself that one is mortal, one will find it out soon enough." He found it out in 1922. He was sixty-four years old.

The greatest of the theatre celebrities who came often to the Napolitain when he was not off on tour was the magnificent actor Lucien Guitry. A colossus of a man, he walked with his head bent forward, making a curve at the back of his massive neck, and his friend Jules Renard remarked that "Lucien Guitry has started the style of carrying the goiter in the rear." A glass of fashion and mold of form, he was a sort of Gallic John Drew and a great ladies' man whom women went wild over. There was the quality of a vigorous Roman god about him. When he said "Bonjour!" it was with the expansive manner of giving one the day itself. Someone, and again it was Jules Renard, spoke of "what a pleasure it is to place one's hand in his big one!" There was something ruthless about Guitry too. He didn't have that neck of a charging bull for nothing.

According to his son Sacha, Lucien Guitry "seized upon life and embellished it, seeking always to make it continually more beautiful." It was with the same vigor that he seized upon his art and made it continually more amazing, for he was one of the great actors of all time. In his own time, his particular form of acting had been a startling innovation to a public accustomed to artificiality and superfluous gesture, for Guitry's method was one of naturalness and powerful simplicity. He had a magnetism that seemed almost supernatural and when he walked onto a stage, the audience was hypnotized by a Presence as when Chaliapin made one of his simple yet astonishing entrances. Even during scenes of intense emotion he hardly moved, conceding to gesture only when it was inevitable. He would study a part while going through routine activities. "This morning at breakfast," he told a friend, "I worked up the big finale of the second act and all the time I was eating an egg. You see? Gestures are superfluous!" He was fully aware of his own magnetism, scorned its absence in others and said of one inadequate performer, "The moment he comes on stage, he seems to have just left it." He had a fine contempt for artificial acting. Once when a rehearsal was going on in the Français he started walking across the lobby on tiptoe, not wishing to disturb the players, then suddenly went into his normal firm tread. "The rehearsal must be over," he said. "They're talking like human beings."

Guitry himself directed at the Français for a time. He was an excellent director, a tough taskmaster and a keen critic who could lacerate a bad performance with brutal ridicule. During one rehearsal he told a certain actor to go off and try his entrance again. "This time," he said "come in with an air of dignity." The actor tried again and, owing to nervous tension, walked on with his legs quite far apart. Guitry halted him. "Monsieur!" he shouted "I asked you to make your entrance with an air of dignity, but not on horseback!"

Lucien Guitry had learned most of his art during the nine years he lived in Russia, playing at the Saint Michael Theatre in St. Petersburg. He was tremendously popular with the Russians. They admired his artistry and delighted in his offstage cavalier charm. He was a brilliant raconteur, yet told his stories with a disarming manner of apologizing for telling them. He always put people at ease and could handle the most awkward situation with grace and a certain amount of bravura. One evening when he and his leading lady, a pink and plump little blonde named Angèle, were dining at The Bear in a *cabinet particulier,* Grand Duke Wladimir barged in accompanied by his wife. The grand duke, who was considerably buzzed, began making outrageously amorous advances toward Angèle which Guitry put a stop to by starting to make equally outrageous advances toward the grand duchess. Their Highnesses departed from The Bear in dignified haste.

The theatre and the labor it entailed was Guitry's joy. He lived it constantly. When Sacha was once rash enough to say that he dreaded the day when his father no longer acted, Lucien thundered out, "That day will never come! I'm acting all the time! In a restaurant, if I ask for more bread, I'm acting. If I ask Mr. X after his wife's health, I'm acting and my double, The Actor, looks on from the wings. Why? Because I love my art . . . that word has become degraded . . . my *métier*. I adore and serve it with my life. Blessed work which intoxicates and fills me with joy. For me, the actor's *métier* is the most beautiful in the world, and if Claude Monet and Vuillard thought differently of theirs, I'd be surprised. Vive la travaille! Each to his own! To work is to live!" Sacha in his memoirs recalls the time as a small boy, after he'd been put to bed, when his father strode in to kiss him good night and the child asked, "Where are you going?"

"I'm going to earn your living," his father answered gravely. "I'm going to play."

"That evening," wrote Sacha, "I understood his way of living. To earn one's livelihood by playing. What a beautiful destiny!"

Sacha's book is filled with delightful souvenirs of his father. One afternoon when Sacha was small and they were out for a stroll together, they passed a beggar. Lucien handed the boy a fifty-centime piece to run back and give the man. When Sacha caught up with him again, Lucien asked, "Did you bow after you'd given him the ten sous?" "Why no," said young Sacha. "Why should I?" His father explained. "Because one should always bow after making a gesture of charity. It's more gracious."

"But Papa!" the boy protested, "the beggar was blind!" "How do we know?" said Guitry.

Lucien Guitry dressed the part of the actor offstage as well as on. His city clothes were elegant but dramatic and at his Normandy house near Honfleur, he went about in a huge Buffalo Bill hat, beautifully tailored corduroy trousers and silk peasant blouses made by his Paris shirtmaker. Here in his country estate, he kept sheep, some thirty dogs, an eagle and a small lion. There was also a chimpanzee named Lakmé who took long walks with her master, holding his hand and listening to his lines with sad attention. Lakmé sometimes sat at table with Guitry and his guests. It was said that her manners were exquisite. Alphonse Allais, the quaint humorist whom Guitry called by the affectionate name of Alphi, used to spend his summers in a nearby village. Allais speaks of the day during a fierce tempest when the great actor took shelter in his local bistro and shouted above the storm, "Garçon! One Pernod and less wind!"

Guitry always spent his salary in advance and he lived sumptuously. His town residence was the fifth floor of an apartment house on the Place Vendôme. It was spacious and luxurious and had a large terrace which was open to the sky and was planted with small trees and flowers. He entertained with expensive simplicity . . . fellow actors, writers, members of the smart set and visiting Russian grand dukes with their voices of thunder. Twice a week, Guitry would hold his *Three Musketeers* luncheons. The three musketeers were four — himself, Tristan Bernard, Alfred Capus and crotchety little Jules Renard. A *déjeuner des mousquetaires* would last well into the late afternoon and continue into the apéritif hour at the Napolitain. Sometimes they'd merely sit out on Guitry's terrace and talk, sometimes they'd go on a long aimless stroll about the city. Guitry loved to wander through side streets and ancient *quartiers* and enjoyed noting down the quaint names of small bistros and obscure cafés. On a single street in Belleville he found:

> *Au Perroquet Populaire*
> *Au Chien Sauveteur*
> *Au Lapin Vengeur*
> *Au Lavatory Club\**

Lucien's wit was that of the *boulevardier* and it was also an actor's wit as he made a production of his best stories. After Sacha had married Yvonne Printemps, he'd entertain his delectable daughter-in-law with his repertory, then ask her please to forget every anecdote immediately so that he could repeat them all to her again.

The elder Guitry was that social phenomenon, an actor who — and in this again he was like John Drew — was received everywhere. However, society, as such, didn't in the least impress him and he abhorred any sort of snob. There was an arrogant clubman who had invested in one of his productions and Guitry felt obliged, at one time, to make a luncheon engagement with him. The snob got out his date book and said with weary elegance, "Let's see: Monday I lunch with Princess Murat, Tuesday with the Clermont-Tonnerres, Wednesday Prince de Beauveau, Thursday the Duc d'Assouville, Friday the British Embassy, Saturday Count Goutant Biron, Sunday Count Primoli. Do you want the next week?" Guitry got out his own book, thumbed the pages carefully and said solemnly, "Week after next I lunch Monday with my butcher, Tuesday the grocer, Wednesday the *boulanger,* Thursday the milkman, Friday the pedicurist and Saturday my bootmaker. Would you want the following?" He was intolerant

---

\* *At the sign of the Popular Parrot*
  *At the sign of the Lifesaving Dog*
  *At the sign of the Vengeful Rabbit*
  The last hardly demands translation

of empty conversation and compulsive talkers drove him from the room. A silly chatterbox countess once told him, with a giggle, "You know, I simply talk the way I think!" to which the actor's comment was "Yes, but more often." He could be equally deflating to members of his own profession. A fellow actor sent him a play he'd written, with an accompanying note saying, "I'll bet you a louis you don't read this script!" The man's script was returned unopened and attached to it an envelope containing one louis and the message "You've won your bet."

After the death of Coquelin, Lucien Guitry was the leading actor of his native theatre and could play any role in the repertory of France, classic or modern. At the height of his career, he chose what were then the moderns . . . Anatole France and Zola, the drawing-room love dramas of Porto-Riche and Bernstein and the comedies of Capus. He played Rostand's Chantecler (it was while studying for this role of the farmyard cock out in his Normandy country place that he remarked, "Have you ever observed that a rooster runs with his hands in his pockets?") and later he made a hit in *Kismet* and a special Molière series, his Tartuffe having become legendary. Whoever was fortunate enough to have seen him during the 1920's at the Théâtre Edouard VII in those delightful plays written by Sacha and acted by the three of them, Lucien, Sacha and Sacha's wife Yvonne Printemps, could never forget *Le Comedien, Mon Père Avait Raison* and his great portrayal of *Pasteur*. He continued to play with simplicity, power and profundity. Henri Bataille said of him, "Guitry is the first real man who has trodden the stage." And Boston's famous critic, H. T. Parker, who signed his reviews simply H.T.P. and was so severely exacting that actors sometimes referred to him as "Hell To Pay," wrote that "the firmness and exactitude of Guitry's acting make it a man's job" and he went on to say that it was the ladies in the audience who seemed the most swayed. Even Guitry's comedy, which was delicious, had depth and masculine strength. One day after a matinee of Molière's *Misanthrope,* an ecstatic woman fan rushed backstage and up to his dressing room puffing like a school of porpoises. "Ah, maître!" she cried rapturously. "How difficult it must be to play comedy!" To which the superb comedian replied, "Difficult, madame? It's impossible!"

Lucien Guitry worshiped Sarah Bernhardt. Ever since he had been her leading man at the Théâtre de la Renaissance in 1894, they had been warm and loyal friends. Sacha in his memoirs recalls how, as a small boy, he'd be taken backstage before every Sunday matinee "to kiss Mme. Sarah" as she sat waiting for her cue in her impressive dressing room, entrance to which, only for the elect, was through an overheated vestibule, across a tropical salon and on into the dressing room itself, torrid as a hothouse and banked with masses of flowers gasping their last. The Guitry family always called her "Madame Sarah" but Lucien spelled it "Ma Dame" because to him she was "Notre Dame du Théâtre."

He was right. Sarah Bernhardt was the theatre and the theatre was Paris. She had absolutely no private life, but belonged to the French public as completely and inviolably as the Eiffel Tower or the Cathedral of Notre Dame. She went her triumphant way like an empress, trailing a retinue of willing servitors and adorers who got to be called "Saradoteurs." In the theatre she was so idolized that when notified of the first-act curtain the callboy would knock on her door and say, "Madame, it will be eight o'clock when it suits you." Be it to her professional integrity that she was never late!

During the '90's Bernhardt was in her fifties, but her tireless vigor, like that of a non-stop dynamo, was as driving as ever. She went on the principle, to quote her own words, "that life engenders life, energy is the source of energy. It is in spending one's self that one becomes rich." She lived to the letter this active precept. As director, theatre manager and scenic designer of the Renaissance and later of her own Théâtre Sarah Bernhardt, she led an existence that would have killed off persons half her age. Every evening she'd play an exacting stellar role, every afternoon she'd rehearse a new play, doing all the directing herself. When she got hungry, she'd knock off work for what she called a *déjeuner sur l'herbe,* the *déjeuner* being a picnic luncheon of cold meats, salad, cheese and wine, and the *herbe* being the floor of her dressing room where she and whomever she chose to invite sat sprawled on a large green carpet. After an hour of this pastoral repast, they'd get back to work.

At one time, she suddenly called upon an actor named Brémont to replace another player in *Lorenzaccio* in a scant four days' notice. Brémont was panic-stricken at the prospect but Bernhardt assured him that she'd rehearse him thoroughly. She was playing *La Dame aux Camélias* that week. Every evening after the lady of the camellias' final death scene, she'd whip out of her costume, order the stage cleared and, starting at midnight, would rehearse with Brémont straight through till 5 A.M. The next morning at nine, she'd be back at the theatre for conferences with costumers and scenery builders. Brémont attributed her physical resistance to her ability to sleep whenever and wherever she wanted, either in short naps or for interminable stretches. When fatigue would hit her, she'd fling herself down onto the nearest couch, go into ten minutes of oblivion, then rise looking radiant and twenty years younger. Victorien Sardou, who wrote so many of her successes, said of her, "If there's anything more astonishing than to watch Sarah Bernhardt act, it's to watch her live." And Jules Lemaître went further, saying, "She's not an individual but a complex of individuals. She could enter a convent, discover the North Pole, inject herself with rabies microbes, kill an emperor or marry a Negro king and it would not surprise me."

When people marveled at her indomitable energy, she'd laugh and say "It's my métier!" and if friends advised her to slow down she'd reply scornfully, "Slow down? Rest? With all eternity before me?" One place however, in which she would take an occasional rest, was that much publicized rosewood, satin-lined coffin which she kept in her boudoir — one can be sure for a theatrical effect. The *Theatre Magazine* for December 1901 shows her lying prettily in this cheery piece of furniture, and under the photograph the information that "When Mme. Bernhardt is world-weary, she gets into this coffin . . . and covering herself with faded wreaths and flowers, folds her hands across her breast and, her eyes closed, bids a temporary farewell to life. A lighted candle on the votary table at her left and a skull grinning on the floor add to the illusion. It is only when dinner is announced that the tragedienne languidly opens her eyes."

For all her languid pose, Bernhardt had the health of a dray horse. When she was in the mood for sculpture . . . and she was not at all a bad sculptress . . . dressed in trousers and artist's smock, she could whack at a block of marble with the power of ten Rodins and take huge bites of bologna sausage between whacks. And yet her public pose was one of delicate exquisiteness and touching fragility as though, like the Marguerite of her portrayal, she was not long for this world. She'd arrive at her theatre in her large open carriage, semi-swooning on the back seat and swathed in chinchilla up to the slim neck which emerged like a flower stalk from the tulle folds of her upstanding collar . . . that "ruche à la Bernhardt" in which she was always painted. As late as the warm month of June, she'd be bundled in furs. Her apparent state of constant chill may have been a part of her frailty pose, although it might also have been due to her skeletal thinness. Sarah's chronic state of emaciation had always been a gold mine for the *diseurs-de-mots*. Aurélien Scholl remarked that "an empty barouche drove up to the door of the Comédie Française and Sarah Bernhardt got out," and a doctor who had taken care of her when she was a young girl recalled that she was so skinny, if she swallowed a pill she looked pregnant. That Sarah was given to wild exaggeration was common knowledge and Dumas *fils* commented to Ganderax the dramatic critic of the *Revue des Deux Mondes,* "You know, she's such a liar, she may even be fat!"

Her apartment on the Boulevard Pérèire was a cluttered congeries of innumerable portraits and busts of herself, white bear rugs, oriental lamps, stuffed snakes, potted palms with electric lights under the fronds and, maquettes of her latest clay modeling wrapped in damp cloths, plus a mass of trunks and suitcases waiting to be packed for her next tour. Jules Renard in his journal gives an account of going there for luncheon. He says that the guests didn't sit on normal chairs, they perched on ottomans, stretched out on canopied Baudelairian couches or sprawled on wild animal skins on the floor. During luncheon in the adjoining dining room, the Divine Sarah sat in a throne chair slightly raised on a low daïs and drank her wine out of a large golden goblet. Renard was so confused he did everything wrong . . . used a fruit knife for his roast, upset a flower vase, at which Sarah dipped her lean fingers into the spilled water and rubbed his forehead while she shrieked with laughter . . . which for some reason seems to have delighted Renard. After the meal, they returned to the bear-skin-strewn salon where their hostess held forth amid heavy sighs about how she had always wanted to do everything . . . scale mountains, write poetry, compose music. These wistful yearnings were cut short by the entrance of her newest pet, one of five pumas she'd just purchased. It was brought in on the end of a leash and introduced to the unhappy guests one at a time. When the creature sniffed at Edmond Haraucourt's watchfob, that poet closed his eyes and appeared to go into prayer. After this, two ferocious-looking mastiffs bounded in but they turned out to be playful puppies. Renard winds up his account of the day saying that as he left, he didn't look for his hat (it happened to be on his head) but left serenely carrying away in his hand the hat of someone else.

Sarah's pet menagerie was varied and spectacular . . . undoubtedly intentionally so. She once returned from a triumphant London engagement with a monkey named Darwin, a parrot named Bouzi-Bouzi, a cheetah and seven live chameleons on a gold chain about her neck. Michel Georges-Michel gives an account of her adding an alligator to the collection. She acquired it during an American tour when she was the guest of a millionaire, staying on his vast Florida estate which boasted a river and rare specimens of birds and animals. Sarah insisted that there must be crocodiles (she didn't know they were alligators over here) and that they organize a crocodile hunt. As there wasn't a trace of either crocodile or alligator on the estate, the compliant millionaire sent off telegrams in all directions and managed to get hold of a baby 'gator. Next morning Bernhardt emerged from the guest house dressed as for an operetta safari, high-heeled shooting boots, wide-brimmed hat with pheasant feathers, white suede jacket on the lapel of which was pinned a wilting hibiscus blossom, and shouted dramatically to bring forth the "pirogues." There being no pirogues, they had to make do with a motorboat but could track down no prey. A gardener finally located the baby 'gator, tied its foot to a line, handed the other end to Bernhardt and she hauled in her trophy only to find out that it was in a state of hibernation. On being informed that it would in all likelihood sleep for three months, she had it shipped via freighter to her country house at Belle-Isle while she took a fast steamer back to France. When the creature arrived, as it was still in its torpor, Sarah uncrated it herself. Her tiny Manchester terrier, excited by the strange reptilian, barked madly and started snapping at its nose. The alligator, alas, came suddenly out of its long winter's sleep and snapped back and the small dog disappeared down the tooth-lined maw. Madame's secretary, Pitou, grabbed a gun and shot the beast and Sarah, grief-stricken over the loss of her pet, had the 'gator's head dissevered, mounted and hung in her hall. She would point it out to her guests and say mournfully, "My beloved little dog . . . his tomb!"

Michel Georges-Michel writes with affectionate amusement of Bernhardt's melodramatic impulses. He first met her when he was a lad of sixteen and begged her for a photograph which she promised to send him. When it arrived, she had written on it "To Michel Georges-Michel, a charming friend to whom I owe all." In his highly amusing book *Un Demi-Siècle de Gloires Théâtrales,* Georges-Michel tells of the time she spent two thousand francs for rolls with which to feed the sparrows of Paris. There was also the time when an elderly colonel came backstage filled with emotion over her performance. She in turn became filled with emotion upon learning that her visitor was adding to the glory of France not only by serving in the army, but by having fathered six children. "There's a colonel who gives his all for the Patrie!" she cried and insisted that he, his wife and all six children spend their next holiday with her at Belle-Isle, even forcing him to swear on his sword that they'd come. The colonel swore, departed and a month later turned up bag and baggage, wife and children at Belle-Isle only to be informed that the great lady could not be disturbed by tourists, that she had injured her knee, that all rooms in the house were already filled with guests and that at the moment, Madame was in the midst of a croquet game.

These are merely a few examples of Sarah Bernhardt's off-stage performance, seemingly undisciplined yet maybe deliberately calculated, for she had the flair for publicity plus a good showman's sense of perfect timing which had more than once gained her the epithet of "Sarah Barnum." Her onstage performance was another matter . . . always disciplined, always professional, always the superb actress of that magnetic, incandescent allure which made the public the world over call her "The Divine." Lucien Guitry loved her as a person and worshiped her as a consummate artist. In 1900 at the Théâtre Sarah Bernhardt, he played Sergeant Flambeau to her L'Aiglon. Bernhardt was fifty-six when she undertook this role of the young Duc de Reichstadt, yet the moment she stepped onto the stage, she became the ill-fated eighteen-year-old boy. Guitry used to stand in the wings every performance to listen to her great speech of the last act. It became great only when she spoke it, for Bernhardt could turn the utmost banality into Homeric poetry with her famous Golden Voice, which seemed to float about her and she appeared to follow it with her eyes. During her early days the poet Théodore de Banville had written, "You recite as the nightingale sings, as the wind sighs, as water murmurs, as Lamartine wrote." In later years, its curious quality was still there. Graham Robertson described it as "the cooing of doves, the running of streams, the falling of spring rain." After the 1914 war, Guitry was asked to take part in a charity benefit, playing a short scene opposite Sarah. They met to go over the script and started a reading run-through. Bernhardt was old and minus a leg. Her face was haggard, her hands like ancient claws, but her voice was still the *voix d'or* and she still glowed with that unique incandescence when she spoke a line. She read through her first long speech, at the end of which Guitry was supposed to come in with a reply. There was no sound from him. Bernhardt paused, then looked up. Lucien Guitry was dissolved in tears.

In 1900 Bernhardt started her own theatre in the Place du Châtelet and Guitry took over the management of the Théâtre de la Renaissance. He had moved there from the Comédie Française, taking with him as leading lady Marthe Brandès, an actress of sensitivity and powerful emotion. The Guitry-Brandès team eventually broke up, although it had been highly successful, and Guitry took on as co-star Jeanne Granier, a seductive and sparklingly malicious little actress. Her laugh sounded stifled, as though it were always under a pillow. She was pretty and extremely curvaceous, and Jules Renard, in whose play *Le Plaisir de Rompre* she appeared, wrote enthusiastically of "Jeanne Granier with her bosom swollen with talent." She had started out in operetta and when she appeared at the Capucines she captivated the Prince of Wales, who went backstage to present her with the flower from his buttonhole. Later he presented her with a collection of rare blue china, Granier undoubtedly presented the prince with a fair exchange, and her reputation was made. She was no longer young when she teamed up with Guitry to play in Maurice Donnay's *Amants* but she made an instant hit as a comedienne and was in demand for all the plays of the popular dramatists. The plays in which she appeared ran for months. Guitry found Granier vastly amusing and took a fiendish delight in playing tricks on her. One night during the middle of a scene, Jeanne was struck by one of those hellish mental blanks which will suddenly hit a performer during the course of a long run. The text called for her to cry out the name of the character Guitry was playing and she could not for the life of her think what it was. In a sweat of panic she waited for the moment when another player had a speech, then sidled over to Guitry and hissed in desperation, "What's your name? Quick! Quick!" and Guitry solemnly whispered back "Lucien Guitry."

A man warm in his friendships, he was never given to sentimentality. An acquaintance of his who had been a person of public distinction died and Guitry was asked to be an honorary pallbearer. There was the usual Requiem Mass followed by the customary funeral procession to Père Lachaise cemetery, the hearse leading the way at slow pace and the mourners following on foot. The church was miles away from the cemetery but Guitry plodded doggedly along with the rest. Halfway there, he turned to the man walking beside him and said, "You know? I'm already beginning to miss him!"

Lucien Guitry had a fine disregard for his own health. He had a bad heart but refused to believe it. His doctor, paraphrasing Molière, told him he was not a *malade imaginaire* but a *bien-portant imaginaire*. He was warned to slow down his super-abundant pace, that he had an extra systole. Guitry snorted: "As they don't know how to cure our illnesses, they baptize them!" and continued in his pace. That pace, free in its stride, high in its courage ended in 1925. He was sixty-five years old.

# 5

## TRISTAN BERNARD

### *Paris' Best-Loved and Fullest-Bearded Wit*

ᴘᴇʀʜᴀᴘs the last of the great *boulevardiers* . . . certainly the most endearing and the most popular . . . was the writer Tristan Bernard. Whenever he'd put in an appearance in any public place, people would call him by his first name whether they knew him or not, and even now, fourteen years since his death and some fifty since the height of his success, mention of "Tristan" could refer to only one person . . . Tristan Bernard whom Sacha Guitry called "Paris' best-loved and fullest-bearded wit."

He was born in 1866 at Besançon and he used to say there was a plaque on the house — that of a gas company. The house was on the Grande Rue, the same street as that on which Victor Hugo first saw the light of day . . . "only," as Bernard explained, "I was born at No. 23, the Master at No. 138 . . . to mark the difference." But if Tristan Bernard was not of Hugo's Olympian heights, he was a master of lighter and more down-to-earth creativity. His plays are joyous nonsense based on honest reality. The best-remembered of his many successes are *Le Petit Café, Triplepatte,* which, after months of sold-out business in Paris, ran for a year in London under the arch name of *Toodles* with Cyril Maude in the title role, and that hardy perennial *L'Anglais tel qu'on le parle* which, translated into "French As It's Spoken" has been revived by British and American amateur groups almost as many times as *Charley's Aunt.*

Bernard used to advise young authors to write for their own

pleasure, without hope of reward or assurance of the future. But he didn't at all abide by his own advice, for he frankly hated the effort of writing. To him it was a form of self-imposed torture and behind his seemingly effortless output, was a grim, plodding labor which it delighted him to postpone whenever in all conscience he could. If someone suggested coming by to see him, he'd say, "Please do. And preferably in the morning. That's when I work." One evening before turning in for the night, resolved to start work early the following day, he told the maid, "Elisa, wake me at seven. If by eight o'clock I'm not up, don't disturb me before noon." Mental discipline bored him. It reminded him of his lycée days when he was a notoriously lazy student and when his professor would try to inspirit the class with the noble example of Pascal who, as a young scholar, used to fight off his excruciating headaches with geometry whereas the youthful Tristan used to fight off geometry by pretending to have excruciating headaches. A member of Bernard's club made a remark which is pretty revelatory of the average man's club when he said, "There's nowhere that I sleep as well as in our big reading room," to which Tristan countered, "That's because you haven't tried my work study."

Hating to buckle down to work or not, the results of his labors were amazingly successful. He had only one big flop . . . some piece whose title is mercifully forgotten, but as flops go, it was spectacular. Coming into the theatre one night at eight-thirty as the hammer was pounding to announce the rise of the curtain, he looked about and said blithely, "Ah, the three blows! They're counting the house." Later during the brief run of this dismal little failure, a friend phoned to ask for a free seat. Bernard told him, "We give away entire rows only. But be sure to bring along your revolver as the place is deserted."

Tristan Bernard loved every aspect of the theatre. Generously appreciative of the good plays of rival dramatists, sympathetic over their failures, he was even indulgent over a bad performance and, if he were obliged to go backstage, would say to whoever was with him, "Come along, let's go lie." One show, however, was too atrocious for even his indulgence, and during the intermission he grabbed the opportunity for sneaking out. The doorman, recognizing him, hurried over to intercept him, saying, "Surely you're not going, maître? There's still another act!" Tristan, finger to lips, said, "Sh! That's why I'm leaving!" In his great good-nature, he actually felt kindly toward dramatic critics (they'd been kindly to him too on the main). He felt sorry for them, having to go to the theatre night after night not for purposes of pleasure, but as stern judges.

As a dramatist he himself was an excellent craftsman and his rules of playwriting are sound. "The audience always wants to be surprised," he stated, "but surprised by what they're expecting." Another rule was "Write any sort of play as long as the subject amuses you. But if you burn Moscow and upset thrones, do so because the little blonde no longer loves her husband on account of the dark young man who lives on the third floor of one of the houses you intend to burn." And a further good hint, "The principal quality of the successful author is a special gift for handling subjects which are not new, without being stale."

Budding playwrights were frequently coming to him for advice and he was humorously kind to them. One young hopeful disturbed his morning work hours entreating him to help him put a title to his play. Bernard, who had not read the play, thought for a moment then asked, "Are there any trumpets in your play?"

"No, maître," answered the young man, somewhat taken aback.

"Any drums?"

"Why no!"

"Then call it 'Without Drums or Trumpets.'"

In addition to his plays, he wrote a number of excellent novels and short essays for the *Nouvelle Revue,* a literary magazine of much distinction which paid its contributors such meager remuneration that whenever Bernard signed a receipt for the amount of pay, he wrote his name with a lower-case *b*. In collaboration with his brother-in-law Pierre Veber, he turned out a humorous supplement called "Chasseur de Chevelure"* which appeared at the end of each issue of the *Revue Blanche* and wrote sports articles for various newspapers. He was an expert on horse racing, an enthusiast of the prize ring, and ardently keen about the current bicycling craze. So keen, in fact, that he edited a weekly cyclist's publication called *Le Journal des Vélocipédistes* and was the director of two arenas, the Vélodrome Buffalo at the Porte de Neuilly and the Vélodrome de la Seine at Levallois-Peret. A well-known lithograph by his friend Toulouse-Lautrec shows him at the Buffalo, in knickerbockers, small "melon" hat, legs wide apart as if to balance the protruding black beard as intently he watches the track. He himself took no part in any sports. "I am," he'd say, "a fervent spectator of the efforts of others."

New inventions intrigued him and he was all for the daring delights of the automobile. Lucien Guitry one of his closest friends, owned a "tuff-tuff," the latest Panhard model with high wheels, rear entrance to the back seat and a wicker umbrella holder strapped to the side. It was bravely open to the elements and was driven by an impressive chauffeur with goggles, a bearskin coat and a talent for crawling under the car at the first breakdown. Bernard's other close friend was Jules Renard. Renard was a touchy, petulant little man, prone to temper and nervous tics, but Bernard and Guitry were fond of him and the three went about a lot together, with the occasional addition of Alfred Capus. They'd venture out into the country in Guitry's motorcar, Guitry

* The Scalp Hunter.

running everything as though he were directing a play. There were, of course, no road signs in those unencumbered days and Guitry conducted their course with a crude map and a primitive Michelin booklet of landmarks, shouting out directions to the chauffeur in his mighty actor's voice. During one trip, as they drove into a town, Guitry in a theatrical tone of triumph announced, "We have arrived in Cervic!" Tristan, who had caught sight of a name over a town hall said quietly, "Yes. But the local inhabitants call it Villeneuve."

Tristan Bernard was that rare individual, a successful man who never had an enemy. He wrote somewhere that "one forgives an author for having a success. One never forgives him for making money." Yet Bernard made money and all the world forgave him, for he was a man of genuine *bonhomie*. He had friends everywhere and was equally at home in the literary scene, the world of sport and that chic stratification known as *le Monde*. He was a highlight in some of the intellectual salons, and warmly welcome on the turf or at the ring. Every summer he'd spend two or three weeks at Deauville where along with the Prince of Wales he lost royally at baccarat. One afternoon he appeared on the grand promenade in a jaunty yachting cap which he said he'd won from the previous night's winnings. Upon being congratulated, he said sadly, "But what I lost would have bought me the yacht."

Tristan Bernard was the last of the widely quoted *diseur-de-mots*. But like those of his fellow wit and playwright, Georges Courteline, his were neither surface smart nor deliberately cruel. It is surprising that his humor came so readily, for he himself said with some truth that "it's not difficult to be witty if one is malicious." But Bernard was never malicious, he was essentially *bon*. Even his occasional jibes were good-natured and no one took offense. A young author who was about to give his first conference before a literary group came to him for advice and asked how one should wind up a lecture. "Very simple," said Tristan. "You pick up your papers, you rise from the reading table, you bow to the audience and then go off on tiptoe."

"Why on tiptoe?"

"So as not to wake them up!"

Any and every amusing remark that went the rounds was automatically attributed to Bernard. He found it vastly amusing and somewhat absurd that his *mots* should be so widely quoted, and claimed that most of them were apochryphal . . . another case of Talleyrand never having uttered so many brilliant comments until after his death. He once made a funny observation to a friend who roared with delight and declared that only he could have said it. Bernard then admitted that he'd read it that morning in a paper.

"But you used it as your own!" the friend protested.

"Yes," said Tristan. "To make it authentic."

But his own spontaneous wit bore the stamp of authenticity. It was he who one day on a busy street was accidentally hit and knocked down by an immense grandfather clock which a workman was carrying on his shoulders. Instead of being angry, he got to his feet, brushed off the dust and said to the workman, "Why don't you wear a wristwatch like everybody else?" And then there was the time when Emile Bergerat, the chronicler of the *Figaro,* who was about to get married, confiding in him the story of his life, admitted the awkward fact that he was a natural child. Bernard tried to reassure him by saying that we are all more or less natural children. "But," Bergerat went on, "my mother was living in marital relations with a priest." Bernard paused then said earnestly, "With whom more honorable would you want your mother to live?"

He had an exuberant zest for living, an irresponsible love of nonsense and the joyousness of a child let loose to play. When he traveled (and being a Frenchman, he seldom did) and stopped for a meal in a strange hotel, he'd summon the chief porter, give his name and order any telegrams or urgent messages to be brought to him immediately. If the porter asked if he were expecting any such communications, Tristan would say no, he wasn't expecting any at all as nobody knew he was there. In one restaurant, when his soup was served he told the waiter that he was sorry but he couldn't eat it. The waiter took it away and returned with the other *soupe du jour* and Bernard said he was still sorry but he couldn't eat that either. At this the proprietor hurried over, protesting that no customer had ever complained about their soups before, they were excellent. "I'm sure they're delicious," Bernard agreed, "but I haven't got a spoon." After the success of Rostand's barnyard allegorical drama *Chantecler,* Bernard found himself one evening sitting in a theatre box next to its author who was one of his good friends. Reaching into his pocket to extract a handkerchief, Tristan discovered some stray bread crumbs. He tossed them into Rostand's box, saying, "Pour Chantecler."

Jules Renard in one of his journal entries speaks of spending the evening with a group of friends at the Napo, including "Bernard with his mouth like a frail pink boat in the black river of his beard." As the river of beard disguised his features, the "pink boat" wore a warm and constant smile that disguised an inner sensitivity which only his intimates knew existed. Jean-Jacques Bernard, the son, in a charming and tender book, *Mon Père, Tristan Bernard,* says that his father's wit was "the mask of emotion, even sometimes the laughter of anguish, nearly always the outflow of profound truth. It was honest humor, plunging its roots into the depths of the human heart, and the sap that rose was made up of all that the human heart contains." He had the gift of making and keeping friends, and he had a great capacity for love. "One talks about the illusions of those who love," he wrote somewhere. "One would do better to talk about the blindness of those who don't love." Bernard knew no such blindness. He had no cautions, no inhibitions with his affections. "What resembles love," he said, "is always love." He adored his family. Jean-Jacques' memoirs show him as a gay and enchanting parent. Tristan had his own racing stable and his wife had hers. In order that his sons should not feel left out, he organized a third stable the horses of which were lead and they raced on a track of green baize cloth spread on the dining-room table. Each spurt was determined by a throw of dice and the whole affair went by the impressive name of the "R.P.C." or "Racing Plomb Club" . . . *plomb* being French for lead. He'd put on unpredictable, idiotic acts at home, such as rising in the middle of a meal to throw a napkin over his arm and imitate a pompous maître d'hôtel, or, during a dinner party, disappearing from the room to return a minute or two later as a trapper from the frozen North, swathed in the furs of the lady guests which he'd purloined from the cloakroom. "I'll never grow into second childhood," he admitted. "I've never emerged from first."

He had a naïve way of writing out maxims for himself and pinning them up on the walls of his study. "Don't count on anybody but yourself . . . and not too much on that!" or "People are always sincere. They simply change their sincerities." Some of them seem worthy of La Rochefoucauld. "If an individual insists upon walking straight in the midst of a crowd that's walking zigzag, it's he who'll give the impression of walking zigzag," and "Love affairs are like mushrooms. One doesn't know if they're the safe or the poisonous variety until it's too late."

There was a scholarly side to this worldly humorist. Jean-Jacques says that he first began really to know his father when he was ten and Tristan placed a book in his small hands, saying,

"Read this aloud. It's *The Cid.*" Up till then the boy had read of the classic dramatists only Molière, "a heady brew which intoxicated me for life and raised for me the curtain of the theatre." His father's sudden command to start in on Corneille came as a shock and a subsequent delight. Tristan had a passion for Corneille, whom he called "that illustrious little-known . . . and *human!* so terribly human in spite of the professors!" He had reverence for Victor Hugo too, but it paled before his veneration for Corneille. Jean-Jacques recalls that after the opening night of a revival of Hugo's *Hernani* at the Comédie Française . . . a classic Tristan knew by heart . . . he paused on the way out before the bust of Corneille and said, "It's all right, my friend, you may sleep tranquilly." He loved the great French poets . . . Ronsard, Villon, Marot, the fables of La Fontaine and the Verlaine of *Sagesse.* He was enchanted with Verlaine's utter disregard of the traditionalists, "one poet who, thank God, did not spring full-grown out of the flank of Papa Hugo." Poetry moved and exalted him. Jean-Jacques writes of summer evenings in their Brittany cottage, remote and silent except for the pounding of the distant sea and the occasional cry of a curlew when his father would recite some of the countless poems he knew by heart. He'd speak the familiar lines with love and as he'd finish, there would be tears in his eyes.

He had wanted to be a poet himself. As a young man, he'd written a fair amount of verse which, in those days, had come easily. Thinking back on that facility he burst into this wistful quatrain:

> *Où donc est-il, ce temps charmant*
> *Où le mot m'arrivait si vite?*
> *Le mot venait d'abord et la pensée ensuite —*
> *J'etais un poète vraiment.**

---

* Where has it gone, that charming time when the words came to me so readily? The words came first and the thought afterward. I was a true poet.

Even in later years he had not lost the gift. One of his happiest verses is "The Amazon and the Centaur":

> *L'Amazone passait. Sur le bord de la route*
> *Un Centaur y pensait, dès plus visiblement,*
> *Mais l'Amazone triste, et qu'assiège un doute:*
> *"Est-ce à moi qu'il en veut ou bien à ma jument?"**

The first of the World Wars broke out and Jean-Jacques enlisted. He was stationed at Compiègne and before starting for the front, he got leave to go as far as Creuil for a few hours. Tristan journeyed over to be with him. It was January and father and son sat up all night in the freezing bedroom of a small, unheated hotel. There was a lump of ice in the water pitcher. They talked and talked, recalled family events, laughed a bit, but mostly they just talked . . . of any and everything except what was in both their minds. At dawn they went to the bleak station where they waited two hours and watched the endless flow of trains loaded with munitions and provisions going out, the empties rattling back to be reloaded . . . "the veins and arteries of the war in double circulation. One learns that one is of use." The son asked if he believed in God. "Yes. These days." he answered.

During those war years, Bernard's chief consolation was his grandchildren. He took particular delight in one small grandson who asked him, "Dis, Grandpapa, is it true that Clemenceau has saved France?"

"Yes, mon cheri."

"Like Joan of Arc?"

"Sort of."

"Then why don't they burn him too?"

Tristan had two wives. Of the first one hears little. It must have

---

* The Amazon passed by. On the edge of the road a Centaur thought about her . . . and most visibly so. But the Amazon, sad and filled with doubt: "Is it me he wants, or is it my mare?"

been a marriage which had its ups and downs. One afternoon of pouring rain, Louis Verneuil came across him standing forlornly in front of a shop window and asked if he were waiting for someone. "No," said Bernard. Verneuil suggested that he dine with him and Bernard again said no. "Then at least have a drink with me at the Napo." Tristan thanked him and said he wasn't thirsty. "But you're not going to stand out here in the rain! Why don't you go home?" "I don't dare," came the lugubrious reply. "Don't dare? Why?" "Because my wife's lover is there. And . . ." he added with vehemence . . . "he's a goddam bore!"

Tristan Bernard was a man who could never take himself seriously. After he had become one of the top playwrights and humorists of his country, Maurice Donnay talked him into applying for admission to the Academy. The complications of putting oneself up for membership among the forty Immortals are well known. Not the least of these is the initial letter of application, which should be a gem of brevity and exquisite composition, carefully handwritten on fine stationery and formally presented to the Permanent Secretary who at the time was René Doumic, director of the *Revue des Deux Mondes*. Tristan couldn't be bothered with any such ceremonial. He scribbled off his letter on the blue, lightweight blank of a fifty-centime *pneumatique* which shot its way through the network of those mysterious underground tubes of compressed air and onto the desk of the Permanent Secretary. Doumic had hardly recovered from the shock before a second *pneu* arrived saying that after further thought, the writer had decided not to present himself for membership in the Academy. Later he said to Donnay, "Me Academician? No! The costume costs too much [it does mount up into the thousands]. I'll wait till someone dies who's my size."

This was not an act of bravura, it was typical of his inherent casualness. He was casual about formalities and shockingly casual about his clothes. It was nothing for him to arrive at a smart dinner party in evening jacket and a pair of old trousers he'd forgotten to change. His tie was always crooked, his shoes often unpolished, and nothing fitted him properly. At one formal soirée he listened to an exquisitely turned-out dandy boasting about the fact that his tailor gave him a special discount as being such a good ad for his establishment. Bernard, growing bored, cut in, "My tailor gives me a special discount too . . . on condition that I don't tell anyone where I get my suits." He was also casual about the social amenities . . . never deliberately rude and so candidly frank, one couldn't get angry with him. He'd been invited to dine one evening at a house that was famous for its excellent food. He was late and the hostess, a stickler for promptness, called him on the telephone. "I'm so sorry," said Bernard, "but I'm not coming."

"Not coming?"

"No. I'm not hungry."

He was casual too, and to an alarming degree, about money. He made a great deal and he spent a great deal and he had no idea where it went, since he never kept accounts. At one point, he learned to his utter amazement that he was just about bankrupt. His lawyer scolded him as one would a child and told him that he had to cut down his expenses. "Ah, mais non!" cried Bernard. "I have enough annoyances without taking on privations!" He may not have taken on privations but he did have to withdraw his entire account from the Banque de France in order to settle his debts. On his way out, with the check for the full amount in his hand, he passed the armed guard stationed at the entrance, nodded and said, "Thank you, my friend. You can go home now."

One of the sources of his financial troubles was a prodigal

generosity in the way of charity and handouts. He could never pass a beggar without giving him something and word got around the tramp set that he was an easy mark. A certain filthy old *clochard* used to station himself outside the Bernard doorway at an hour when he knew the master of the house was likely to emerge. One afternoon in early July, seeing him standing in his accustomed spot, hat in hand, Tristan took a sizable bill from his wallet and handed it to him, saying, "We're leaving tomorrow for Normandy. Here's two months' donation in advance. You have a right to your vacation too." Bernard made one mistake when, out of pity, he befriended a presumptuous derelict of a somewhat military appearance who called himself Major Heitner. The man was utterly worthless but he could fake a certain distinction of manner and his very gall amused the good-natured author. He, at the time, had just finished a book, comic but fairly pornographic . . . so much so, in fact, that he hesitated to sign his name to it. By way of a lark, he arranged to have it appear as the work of Major Heitner and the book had the usual short but popular sale of most lightweight but salacious novels. The "Major" made a good thing of it, he not only received one third of the royalties but, in his new capacity as a successful author, he demanded that his living circumstances be worthy of his advancement and Tristan found himself cheerfully footing bills for restaurants, new lodgings, clothing, barber services and even special manicures! Finally Mme. Bernard and the family lawyer decided to call a halt and Tristan himself realized the prank had become too costly. Sending for the "Major" he explained that he felt he had done enough for him "and besides," he added, "I have so many commitments." The panhandler pondered the situation for a moment, then said brightly, "Count me as one of your commitments, monsieur." And Bernard thought this warranted another handout.

Tristan Bernard lived on through the turn of the century and into four of the ensuing decades. His zest for life was as keen as ever. "Death is nothing," he said. "Only old age fills me with horror." There came the Second World War and with it the fall of France. Bernard was a Jew, but he stayed on in Paris until the authorities had him moved to Cannes. Even in this exile he could still joke. "Fifty-seven years ago," he told a friend, "I did my voluntary service at Evreux. Now I'm forced to do my involuntary service on the Côte d'Azur." The involuntary service on the Côte d'Azur did not last long. The Nazis had taken control of the country and the Gestapo was rounding up all Jews regardless of age, rank or distinction. Bernard took his place in the lineup of white-faced men and women, screaming children and silent, bewildered babies. With them, he was crowded into a foul freight car bound for the north and the horror camp at Drancy. During that hideous trip, he was an unforgettable figure of serenity and fortitude. "Friends." He spoke to his terrified companions. "Up to now we have lived in fear. Now we are going to live in hope." At Drancy he continued to set the calm, courageous example he'd shown on the prison train. His memory stood him in good stead and, as years ago with his family in the peaceful Brittany cottage, now in unspeakable confines close to the smoking gas chambers, he'd fill many of the interminable hours reciting the poems of Ronsard, the fables of La Fontaine, the lyrics of Verlaine and the heroic couplets of his beloved Corneille. The listeners were French Jews, many of them persons of intellect. The sound of their native language and their native literature lovingly spoken by this man of simple goodness may have made it quieter for those who were to die.

Tristan survived his horror camp. Not all of his family survived theirs. His grandson François, Jean-Jacques' eldest boy, a promising young painter, perished at Mauthausen. Tristan was released from Drancy and returned to Paris, a defeated man. He had grown very deaf. When friends suggested a hearing aid, he'd repel the idea, saying, "What's the use? One hears only the same things." And yet, exhausted and anguished as he was, he harbored no bitterness. "Sorrow and tribulation have not changed me," he said. "I hate only one thing. That's hatred."

A square in Paris has been named after Tristan Bernard. It is at the meeting section of the Ternes and the rues d'Armaille and Saint-Ferdinand. At the dedication ceremony, Bernard's good friend Roland Dorgelès, who has written beautifully about the man whom he calls "le philosophe du sourire,"* gave the address. He wound it up with:

At night, when the town belongs to its shadows, he will come here to sit between Triplepatte and Monsieur Comodat (two characters from his plays). He will talk with his friends of the past, he'll go back over his memories and when the last night-wanderers and the early morning workers pass by, he'll come forth with a *mot* from force of habit. But that *mot,* alas, we shall not hear.

* The philosopher of the smile.

# 6

## SOME SALONS
## AND THEIR LEADERS

THE BELLE EPOQUE was the twilight era of the French salon. Within a few years there would be no more of those gracious gatherings in settings of tasteful opulence, where on a set day of the week a gifted hostess would receive her coterie of "regulars," along with special celebrities of current distinction and a judicious sprinkling of pretty and well-born women. The tradition of France's salon, over three hundred years old, was primarily a woman's tradition. Except for the literary cénacles of men-of-letters, Mallarmé's Tuesdays on the rue de Rome or de Goncourt's Sundays in his Auteuil *grenier* which were more on the order of men's clubs, the salon had always been run by a woman. It was created by the extraordinary spinster sister of Louis XIV, La Grande Mademoiselle, launched firmly on its way by Mme. de Rambouillet, kept sparkling by the wit of Mme. du Deffand (it was she who remarked apropos of the miracle of St. Denis strolling about Paris with his severed head under one arm, "It's the first few strides that count"). Mme. du Deffand's protégée, Julie de Lespinasse, continued the tradition through her ineffable charm. After the Revolution, Mme. Récamier revived the cultural custom, during the Second Empire Pauline Metternich and Princesse Mathilde kept it staunchly going, and toward the turn of the century there still existed a number of select and stimulating drawing rooms.

The salons of the '90's were the inheritors of those of the two

Empires which, in turn, had inherited those of the monarchy. They had flourished only in periods of wealth and aristocracy. Observers have remarked that one needed a king, no matter how worthless or idiotic, as a figurehead and Fernand Gregh has written, "A Republic, even an Athenian one, cannot have a real salon." However, the republican hostesses did their best which in certain milieus was more than good, flavored as their assemblies were with the graciousness of the past plus a keen awareness of the present. Admission to the leading salons was for an exceptional elite. Wealth and breeding alone did not make for eligibility. The necessary attributes could be literary or political distinction, a high position in the world of the arts, or merely intelligence, charm of manner, an ability to amuse and, above all, to appreciate.

The career of the successful salon leader was an exacting one for even the cleverest of women. She must have grace, sensitivity, a talent for organization and the energy of a field marshal. When a woman embarked on the career of a salon leader, she had time for little else. As one husband remarked, with glum resignation, "Breakfast is the only meal to which no one is invited." She had to keep up a vast social correspondence, in her own hand, of course. Her household had to be run with perfection, her cuisine and wines must be of the best (no mean feat in France). She must keep herself well primed on topics of the day and be up on the latest trends in literature and the arts. Her intimate coterie, the "regulars" who came every week to her dinners and soirées, must get on well with each other and with her special guests. Above all, they must be acceptable to her "Great Man." For nearly every hostess had her *grand homme*. He was her showcase exhibit, the celebrity for whom she ran her weekly gatherings and sometimes her life. The *grand homme* was a further part of the salon tradition. Julie de Lespinasse had planned her recep-

tions for the pleasure of the Encyclopedist, D'Alembert, Mme. du
Deffand had established Horace Walpole as the sun about which
to set whirling her satellites. Madame Récamier, from her Direc-
toire settee, ran her evenings solely for the entertainment of
Chateaubriand, and more recently, Mme. Juliette Adam had built
up one of the most stimulating salons of the century around her
lion . . . and lion indeed he was, that nineteenth century Danton,
man of the masses, Léon Gambetta. The *grand homme* was the
star performer and the hostess was his producer, manager and
devoted slave. She exerted every effort to keep him within the
confines of her special circle with the ferocity of a mistress
guarding her lover . . . which was sometimes the case. Any
invitation from a rival hostess was the signal for social warfare.
She would even go so far as to get her intimate friends to act as
spies and keep her informed about the activities in other houses,
whether her pet lion had been there and whether he seemed to be
overly enjoying himself. How the salon leader's husband, if she
had one, counted in the situation, is subject for speculation.
Sometimes his was the ignominious position of the spouse of the
militant American clubwoman. Sometimes, though rarely, he
shared his wife's enthusiasm for the captive lion and acted as
joint host. But more often he left her to carry on her own incense
burning while he spent a pleasant evening at his club or an even
pleasanter one in the arms of his current *chère amie*.

The running of a successful salon required many things, one
of which was money, for it was an expensive business. The setting
was also vastly important. The salon itself, the drawing-room set
apart for these gatherings, must have its individuality and special
charm. Paul Hervieu in one of his gracefully worldly novels
calls this room "a place of civilization from which all material
utility has been banished . . . whose sole use is that of being useless,
a place of perpetual parade where all acts are leisurely and all

words suitable, in which the time spent is a luxury. Can't one conceive that there is a state of art in this completely artificial atmosphere?" In addition to the large drawing room, it was almost imperative to have a ballroom or what was termed by smart Parisians in their fad for anglicizing words, a "hall." A "hall" wasn't a hall at all, but a formally impressive area that could serve as both ballroom and auditorium. During the '80's and '90's it was unthinkable for an up-to-date *hôtel privé* not to have a "hall." They were used most often for musicales and a particular feature of their charm were the fashionable women who adorned the audience. Alluring as Boldini portraits, tulle scarves billowing off bare shoulders, necks arched and vulnerable beneath the stray wisps from their soft hairtwists, they sat on gilt chairs in carefully rapturous poses. Edmond de Goncourt writes in his Journal, "What I love about music are the women who listen to it." And Jules Renard in his daily diary said that there was no prettier sight in town than an audience of young matrons at an evening concert. He only regretted that nature had not endowed them with ears like little racehorses which they could prick forward in unison the better to hear.

Concerts, theatricals and whatever else might be held in the "hall" were extracurricular to the regular salon gatherings which depended for entertainment solely on that amenity which the French have developed into a great art . . . conversation. The trend of conversation varied according to the nature of the salon . . . political, literary, artistic. The hostess of the political salon had not only to keep up with French politics, she had actually to understand them. The literary hostess had to do a great deal of homework, reading the best of current books and articles, wading through the Academy prizes and skimming the pages of the literary reviews, the *Revue des Deux Mondes,* the *Revue Blanche* and the countless others. There were salons of Old

World formality, as stiffly ceremonious as eighteenth century Versailles, there were others of ease and lively stimulus and there were a few determinedly highbrow houses into which the visitor entered with the awed sense of entering a church. There were salon queens who ruled with wit and charm; others who justified the contention that "women don't become bluestockings until men are no longer interested in the color of their stockings." And there were a few who seemed less like hostesses than schoolmistresses, the sort who, according to Paul Morand, "maintained rigid rules of discussion and directed the conversation with all the softness of a president of assizes." Morand was clearly referring to Mme. Aubernon.

Mme. Aubernon whose mother, Mme. de Nerville, had been a salon leader before her, was a formidable lady with the Christian name of Euphrasie-Héloïse-Lydie although it's doubtful if anyone ever called her that. In her house on the Square de Messine, she ruled over a choice literary coterie and she ruled with the aid of a large silver bell which she'd clang vigorously when she wanted the company's undivided attention or when conversation threatened to break up into pairs. Any side talk was strictly forbidden at Mme. Aubernon's and the slightest whispered word to one's neighbor brought a reprimand. Her silver bell was surmounted by a statue of Saint Louis and inscribed about the edge with a precept of that sanctified monarch, "If you have something to say that will interest the entire company, then speak up . . . otherwise, be still." It was her purpose to see to it that everybody abode by this rule.

There was never any carefree chatter at Mme. Aubernon's. Conversation was general in the sense that everyone participated, but with no fluent give and take. She obliged her guests to speak one at a time as though at a board meeting, to speak well and preferably brilliantly. While one person held forth, the rest listened with the attentive respect an audience pays to a violin virtuoso at a concert. It could be an ordeal for both listeners and speakers. Mme. Aubernon would toss out a subject to someone, give him or her the floor until she felt they'd all heard enough, then she'd ring her bell and the subject would go the rounds of the table after which she'd toss out another subject. It was a system which incensed some, amused others and terrified more than a few. During one dinner, a young woman was so panic-stricken at the thought of having to speak that she pulled her rosary out of her reticule and started saying her beads. Guests were expected to come more or less prepared with a subject for general discussion. It was a little like attending an esoteric debating society. Not all of Madame's guests were as cowed as the young woman who said her beads. The attractive Mme. Baignières, a spirited lady whom gossips called "Le tour qui n'a pas prit garde,"* arrived a bit late one evening and before she had time to be seated, her hostess called out to her, "You've come just in time, my dear. We were discussing adultery. What do you think of it?"

"So sorry," replied Mme. Baignières. "Tonight I've come prepared only on incest."

It is amazing that with such roughshod tactics Mme. Aubernon could attract the distinguished people who came to her house. Among these were Edmond de Goncourt, Leconte de Lisle, Ferdinand Brunetière, editor of the *Revue des Deux Mondes,* Hèredia the poet and the author-diplomat Maurice Paléologue. The critic Jules Lemaître used also to come until he was spirited away by another salon leader, Mme. de Loynes, and so did Anatole France until Mme. de Caillavet took him under her smothering wing. In earlier days the Olympian god of them

---

* The Tower that wasn't on guard, a reference to the old nursery song "La Tour prend garde."

all, Victor Hugo, had occasionally been her guest. Philosophers, playwrights, scholars, Academicians, she gathered them all in and was not overimpressed by any. She'd call the great ones to order with as much severity as the lesser. "Keep quiet, Pailleron!" she barked at the author of *Le Monde ou l'on s'ennuie.* "You'll speak when your turn comes!" During her dinner in honor of Ernest Renan, she overheard the eminent sage muttering some side comment and started energetically ringing her bell. As the company became obediently silent she announced, "Our illustrious friend is expressing some valuable ideas which I'm sure we shall all want to hear." France's great apostle of Free Thought meekly explained, "I was just asking for another helping of peas."

Apart from the lady's aggressive tactics, a further reason for amazement that these remarkable personages should attend her dinners time and again is the fact that her food was lamentably inferior. It had the dismal quality of that of a second-class Grand Hotel in the provinces. For her, the only food of any importance was that of the intellect and she didn't see why it shouldn't be so for everybody else. She left the arrangements to her chef, told him there'd always be twelve or fourteen people to dinner twice a week and paid him twenty thousand francs a year with which to do the marketing. Either the chef didn't recognize quality when he saw it or he made a good thing of matters by purchasing inferior produce and pocketing the difference. It became a cliché among the literary set to say, "I'm off to Mme. Aubernon's to dine badly." And yet, Madame had a curious way of speaking of her guests who conversed particularly well as "dining well." If one was a "good diner" . . . in other words, if one said one's say clearly and with aplomb, one was invited back. The charmingly patrician and courteous poet, Henri de Régnier, official representative of Symbolism in the French Academy, apparently didn't make the grade. "He eats well, but he dines badly," she said of him. The only celebrity who blandly ignored her militant rules of order was Gabriele D'Annunzio, who visited Paris amid considerable fanfare and whom she was able to grab for one of her dinners. Feeling that the moment for the high point of the evening had arrived, she rang her bell and asked exuberantly, "Signor D'Annunzio, what do you think of love?" Italy's literary giant gave her a withering look and quelled her with "Read my books, madame, and let me finish my meal."

Mme. Aubernon was a flamboyant lady of Rubens-esque proportions who dressed in clothes of pastel shades trimmed in bright braid and flying ribbons. She wore pompons on her shoes and giddy little ornaments in her hair. She claimed that these gay colors banished gloom. Her absurdity at times could be almost endearing. If she were invited to the Academy to hear the reception address of a newly elected member, she'd arrive in the visitor's gallery resplendent from head to foot in the royal purple of the Institute. She called it her homage to France's forty Immortals.

She was quite cavalier about the things she said, and she said a great deal, for this strenuous lady could talk for ten, even twelve hours at a stretch. She hated pretty women who, she claimed, drained men of both money and character. Worse, they distracted them from stimulating general conversation into frivolous side talk. She bluntly told one young matron who came to her for advice on how to run a salon, "Don't try! You have too luscious a bosom to keep the conversation general." She was agitated about the expanding birth rate and all against large families. A group of visitors arriving one evening were greeted by the jubilant announcement, "My daughter-in-law has just had a superb miscarriage!" There had been a Monsieur Aubernon, but only briefly so. After a scant few years of marriage, George Aubernon, a states councilor, could stand the strain of his wife's exuberance no longer and went off to spend the rest of his life in Antibes. As she blithely told one gathering of diners, "My husband and I will soon be celebrating our golden anniversary of cloudless separation."

There could be rather bawdy moments in the conversation at Mme. Aubernon's table. There was one guest who, talking about his little boy, spoke of the child asking him, "Papa, when you and Maman went on your honeymoon in Italy, where was I?" "And what did you tell him?" asked Mme. Aubernon. "I thought for a moment," the man answered, "then I said, 'You went there with me and came back with your mother.' " Paul Bourget brought Barbey d'Aurevilly there one time. The eccentric author of the fantastic *Les Diaboliques* was a deliberate vulgarian. After dinner when Mme. Aubernon tactfully suggested that he might care to join the gentlemen for a smoke, Barbey d'Aurevilly said in a loud voice, "Madame, I have a bladder of brass. I pee only twice a day . . . once in the morning, and again at night when I pray." Barbey d'Aurevilly could be amusingly perceptive about other authors. He dismissed the satirical novelist-publicist Edmond About as "a *gamin* who runs after the stagecoach of Voltaire without ever catching up" and of Voltaire himself he said, "His punishment is to have become the god of imbeciles."

For all her bumptious dictatorship, Mme. Aubernon had a kind heart. From the salon of her mother, Mme. de Nerville, she had inherited three or four "stray cats," pitiful old horrors, badly dressed and grotesquely made up. But she was good to them and invited them occasionally to the receptions which followed her Wednesday dinners or to the theatricals presented in her "hall," explaining with a good-natured shrug to any raised eyebrows, "Oh well, I have my sacred monsters as I have my charities."

With her abounding vitality, she had an unquenchable thirst for matters of the intellect and worked constantly at culture as an Olympics contestant at training, keeping strident pace with all trends in literature, drama and the arts. During the Russian literary invasion when Tolstoy and Dostoevsky had crossed the European borders, she joined the faddists who called one another pet names like "my pigeon" and "little father." She went in for Ibsen with determination and appropriate gloom. A friend calling on her one rainy afternoon and finding her deep in *The Lady from the Sea* was peremptorily admonished, "Shhh! Don't disturb me! I'm in the midst of acquiring a Norwegian soul!" She called her "hall" the Théâtre de Messine, after the name of the square on which she lived. Here she put on several of Ibsen's plays and she put them remarkably well. They were meticulously staged, tirelessly rehearsed and played by talented amateurs with almost professional excellence. For the three performances she gave of *John Gabriel Borkman* there had been one hundred and sixteen rehearsals over a period of fifteen months. Molière and Racine were given first-rate productions and so were the contemporary playwrights Henri Becque and Victorien Sardou. Sometimes she engaged professional casts with big theatre names. On one glamorous occasion, Réjane and Antoine starred in Becque's *Parisienne*.

Her chief pride was to put on a play by Alexandre Dumas *fils* . . . *Françillon* and, of course, *La Dame aux Camélias*. For Dumas *fils* was Mme. Aubernon's *grand homme* in whose honor she ran her dinners, her receptions, her concerts and theatricals. In her adulation of Dumas she tried to run him too and she all but ran him to death. Dumas took her expansive incense-burning as his due just as he took his unwavering success as a matter of course. He had hit on a surefire formula and seemed never to have had a failure. His plays all follow the same pattern, harp on the same piously moral theme, and Bernard Shaw dismissed them as the stereotype "Dumas filial drama." They are smoothly written, perfectly constructed diatribes against illicit love (with which their author was considerably familiar through many early liaisons plus the constantly galling reminder of his own illegitimacy). They deal with the frail and repentant sinner, the good woman wronged by the heartless rake, the decent young man ruined by the venal courtisane. The sermonizing content of Dumas' works is so much sentimental trash. Their unerring sense of theatre and superlative construction is quite a different thing, which makes one realize why to this day they still enthrall their audiences at the Française. Even Shaw had grudgingly to admit in regard to Dumas *fils* that "a man without any worth as a thinker, whose imagination is weak and whose culture is mediocre can, nevertheless, be a first rate playwright."

For all the tiresome moralizing inherent in his plays, Alexandre Dumas *fils* was a worldly man of charm and delightful small talk. One evening at Mme. Aubernon's when old Marshal Canrobert, who had retired from military life to take up politics, apologized for not hearing what someone was saying and added, "I am deaf, although I'm a senator," Dumas congratulated him, saying: "What a happy fate for a senator!" In reference to a former beauty he'd known in the past, now grown faded and raddled, he remarked wistfully, "When I saw her, she reminded me of my youth . . . but not of hers." Before one of his openings at the Gymnase, a giddy little actress fluttering with stage-fright rushed over to him and chirped, "Oh, Monsieur Dumas, feel how my heart's beating!" Dumas was of course glad to oblige. "How does it feel?" quavered the soubrette. "Round," answered Dumas.

Dumas was attractive to women. They, in turn, were attractive to him but not obsessively so. As for the great national pastime of "galanterie," he was always pronouncing its death sentence. "All that adultery amounts to," he wrote, "is for the woman, hatred, and for the man, contempt." Not that he was above occasionally practicing it himself. Once at Trouville,

Dumas found himself not only in the same hotel but on the same floor as a young married woman whose husband came down only on weekends. The lady had met Dumas at Mme. Aubernon's, hadn't liked him and had told someone within his hearing that she considered him a boorish man with whom one could never spend more than an hour. During the midweek at Trouville, Dumas laid siege to the young woman, broke down her defenses and managed to have a rendezvous with her in her room. At the end of one hour's dalliance, he walked to the door. "Madame," he said, "you called me a boorish man with whom one could never spend more than an hour. Your time is up!" and with a formal bow he departed.

Mme. Aubernon was a jealous hostess. She hated to hear about any of her celebrities starring in other salons and if Dumas occasionally managed to stray from her clutches, she'd be highly indignant. "Dumas is never as witty with others as he is with me," she'd boast. Her ego was as enormous as her body and her tact nonexistent. She claimed that brilliant people were brilliant only at her table and she blithely told two well-known hostesses, Mme. Buloz and Mme. Janzé, that she loved dining in different houses because it proved to her how much more people enjoyed themselves in hers.

When Mme. Arman de Caillavet, the future friend and guide of Anatole France, was in her youth, Mme. Aubernon had taken her on as a protégée. The young woman was keenly intelligent and the ever possessive Mme. Aubernon tried to keep a firm hold of her as an ornament to her salon and a useful companion to herself who could be counted upon to run errands and help her with her heavy correspondence. However, the youthful Mme. de Caillavet had ambition and a strong will of her own and her will was to start a salon herself in her handsome house on the Avenue Hoche. She managed her evenings with grace and gaiety.

Some of Mme. Aubernon's lions began going there and before long the attractive hostess had acquired a considerable pride, including Jules Lemaître, Sardou and, of course, Anatole France. Mme. Aubernon's resentment was intense. "Léontine de Caillavet?" she snorted. "Why, I invented her!" Hers was like the bitterness of blind old Mme. du Deffand railing against her former disciple Julie de Lespinasse for stealing her friends. She was also jealous of Mme. de Loynes, the aging but still seductive ex-courtisane, after she had appropriated Jules Lemaître and would crow with triumph if she could lure Lemaître or Anatole France back to one of her dinners. When in 1887 she found out that her beloved Dumas was a steady caller at the Avenue Hoche, she severed diplomatic relations with Mme. de Caillavet forever.

It was a bit late for such a gesture because Dumas had severed his own diplomatic relations with Mme. Aubernon two years previously. It was over a trifling situation involving an alleged offense to Dumas' daughter and the son of one of Madame's "regulars." Dumas, behaving with stupid pride and stubbornness, demanded that Madame ostracize the man from her coterie. Madame, feeling that Dumas' petty grievance by no means warranted disloyalty to her other guest, stoutly refused to take sides. Dumas gave her the alternative of banishing the man or of losing him. In an agony of warring emotions, deep affection against high principles, Madame stuck to her standards and Dumas shed the dust of her salon from his heels (and in the casual Aubernon household, there may well have been dust). Madame, shattered and brokenhearted, let him go.

There is little doubt but that Dumas was relieved to go. His adoring dictator was not only overpoweringly possessive, there were moments when she could be painfully mortifying. The most embarrassing of such moments was at a grand gala she held in his honor in her "Théâtre de Messine," where a performance of his *Diane de Lys* was to be given, performed by professional actors. Just before the rise of the curtain, the lady of the house came out before the audience, large, beaming and robed in an inspired allegorical costume as "The Apotheosis of the Glory of Alexandre Dumas, *fils*." Streaming from ample bosom to shoe pompons were moiré ribbons in Legion of Honor colors bearing in gold lettering the titles of all Dumas' plays and novels while on top of her head in gilded papier-mâché was a bust of the famous author. She unfurled a parchment scroll and read a poetic eulogy of her own composition and, as she read, the bust wobbled to a precarious angle over her left ear. Most members of the audience tried their best to stifle their mad hysterics. Dumas, in tortures of embarrassment, hissed to the person beside him, "One must have strong kidneys to live through anything like this."

After the departure of Dumas, Mme. Aubernon chose Henri Becque for her *grand homme,* but Becque, excellent naturalist playwright that he was, never attained the stature of Dumas *fils*. However, the flamboyant lady held her indomitable head high and kept her salon going with flying colors and fluttering ribbons. Her zest and enthusiasm were as bouncing as ever and when her friends asked if she never got bored, her answer was, "Sometimes at night, in bed." She continued to rule over her intellectual assizes, to clang her silver bell and to talk, talk, talk undauntedly until 1899. In that year, Mme. Aubernon went to her glory. The cause of her death was cancer of the tongue. There is no need to quote the heartless remarks of the boulevard wits.

The salon leader whom Mme. Aubernon claimed to have invented, Mme. Arman de Caillavet was born Léontine Lippman and came of wealthy Jewish aristocracy. So much has already been written about this remarkable lady and so much more about her remarkable *grand homme* Anatole France, that this resumé can be only a brief and sketchy one. She had a great deal more feminine appeal than her aggressive "inventor." The letters written to her by Dumas after he defected over to her salon are far more gallantly effusive than any he ever wrote to his first patroness: "I am very happy to have your delightful letter and I kiss the hand that wrote it. If the other hand is anywhere about, I kiss it also."

However, Mme. de Caillavet, or Mme. Arman as she was usually called, was not interested in hand-kissing or attracting adulation for herself. She was neither an egotist like Mme. Aubernon nor a deliberate charmer like Mme. de Loynes. Mme. Arman's only coquetry was her intellect, which she possessed to an astonishing degree. Her brightly alert mind was restless and continually inquiring, yet at the same time she was a womanly woman, wise and warm. She was also an honestly forthright woman with a will of iron, witty, completely intolerant of dull or silly persons and blunt, sometimes to the degree of wounding. According to Robert de Flers, the playwright who so successfully collaborated with her son, "she preferred to understand rather than to please." She was essentially a modern and her salon was modern, lively and liberal. It was mainly literary, but a few politicians were her steady guests . . . Raymond Poincaré, Jean Jaurès the radical leader and Clemenceau with his tufted eyebrows, prominent cheekbones and Asiatic appearance, which in 1914 was to earn him the title of "The Tiger of France." But the outstanding visitors at the Avenue Hoche were men-of-letters . . . editors like Ferdinand Brunetière of the *Revue des Deux Mondes,* that "antichamber to the Academy," foreign writers when they came to Paris such as D'Annunzio and the Danish literary historian Georg Brandes . . . current novelists of stature, Marcel Prévost and Paul Bourget. It is hard to reconcile Paul Bourget, the elegantly complicated *psychologue* of the feminine heart, with Mme. Arman's broad-minded salon, for he moved much in circles which were snobbishly fashionable, royalist slanted and definitely anti-Semitic. Madame was a staunch Republican and took a courageously pro-Dreyfus stand during the heat of the Affair.

It was a warm and unselfconscious salon where everyone felt at ease. Madame's son, Gaston de Caillavet, would invite in his friends. Sometimes he'd bring along a young man he'd met during their joint military training. He was three years younger than Gaston and still in his uniform and it looked incongruous on his frail body. He was pale and had the big sad eyes of a Persian prince and was constantly racked with a hacking asthma. His name was Marcel Proust. Proust worshiped Mme. Arman with that obsessive infatuation he felt for all great ladies and called her "one of those women who, nurtured in luxury and the arts, contribute to life, by the salt of their intelligence, a fine flavor which one didn't taste before."

Entertainment in the Caillavet household had none of the Aubernon regimentation. Some evenings were of profound mental stimulus, others frivolously gay. Authors might read from their latest works, poets recite their verse, musicians play their newest compositions. Pierre Loti with his high heels, corseted waist and far-off manner as though gazing out on tropical seas would tell of his travels. Loti had an unusually musical voice, a *voix d'or* which listeners often likened to Sarah Bernhardt's fourteen-karat organ. The youthful little Comtesse de Noailles would shyly recite some of her exquisite poems. Anna de Noailles was a delicate, fairylike creature whom Mme. Arman called her "child of genius." Madame loved to encourage fresh or latent talent and would say she wasn't interested in people who had already arrived because they usually arrived worn out.

This hostess of tireless energy held a weekly dinner on Wednes-

day and every Sunday a reception at which she'd receive as many
as a hundred guests. In addition to this, she arranged for any
number of concerts and theatricals to be put on in her "hall."
The plays given were usually works of the best Boulevard playwrights since she and her son were good friends with many of
them ... Alfred Capus, Georges Feydeau, Tristan Bernard. They
had theatre friends too and this was considered rather daring in
a society which still regarded actors and actresses as socially
taboo. The ultra-chic Julia Bartet came often. She was an actress
of exceptional artistry. She was known as "la femme la plus
elegante de Paris" and was always so beautifully dressed that her
very smartness seemed, in certain roles, to be almost a detriment
to her performance . . . as someone remarked, "Hand Bartet
Racine and she'll give you back Paquin." Lucien Guitry might
drop in after his evening performance or the joyously enchanting
Gabrielle Réjane. Loïe Fuller, the American dancer of the
shimmering scarves and Tiffany glass lighting effects occasionally
fluttered her China silk butterfly wings on Madame's stage and
Reynaldo Hahn came time and again to play and sing his
*Chansons Grises* and other compositions. It may well be that
Marcel Proust found in Hahn and his music the prototype for
his musician Vinteuil and that haunting "little phrase" which
permeates his *Coté de chez Guermantes*. Hahn composed musical
scores for some of the early satirical plays Gaston wrote in
collaboration with Robert de Flers. The two young men were
skillful showmen and the team of *Flers et Caillavet* was already
making its highly successful mark. Gaston and his wife brought
youth and gaiety into a house which even without them would
have been lively and up to date.

Jules Lemaître had been a frequent guest until the Dreyfus
ruckus when Lemaître, who was a rabid anti-Dreyfusard, cut
short his visits to the broad-minded salon and sought more

restricted refuge in the loving arms of Mme. de Loynes. Léontine de Caillavet was hurt by Lemaître's rebuff, but Anatole France bore the critic no grudge. Lemaître had been France's early champion and France, with amused indulgence told Madame, "You must not speak ill of him. It's offending the muses."

It is, of course, a matter of literary history that the *grand homme* Léontine de Caillavet discovered, adopted and cultivated until in his day his reputation as author and thinker was second only to that of Voltaire was Anatole France. At the time of his discovery in 1883, he was anything but a *grand homme*. Awkward, shy, sloppy in dress, he was utterly lacking in the social graces and people meeting him for the first time thought him a lout. But Léontine sensed the fire and genius simmering behind the loutishness and, for the next twenty years, this dynamic woman devoted her every waking hour . . . and very possibly a fair number of her sleeping ones . . . to the creation of Anatole France. His success, his fame, was the chief goal of her life. Charles Maurras writing of her complete dedication said, "It was an exemplary but very rare case of a vigorous personality, a superior soul and mind, content to identify itself with another person."

Mme. Arman de Caillavet took Anatole France firmly in her steady hand and educated him from the ground up. She was responsible for the success of all but three or four of his many books and it was through her efforts that he was eventually admitted to the Academy. She turned herself into a secretary extraordinary for him, editing everything he wrote, gathering endless research material for him, translating useful articles from foreign publications, for she was an accomplished linguist. She took notes during his conversations and filed them for future use. She brought him new ideas, new facets of erudition, new plots for his novels, new topics for his essays. She worked along with him and literally so, her writing desk next to his, writing his prefaces for him, sometimes entire chapters of his novels. She herself was a fine author and could imitate his style. It is not unlikely that France occasionally imitated hers, for he would unconsciously borrow her turn of phrase, accept her ideas, work with them, put them down on paper and eventually believe them to be his own.

France was well aware of her invaluable assistance and duly grateful. His dedication to *Crainquebille* reads: "To Mme. de Caillavet, this book which I should not have written without her help, for, without her help, I should not write books." One day Pierre Loti thanked him for mentioning him favorably in *La Revue.* France pointed at Madame. "Thank her," he said. "She was the person who wrote the article."

Léontine de Caillavet's task in creating the country's great author was not an easy one. Anatole was a naturally lazy man who hated to get down to work and, like most good honest writers, would find any excuse not to . . . only with him it was worse than with most. He'd complain that the sight of a blank sheet of paper made him acutely dizzy. Mme. Arman cured the vertigo by forcing him to fill out the sheet. She'd keep after him night and day, until, possibly in exasperation, he would create a masterpiece. During the twenty years prior to their meeting, he had written only two or three books. Thanks to her persistent goading, in a scant five years he produced *Thaïs, Balthazar, L'Etui de Nacre, La Rôtisserie de la Reine Pédauque, Les Opinions de Jérôme Coignard, Le Jardin d'Epicure* and *Le Lys Rouge.* She helped him not only in literary matters but in personal ones as well, taught him to dress better, bought his vests and ties and spruced him up for occasions such as receiving an honor or attending a meeting at the Academy.

Anatole France had a wife, a disagreeable, domineering female in whose presence he used to tremble and stammer. It was only due to his inherently indolent nature that he remained married to her as long as he did. His ultimate release came through an argument involving some hangings of ancient Genoese velvet. Mme. Arman had purchased the hangings during one of her trips to Italy but having no suitable place for them either at the Avenue Hoche or in her country house in the Gironde, she gave them to Anatole to put in his study which was on the upper floor of his place in the rue Chalgrin. When the curtains were delivered, Mme. France shouted in loud indignation that she would have nothing from Mme. de Caillavet in her house and stormed out to do some shopping. France calmly summoned a draper and ordered him to install the curtains. The draper climbed up onto a ladder and started his work. France, at his desk, continued writing an article. It was France's literary affectation to wear a dressing gown when he wrote. Voltaire and Diderot had always worn theirs, so did Flaubert and it is impossible to think of Balzac dressed any other way. When Mme. France returned from her shopping and saw what was going on, she ordered the curtain hanger down off the ladder. France told him to keep on with his work and the man, obeying the supposed master of the house, remained on the ladder. Mme. France, shrill with rage, whizzed out of the study, slammed the door, locked it and pocketed the key. She then marched out of her house and went off to dine with and tell her woes to the Comtesse de Martel, a popular authoress who wrote under the pen name of Gyp.* When she returned a few hours later, in company with Gyp, a crowd had collected on the rue Chalgrin and were gazing with fascination up at a third-floor window through which came

---

* Sybille-Gabrielle Marie Antoinette de Riquetti de Mirabeau, Comtesse de Martel de Janville (little wonder she chose the shorter pen name) was a grand-niece of Mirabeau, a Boulangist, an anti-Semite, but an excellent satirical novelist.

the desperate yells of the curtain hanger calling for someone to break down the door and let him out. Mme. France and Gyp went into the house and up to the study. Madame unlocked the door and the curtain hanger fled into the night. The great author, elaborately unperturbed, kept on writing. His wife screamed that he and his lady friend were dirty pigs and at that, France rose, picked up his work, walked out of the house and across to the Hôtel Carnot. Gyp described the scene: "He was still in his dressing gown and his skullcap. The tassels of his belt were dragging in the ground behind him and on a portfolio he carried an inkpot, his pen and the article he'd begun. An hour later, he sent a messenger from the Hôtel Carnot with a note asking for some clean underwear." He never returned to his wife, and in 1892 they were divorced.

In 1894, Anatole France purchased his well-known Villa Saïde on the Avenue du Bois, an easy distance from the Avenue Hoche. By now, Mme. de Caillavet ran her house entirely for his pleasure and convenience. He lunched there every day. He was the focal point around which she arranged her Wednesday dinners and her Sunday receptions. And she arranged them with a good sense of showmanship, getting all of her guests assembled, then producing Anatole France in an entrance as though preceded by a flourish of trumpets.

Gradually she had changed him from the boorish lout he'd been into an easygoing man of the world. He had become polite, in a vague ecclesiastical sort of politeness saluting everyone as he entered a room, even the empty chairs. His talk seemed eighteenth century, witty and graceful, ironic and kindly, erudite and fanciful. Fernand Gregh says it might have been the conversation at La Fontaine. He had an endless store of good anecdotes and told them well, but never merely for the sake of telling them, never out of context with whatever was being discussed.

His wit could be both cynical and delightful. One of Madame's guests, a collector of antiques, brought along an old Roman cameo he'd come across, for the opinion of France, who was himself an amateur antiquarian. "Whose head do you think this is?" the collector asked him. France inspected the carving for a moment then asked politely, "Well, whose do you want it to be?"

France had a superb antique collection of his own and specialized in early Gothic. His house was generously cluttered with Madonnas, saints, ancient altar cloths and church vessels — an enthusiasm which seems strangely ironic when one remembers his bitter anti-clericalism. An early education by some exceptionally harsh Jesuits had soured him on religion and the clergy for life. He'd take a sardonic glee in making sly fun of any priest or abbé who might be present, by treating him with mock deference and sanctimoniousness. Once when he and Mme. Arman visited Lourdes together, purely in a spirit of sightseeing curiosity, he stared in astonished disbelief at the ex-voto offerings left at the shrine in gratitude for miraculous cures . . . crutches, canes, eyeglasses, wheelchairs and exclaimed, "What? No wooden legs?"

Anatole France liked pretty women but deplored the insistently highbrow ones who would try to discuss literature with him. "Oh for a young and pretty woman," he bemoaned, "who'd think that Hamlet meant some sort of omelet!" At the beginning of their relationship, Mme. Arman herself was young and not exactly pretty but handsome, with finely chiseled features and sparkling blue eyes. She was short and plumpish with appetizing shoulders and arms. Later she was to become extremely heavy, a defect which seems not to have bothered France who admitted to a preference for what he called "feather-bed women."

There was, as one may presume, a *Monsieur* de Caillavet and just how he fitted into the triangle . . . well, one may presume that. He was an affable clubman, florid, shaped rather like a

penguin and bursting with loud jokes. He was the very antithesis of his wife's *cher ami,* a sportsman, jovial and completely
nonintellectual. He was a dedicated monarchist, a geneological
zealot who would spend long hours tracing his ancestry back to
the sixteenth century, a hobby that amused his republican wife
who said: "We must encourage him. While he's busy with this
nonsense, he leaves me in peace." He and France got on well
enough together although they disagreed on most matters, often
violently so, but always with underlying good humor. Madame
very wisely never allowed the two to discuss politics at the
luncheon table. "Spare me your political quarrels, gentlemen!"
she'd say. "Reserve them for the smoking room." M. Arman's
chief hobbies, in addition to his ancestry tracing, were wine and
the culinary arts. On the country estate at Capian near Bordeaux,
he took great pride in his vineyards, and always remained through
the vintage season to supervise the gathering, the bottling and
the storage. Owing to him the Caillavet *vins de maison* were of
unusual excellence. Monsieur also supervised much of the family
cuisine, for he fancied himself as an authority on food. It amused
him to look up seventeenth and eighteenth century recipes and
have them tried out at home . . . not that everyone who ate
the results was unmitigatedly amused when these quaint
dishes appeared unexpectedly at table. Some dishes were quite
awful.

Arman de Caillavet was an expert yachtsman and occasionally
wrote articles on sailing for sports publications, signing his name
"Djeb Topsail." Over the years he owned two luxurious yachts,
the *Cymbelene* and the *Mélusine* both of which he captained
himself. Madame too loved sailing. It was one of the few en-
thusiasms she shared with her husband. They'd go on cruises
and she'd bring Anatole in tow, but even on a seagoing holiday
she'd not allow him to idle lazily. Every day, rain or shine, rough

weather or smooth, she'd order him to go inside to the main saloon to write for several hours. On the *Cymbelene,* they visited Cowes for the Regatta, and on the *Mélusine* they voyaged about Sicily. M. Arman was in his element when he was at the helm of one of his smart vessels. He was quite out of it in his wife's sophisticated salon. As a matter of truth, he wasn't often in it. What few times he did happen to be present, he'd greet arriving guests with a rather revealing, "Do come in! I'm not Anatole France!"

The author spent many weeks at the Caillavet house in Capian. Sometimes Monsieur was there, sometimes not. France loved to relax indolently in the sun but his feminine mentor was merciless. She made him stick to his regulated hours of work. Now and then she'd give him the respite of a bit of gardening which they both enjoyed and they'd take long walks about the hills of the grape-teeming Gironde. One of the many likings they had in common was a fondness for dogs. Anatole's love for them shows up in frequent tender passages in his books. Mme. Arman had three small poodles, Mitzi, Riquet and Kiki, all of them overspoiled and overfat. Kiki was a problem dog . . . disobedient, giddy and impossible to housebreak. He seems to have assumed that a library rug, green and needlepointed with pink roses was a section of the garden. One morning when Kiki had been kept outside for two hours in a futile attempt to persuade him to make hygienic use of nature's facilities and was yipping pleadingly at the door, France said, "Let the poor little devil come in! He's been restraining himself so long!"

Anatole France and his Egeria (the classical terminology seems respectably exonerating) traveled much through Europe. Madame, an avid and scholarly sightseer, would visit every museum, every cathedral, every palace and château. In her zeal for expanding her already wide knowledge of art and history, she'd do masses of research in the local libraries, ferreting out new facets of information, any and everything that might prove useful for her great man. The fruitful result of their stay in Florence was France's most popularly successful novel, *The Red Lily*. He had a special copy bound for her in Florentine brocade, and for years she kept it on a lectern, like a Bible, in a conspicuous corner of her drawing room.

Whenever they were separated, they exchanged daily letters. One senses the fervor and passionate friendship behind the words, which are for the most part surprisingly restrained. There is little or no use of the intimate second person singular and in all of them, they address one another as Monsieur and Madame. France seldom terminates a letter with anything more ardent than "I kiss your hands with tender respect." One wonders if it was due to the outward formality of the times or if the two of them had an eye on future publication. Madame's letters from Biarritz where she spent every September and from Saint Gervais where she took an annual cure are filled with humor, grace and keen observation. He realized her talent and wrote, "Do you know, madame, that your letters are miracles of taste and sense (yes, of sense, I know that annoys you, but I find them sensible!) of critique and of irony . . . ah! if only you wanted to be a writer!" His own letters written from the south of France have bright flashes that remind one of the meridional paintings of Matisse. "When I go down the streets, I see between the walls a little bit of the sea waving like a handkerchief."

Mme. Arman wrote countless letters to other people as well. It was one of her ways of keeping up her many friendships. The ones she wrote to Gaston when he was growing up are warmly gay and humorously admonitory. One thinks of Mme. de Sévigné and her daughter. When Gaston was visiting friends at Puys and had written her an ecstatic account of the delicious food he was getting she warned him, "Moderate your raptures, I beg of you, otherwise you will return to us amplified to a colossal degree." Further extracts from her letters to Gaston are revealing of her character:

I have traveled more than half of my road in life and you have almost all of yours to go. And for this journey I want to see you armed and well attired. The spirit is the thing which one must deck and embellish ceaselessly . . . Make your dreams of the future and try to make them as lovely as possible . . . There will always be time to tear them down.

When the lad was off spending an athletic holiday at Dinard she wrote with a certain anxiety:

In the midst of all these sporting gambols does it ever happen that you read a book? Remember that there is never a schoolboy on vacation whose habits don't become lifelong ones and I'd never be resigned to have you become a sort of English sports fanatic, mad for the pleasures of sailing and tennis. All this sporting life is very fine but one must absolutely have something else along with it if one does not wish to be merely a set of muscles and a stomach.

All her life she was possessed with the impulse to prod those she loved into greater and greater achievement. Her zeal was tireless, but it could exhaust others. After twenty years, Anatole France began to chafe under the prodding. He grew irritable and on occasion, vindictive. There were petty squabbles and a few ugly scenes. The story of his ultimate escape from bondage is a familiar one . . . how he fled to South America, how Léontine was to read in a newspaper of his marriage to Jeanne Brindeau, an actress who was touring in the Argentine . . . a cruel rumor which proved to be quite untrue, how she grieved over the loss of Anatole . . . or perhaps over the loss of dominating him. She died in 1910 at the age of sixty-three. The news came as an unexpected and profound blow to France. "Her death is my death," he wrote. In some ways it was true, for ever since he had walked away from her he had written nothing of particular merit.

Some years later, at an age when he should have known better, he married Emma Laprévotte, Mme. Arman's former maid . . . a placid, bourgeois person whom he called by the arch name of Tico, an abbreviation for the yet more arch pet term of *petit coco*. He seems to have been comparatively happy with her. She went everywhere with him and was intelligent enough to keep her mouth shut. "Tico is a rare woman," France remarked to a friend. "She has an opinion on every subject but never gives it." At least Tico was a change from Léontine de Caillavet. It is to be hoped that Anatole France thought often about his remarkable Egeria and thought with the affection and gratitude she deserved. Certainly those of us today who give ourselves the keen pleasure of reading *Penguin Island, The Crime of Sylvester Bonnard, The Rotisserie of Queen Pedauque* or *The Gods Are Thirsty* can pay our own grateful hommage to the extraordinary creator of an extraordinary author.

There were other salons, other leaders. A small and exclusive one was that of the Baroness de Pierrebourg at Number 1 Avenue du Bois de Boulogne. At number 7 of the same avenue lived Paul Hervieu, the playwright and author of delightful novels which, as period pieces, still make for excellent reading. The proximity of the houses was convenient, for Hervieu and Baronesse de Pierrebourg were devoted lovers. She was an aristocrat of beauty and brains who gave up everything and braved the disapproval of society to become Hervieu's faithful mistress. It was an idyllic romance conducted with grace and Old World formality. She ran a literary salon for his friends and fellow writers, Maurice Donnay, Henri de Régnier, Jean Richepin and Alfred Capus. Anna, Comtesse de Noailles, came frequently and a few broad-minded members of the aristocracy, the Duchesse de

Rohan and Princesse Lucien Murat. Occasionally the old Second Empire beau, Count Primoli, would totter in. She received Paul Valéry and Jean Cocteau in later years and she herself wrote historical studies under the pen name of Claude Ferval. The manner of Mme. de Pierrebourg and Paul Hervieu when company was present was above reproach. He was always careful to leave before the others. She would rise, walk with him to the drawing-room door and as he gave her hand a conventional kiss she'd say quietly, "You know the way, don't you?" Theirs was a deep and abiding love. He came to see her every evening and every morning he wrote her a letter, sometimes a long one, sometimes merely a short note, but always some sort of communication. Eventually two days went by during which Hervieu neither called nor sent her a letter and Mme. de Pierrebourg concluded that he must be dead. He was. After that, she continued her salon as a memorial to him and led a life of study and, one trusts, of beautiful memories.

The salon of Mme. Straus on the rue Miromesnil specialized in the theatre and the world of music. It was one of the liveliest and least formal in Paris and she was one of the town's most attractive and spirited hostesses. It is not surprising that Geneviève Straus cultivated the musical world. She was the daughter of Jacques François Halévy, composer of *La Juive*. As a girl she had studied with Charles Gounod and her first marriage at the age of nineteen was to Georges Bizet who had been a pupil of her father. Six years later Bizet died, and for the next eight she remained a rather retiring widow. Her quick wit and gypsylike beauty attracted the attention of Princesse Mathilde, who took her into her Napoleonic salon where the young woman blossomed into a gay, engaging and somewhat wayward person. Emile Straus, a wealthy lawyer and connection of the Rothschilds, fell in love with her and they were married. She was intelligent rather than intellectual, a person of great animation, bold, blunt and beautiful, completely down to earth and able to get by with outrageous remarks. When a lady she knew who had just received a decoration arrived at one of her evenings flaunting the medal pinned to the edge of a low-cut gown, Mme. Straus exclaimed, "A woman's breast is made for other purposes!" And upon encountering a friend who was known as a statuesque beauty and was now in an advanced state of pregnancy, she declared, "Why, you're no longer a statue, you're practically a group!"

Few people took offense at Geneviève Straus's careless exuberance, and her gay dinners and lighthearted soirées were very popular. Anatole France was vastly amused by her as was Victorien Sardou, and in her company Guy de Maupassant found respite from his mental torment. Marcel Proust, who certainly got around the salons a lot, adored her and borrowed her turn of phrase and spontaneous form of wit for his Oriane de Guermantes. He wrote to her in his peculiarly fatuous fashion, "Madame, if I could do no matter what to give you pleasure, go take a letter for you to Stockholm or Naples, I don't know why, but it would make me very happy." Even the grouchy Edmond de Goncourt was charmed by her vivacity and by the excellent taste of her house decoration, a mixture of eighteenth century furniture, oriental bibelots and impressionist paintings. Geneviève Straus was one of the few women of the upper *gratin* who had a perceptive eye for art as well as the courage to collect the moderns of her day. Painters were part of her coterie; Degas and Renoir and even Forain came from time to time.

It is proof of Mme. Straus's attractive personality that Forain went there at all. Forain was a venomous anti-Semite and the Strauses, of course, were Jewish. During the heat of the Affair, Geneviève took a defiant stand on the side of the Pros and the day that Dreyfus was declared guilty, she put on mourning which she didn't take off until Zola's *J'accuse* came out like a trumpet call on the front page of *L'Aurore*. Léon Daudet, the snobbish son of the gentle Alphonse, sneeringly called her "one of those ardent spirits to whom Dreyfus is Christ and Zola is his apostle." However, throughout that period of tension and hysteria, she remained on good terms with all her acquaintances, even the ones who were declaredly in the opposite camp such as Maurice Barrès and Jules Lemaître, and her salon remained as popular as ever. The much loved Abbé Mugnier was her good friend. The abbé had converted one or two Jewish persons in the past and one day he talked in his charming persuasive manner to Geneviève Straus about the comforts of Catholicism. She only laughed gently, patted his hand and said, "Dear, dear Father, I have too little religion to risk changing what I've got!" The abbé didn't try again.

Originally in a palace on the rue de Courcelles, now installed at 18 rue de Berri in quarters of Second Empire splendor was the last of a great salon, famous for over half a century. Its ruler, and rule she did, was the formidably aging Princess Mathilde, daughter of King Jérôme, niece of the first Napoleon, cousin of the third, grandniece of Tsar Paul, with a side grafting from the royal house of England. She was a Bonaparte from her Caesarean profile to her firmly planted feet and majestic stride. Any armchair on which she sat took on the air of a throne . . . not the canopied velvet throne of royalty but the lion-carved seat of the Caesars. Her language was imperial — not courtly, but military and plebeian, brusque and commanding. Her nature was impulsive and unpredictable. She could be both brutal and kind, exquisite or coarse with flashes of bawdy wit and, according to the Goncourts, "rumblings of thunder like an echo of her uncle. Ah yes, she was a true Napoleon!" Her temper was short, and

Sainte-Beuve, who adored her, in one of his many letters to her speaks of "your magnificent rages." And yet, with the guests who came to her house, she was graciousness itself. She was, of course, treated by everyone with the deference paid to majesty, but she'd do her best to brush formality aside. She'd rise to greet every woman who entered her drawing room, make a genial gesture indicating that the lady needn't kiss her hand, but if the guest insisted upon doing so, the princess would gently kiss her brow during the curtsey.

Princesse Mathilde had always been popular with the public. She was the only member of the imperial family who was never the butt of the pamphleteers. Loyal to the cause of Empire, yet never a willing member of Louis Napoleon's and Eugénie's court, she was far too spirited and independent to feel free in the stuffy confines of the Tuileries or the self-conscious formality of Compiègne. "I always felt I was somebody else," she told Edmond de Goncourt. "I longed to get back home and be myself. When I spent a night at Compiègne, they gave me the Pope's bed. It was so vast and chilly, I had to pile my entire wardrobe on top of myself to keep warm." Mathilde's own court in her Paris mansion or out in her summer residence at Saint Gratien was a far warmer and more stimulating one. Her salon had been the most sought after in Europe and her "salonards" the most brilliant personalities of their time. Her generous house was neutral territory for the elegant and the intelligentsia, men of arts and letters, scholars and the more intellectual aristocrats and politicians.

Curiously enough, Mathilde herself was woefully lacking in any formal education. Her mother, Catherine of Würtemberg, had consistently neglected her children's upbringing. "Our governesses," Mathilde told Goncourt, "were all my father's mistresses and when one of them got pregnant, she was dismissed."

BICYCLE RACING IN THE 1890's
*(The bearded enthusiast supporting racer #5 is Tristan Bernard)*

Collection A. Jakovsky, Paris

TRISTAN BERNARD AND GASTON THOMSON
*The dramatist, wit, sportsman and man of good will
with his close friend*

Photo A. Well, Collection J.-J. Bernard, Paris

JEAN LORRAIN
*Journalist, whose brilliant column, "Pall Mall," was a combination
of* belles lettres *and scandal gossip*

SARAH BERNHARDT
*"Ma Dame Sarah, our Lady of the Theatre"*

LUCIEN GUITRY

*Grandest actor of his time: "a colossus of a man who seized
upon life and embellished it"*

Collection Yvan Christ, Paris

LÉONIDE LEBLANC

*"And I, ladies, am sleeping with His Highness tonight"*

Photo Reutlinger, Bibliothèque Nationale, Estampes, Paris

PRINCESSE MATHILDE
*Niece of Napoleon Bonaparte, patriotic and popular
matriarch of the salons*

Photo Nadar, Bibliothèque Nationale, Estampes, Paris

ANATOLE FRANCE AND MME. DE CAILLAVET
*Most distinguished writer of his time with his sponsor at Capian*

Bibliothèque Nationale, Estampes, Paris

According to Victor du Bled, Mathilde "educated herself through the great book of life and polished it off with the conversation of the eminent men she received." She knew no history whatsoever except that of the Bonapartes, on which subject she was an authority. She specialized in an almost fanatical cult of the uncle she never knew, for at the time of her birth in 1820, cancer and St. Helena were taking the toll of that spectacular meteor, but she worshiped the idea of him all her life. In the foyer of her rue de Berri *hôtel* loomed a large bronze statue of him, and the entire first floor was in the nature of a museum to his glory. In addition to the Canova bust of the Emperor, which stood in front of a hanging of purple velvet, there were countless portraits, etchings and miniatures of his likeness. The wall panels were carved with garlanded *N*'s, imperial violets jammed the heavy cut-glass vases and the place was fairly swarming with gold bees. Even at the dinner table, the Little Corporal's presence was apparent. The centerpiece was an immense gilded eagle, surrounded by smaller ones, and at each plate as a menu holder was an individual eaglet. At her request she had been entrusted with her own key to Napoleon's Tomb. During Tsar Nicholas' state visit to Paris, he expressed a desire to pay his homage to that shrine. President Faure, with a good sense of theatre, arranged for Princesse Mathilde to be his only escort. The two entered the big mausoleum and knelt on prie-dieux looking down onto the porphyry coffin. Suddenly outside in the Invalides parade grounds there sounded a clatter of hoofs, a roll of drums, a flourish of trumpets and cries of "Vive l'Empereur!" Mathilde, with her head held like a true daughter of the Caesars, emerged with the shy, pale Russian emperor to inspect the descendants of her uncle's *grognards,* and the *gloire* of Austerlitz, Wagram and Iéna was in the air. The princess's hero worship of the first Napoleon was akin to the blind devotion of the more demented one of those idiotic "Two Grenadiers" and yet she had, at times, a bluntly realistic attitude toward her dynasty. "What bores these Bonapartes can be!" she once exclaimed. "Just because there was one soldier in the family, they all have to consider themselves generals!" And in regard to that one soldier she frankly admitted, "But for him, I'd be selling oranges on the streets of Ajaccio."

Her loyalty to the Bonapartes hardly blinded her to the mediocrity of the one who was then on the throne. As a girl living in Arenenberg with her aunt, his mother Queen Hortense, she'd had a brief flirtation with her cousin and in later years would indulge in the sentimental fantasy that because of him she'd turned down the suit of the elder Duc d'Orléans, the then Pretender, as well as that of the next most important royalist, the Duc de Chambord. There had been other suitors as well, for in her youth Mathilde was very much of a beauty, with great flair and high spirits. In later years, when she had acquired a more mature estimation of the contemporary imperial family, she must have been grateful that it was Eugénie de Montigo who eventually captured Louis Napoleon. "Why, if I'd ever married him," she announced, "I'd have had to crack open his head to find out if there was anything in it!" And yet, some of her warmest friendships had been severed because of adverse criticism of that unmajestic majesty. It was well for the Goncourts that she never read the entry in their journal stating that "the Emperor would be an excellent somnambulist if only he had moments of lucidity," because she remained on terms of affection with both brothers and after the death of Jules, Edmond was her close confidant and she, perhaps, his most faithful woman friend. Sainte-Beuve was not so lucky. That great critic, the Montaigne of his century, had been a shining ornament of the Mathildean salon until his increasingly Leftist leanings in the

Senate, plus an article in *Le Temps* in which he attacked Napoleonic policies, enraged her and she showed him the imperial door, never to speak to him again until just prior to his death when they made up their differences. Victorien Sardou had often been her welcome guest but after the production of *Madame Sans-Gêne* he too was given the brush-off. The princess had attended the opening of that amusing comedy with Réjane playing the carefree Duchess of Danzig, the former laundress who presents Napoleon with his unpaid laundry bill. The scene of the family squabble when the Emperor and his sisters start hurling Corsican invectives at one another was too much for the princess's pride and, gathering her retinue together, she left the theatre in a magnificent huff.

That was in 1893, long after those evenings when her salon had been at its lively height, enriched by the presence of the great conversationalists, the Duc de Morny and the Duc d'Aumale. One sparked to the keen, biting remarks of Gustave Flaubert or glowed to the affable sweetness of Prosper Mérimée basking in the continued success of *Carmen*. Paul Bourget, Guy de Maupassant and Alexandre Dumas *fils* were the young writers then and they brought with them spirit and vitality. Théophile Gautier was on a retainer from the princess as her official librarian . . . "le bon Théo" with his expansive nature and his great ringing laugh. He'd delight everyone with stories of his student days when he led the riots in defense of Victor Hugo's controversial *Hernani* and he'd give readings from his *Emaux et Camées*. Gautier was a happy soul, pleased as a child with the polished perfection of his marmoreal, Parnassian verse. Writing came easily for him. He used to say naïvely that if he pitched his sentences into the air, they invariably fell on their feet like a cat. François Coppée also would read aloud his charmingly sentimental poems of the humble. Sometimes Gounod would be there to play his latest songs of romance or accompany Christine Nilsson or Adelina Patti.

Princesse Mathilde was sometimes called Notre Dame des Arts. Certainly she was an artistic benefactress. In her house one hobnobbed with the fashionable painters Carolus Durand and Ary Scheffer. She was the good friend of those melodramatists on canvas, Gérôme, Détaille, Fromentin and Meissonier, whose military subjects were right up her artistic alley. She owned a few Meissonier battle scenes, including a "Charge of Cuirassiers" regarding which the crotchety Edouard Manet was to snort "Excellent! All steel except the breastplates!" The princess rather fancied herself as a watercolorist and in among the Napoleonic portraits were any number of somewhat distressing examples of her art.

As hers was an academic taste in painting, so were her leanings in literature and she harbored a fine contempt for writers who were not members of the Institute. When a statue to the elder Dumas was unveiled she cried out in disgust, "Why, he wasn't even an Academician!" She cared little about the scientific world and yet sometimes, though rarely, a modest scientist by the name of Louis Pasteur would come quietly in for the respite of civilized entertainment and nontechnical talk.

Pasteur was not the only great thinker of the Mathildean coterie. Two of her "regulars" were the foremost exponents of current French thought of their time, Hippolyte Taine and Ernest Renan. Taine was the daylight-clear writer who brought dead history to life, the artist who wrote of scientific matters with such sensitivity, he "lined the brilliant silk of imagination with the solid stuff of science." The metaphor is that of his pupil, Paul Bourget. Loving bold colors and heroic themes, Titian, Shakespeare and Rubens, Taine fighting a losing battle with diabetes went his stoical way, looking like a medieval alchemist.

Maurice Barrès, another of his disciples, recalled that "Taine's eyes, which were remarkably gentle, full of light and depth, didn't quite match ... in fact, he was wall-eyed ... a man who was always looking at abstractions and who had to rouse himself to see reality."

Taine's fellow giant in matters of the mind, Ernest Renan, the idealistic apostle of doubt, was Europe's most popular iconoclast. Some years had passed since his *Life of Jesus* had burst like a blasphemous bombshell on a smugly pious public. One can imagine the shock effect of his blunt statement that "the high thought of Jesus, scarcely understood by his disciples, has undergone many defeats. In adopting Christianity we have profoundly altered it; in reality it is our creation." It horrified as much as Nietzsche's contention that "the only true Christian died on the cross," and there was a period when Renan's name was linked with that of Anti-Christ. The volatile French, however, recovered from the shock and by the time Princesse Mathilde made a friend of this profound scholar, he was hailed as the greatest intellectual celebrity since Victor Hugo. He was an authority on Sanskrit, lecturer on Hebrew literature, and lecturing in the language itself, Administrator of the Collège de France, and author of the most important book of the nineteenth century *The Origins of Christianity*. For all his encyclopedic brain and intellectual achievements, Renan's nature was a gentle one with much of the Celtic mysticism of his native Brittany. And for all his anti-clericalism, he seemed never to forget that once, as a youth, he had studied for the priesthood. At times he had an air of troubled brooding, as though still haunted by the image of the unfrocked seminarist going through his gehenna of apostasy. "An archangel ruined, who could not forget the heaven from whence he had cast himself down," says one biographer, while Edmond de Goncourt referred to him more tersely as "that disused cathedral."

Of his early break with the Church, Renan wrote with moving simplicity: "The gods pass away like men . . . the faith which we once held ought never to be a chain. We have done our duty when we have carefully wrapped it up in the purple shroud wherein the dead gods sleep."

Taine was another writer who evoked the wrath of the princess. In one of his historical works, he referred to the First Consul as a "superior bandit" and she banished him from her premises. Taine in hurt bewilderment sought out Renan, who after hearing the sad story said, by way of consolation, "My friend, I have quarreled with a far greater lady than Princesse Mathilde."

"Who was that?" Taine asked.

"The Church," answered Renan.

With all her loyalty to the Empire, Princesse Mathilde's true devotion was to France. Whether monarchist or republican, her country came first. She had had four years of a bitterly unhappy marriage to Prince Demidoff, a wealthy Russian who practically owned the Ural mines. He was a handsome creature but cruel and depraved. He treated Mathilde abominably and after he slapped her face with a vicious blow in public at a court function, the Tsar gladly had the marriage annulled and Mathilde fled from Russia. At the border of her homeland, the sight of a French soldier moved her so, she shouted to her coachman to stop the horses, leapt from her carriage and kissed the astonished young man on both cheeks. "It's like embracing a living national flag!" she cried with happy tears. She responded to patriotic emotions as a war horse to a trumpet call. She could be democratic, even liberal up to a point, but not regarding military honor. During the Dreyfus excitement, some of her acquaintances who were fighting for the cause of truth and justice tried to persuade her to come out publicly on their side. "I can't," she said. "I have a Soldier in my family."

After her return from Russia, the princess ran her palace in town and her country house in Saint Gratien on the order of an Italian court. She was a noble lady surrounded by a Decameron of artists, writers and distinguished men. She had her own court household, her major domo, her groom-of-honor, her father confessor, her librarian (Théophile Gautier), her personal reader who read aloud from the classics two hours a day and her bevy of ladies-in-waiting who were always present when she received callers. Goncourt looking in one afternoon said that the main reception room in the rue de Berri was "a veritable academy of design . . . the princess working on a drawing of a terra-cotta figurine, Mlle. Abbatucci hand-tinting a screen with butterflies, Mme. Hébert making a charcoal portrait of Napoleon First and Mme. de Girardi constructing a fan of autumn leaves." They were handsome ladies but not overly intelligent. Their chief distraction of a morning was to walk down the street to purchase toilet articles and scent at the Pharmacie d'Enghien.

The houseparties she gave at Saint Gratien had none of the elaborate formality of royalist château life. In her country manor she was completely relaxed, tending to her household and garden, showing guests all over the place like any bourgeois homebody. Here she could be great fun. She could also be fairly bawdy. At the end of one evening at Saint Gratien, she turned to General Bougenel, her *chevalier d'honneur,* and said, "Now let's go to bed." Admiral Duperré who was standing nearby whispered, "Madame, I wish I were in the general's place." "Why?" asked Mathilde. "Because of what you just said." She whacked his wrist with her bee-embroidered fan. "Mon cher, you'd be cheated!" she said. "In this house we don't give night service." Yet it may well have been that some of her guests did, for on another occasion after everyone had retired and she and one of her *dames d'honneur* were discussing the houseparty as they mounted the stairs, she gestured to the rows of closed doors and said with a sigh, "And to think that not one of them is in the bed he belongs in!"

Mathilde was far too independent a woman ever to have made a good wife. She once gave a woman friend a bit of sound advice. "Marry your lover," she said. "It's the only way to regain your liberty." She didn't follow her own advice, however, for she married neither of her two known lovers. (If there were unknown ones, the fact does not concern us.) Her first had been Count Alfred Emilien de Nieuwerkerke, Minister of Fine Arts and director of the Louvre. In 1871 when the country threw over the Bonapartes, Nieuwerkerke threw over Mathilde and fled the country. She appears not to have mourned the loss.

The man of her later years, in fact of her old age, was Claudius Popelin, an enameler. He was an insignificant person whose only claim to distinction was that of being her Prince Consort *de la main gauche*. Mathilde managed somehow to have him given the Legion of Honor, on what pretext heaven knows unless for services if not to his country at least to an important member of that country. Goncourt, often sour, was especially so over this honor, writing in his Journal, "a pusher, rich, bitter, nervous . . . Popelin, the enameler of fake ancient works of art, has just been decorated." Second rate or not, the little man filled the needs of the princess for many years. He ran all her affairs, her finances, her household, her public duties. He cared for her with devoted solicitude, waited on her if she were ill, gave her massages and acted as a combination lover, husband and nurse. Popelin had somewhat of a flair for writing, and further proof of his unflagging devotion was the fact that he corrected and edited what few articles the princess ever wrote. As she fancied herself a watercolorist, she fancied herself an author. Her efforts in literature were as lamentable as the example of her painting, but Popelin was able to rewrite her material until it was fit for publication in some periodical whose editor was indulgent enough to print it because of her name. As she never read over her published pieces, she didn't know the difference and he never told her.

As the years went by, the salon on the rue de Berri deteriorated. The table there had never been very good and the food gradually became inedible. One guest compared the kidneys to frizzled corks and the butler himself once whispered to Goncourt as he passed the fish, "Don't take any, Monsieur de Goncourt. It isn't fresh!" Goncourt in a further entry writes of someone "going to imbibe poison *chez la Princesse*."

She still kept up the pretense of holding her court about her, still retained her ladies-in-waiting and her dozens of white-wigged, red-trousered lackeys; but by the 1890's the house and its retinue seemed lugubriously outmoded, like an immense arrangement of wax flowers under glass. Léon Daudet, who had never known the place in the spirited days of its glory, dined there and found the experience dismal. "A vast enveloping boredom poured down from the ceiling," he wrote. "It smothered all . . . the table covered with eagles, cut glass and flowers, the guests laboring to make animate this graveyard of what had once been a brilliant society." After dinner they'd all move into the heavily furnished drawing rooms where some played a few doleful games of cards and the princess worked on one of her endless petit-point tapestry pieces, always of a Napoleonic subject. Of the princess herself Léon Daudet said, "She seemed as fossilized as the carved and chiseled eagles that continued to encumber her funereal parlor." When Daudet complained to Goncourt the latter told him, "You're seeing it too late. Even the rats have abandoned the ship."

It was sad but true. And yet, at eighty Princesse Mathilde was still handsome. Her carriage was as erectly superb as ever and her shoulders remained remarkably beautiful. Every evening she wore a formal gown cut daringly low in a *décolletage à la baignoire,* a mid-century fashion term referring to the charmingly bare appearance of a woman as she sat in her opera box. Her historic pearl necklace was clasped about a throat that was still firm and her hands were still shapely. She had always been vain about her hands and refused ever to desecrate them with any rings. She was vain too in regard to the beauty she once had been and was fond of telling the story about when the canal builder de Lesseps saw her for the first time and exclaimed in rapturous sotto-voce to Dumas *fils,* "Ah! If only she were an isthmus!" and Dumas murmured back, "Be continent!"

As she grew older, she coarsened. Her faithful friend Edmond de Goncourt would call on her at dusk and find her bolt upright in an armchair snoring loudly. She'd wake with a start, spring up to greet him and lead him into some other room, jabbering distractedly about this, that and anything. She became subject to black moods of depression. During an evening she'd suddenly put a stop to all chatter with a loud "Je réfléchis!" and the company would be cowed into silence. The poor princess had plenty on which to reflect. Popelin had left her, although she claimed it was she who had dismissed him. Popelin, who was years her junior, had a roving eye and had started up a serious flirtation with one of the young ladies-in-waiting. Mathilde's jealousy and rage were homeric. Over the years, she and Popelin had fought continuously. Apparently he could stand the fights no longer. When he died in 1892, people said he had succumbed because of the scenes she made. Edmond de Goncourt went to see her the day after his death. She was grief-stricken but held her head high. Only as Goncourt was leaving she said to him, "Goncourt, our good years are long passed." His description of Popelin's funeral is vividly touching. The princess, who wanted a princely burial for her lover, had ordered masses of flowers. Goncourt shared a funeral carriage with François Coppée and José-Maria Heredia. On the way to Père Lachaise, Coppée and Heredia talked of their fellow poets. Heredia said that Catulle Mendès looked worn out and Coppée said that Verlaine smelled like an uncleaned birdcage. Once arrived at Père Lachaise, they watched the princess kneel in unabashed sorrow beside the open grave, and be the first to sprinkle holy water. They also noted that the second holy water sprinkler was Mlle. Abbatucci, the lady-in-waiting who had helped bring about the princess's final split with Popelin.

His loss and subsequent death were a bitter blow to Mathilde. She had always been a close friend of Mme. Straus and nearly every afternoon she'd leave the rue de Berri to go sit in a corner of the Straus parlor or dining room alone and with the lights turned off. If Geneviève Straus came in, the broken old woman would say, "Pretend I'm not here. It's *his* time of day. I can't stay at home. When the bad moment has passed, I'll go back. Don't bother about me."

The more eminent Napoleons seem each to have had a sad ending . . . the First, the Third, and the tragic young l'Aiglon. If Mathilde Bonaparte was true to Napoleonic tradition during her life, she remained true to it in her departure. And yet she had made an unforgettable mark on her times. It would have gratified this indomitable lady to have known that after her death, which was in 1902, there was a national mourning.

# 7

## MME. DE LOYNES
## AND HER LIONS

To know how to pay quiet attention and to possess the art of creative listening . . . these are the two secret gifts of the successful hostess." The words were written about Jeanne Detourbey, Comtesse de Loynes, salon leader, political adviser, charmer and courtisane of impeccable respectability. Many further words have been written about this amazing little woman and those published in the memoirs of the men who knew her, even on a purely platonic basis, read like love letters. For men were expected to fall in love with Mme. de Loynes. They did and she took their mass infatuation in her stride, which wasn't a stride at all but a graceful seat on a pink ottoman beside the fire in her mid-century drawing room, from where she reigned with the confidence of an exquisite monarch, the tact of a diplomat, the enchantment of a Ninon de Lenclos and the efficiency of a bourgeois housewife. Her reign lasted for over three decades.

Of all the great hostesses, she had the reputation of being the most feminine and the most Parisienne . . . the adjectives are synonymous. She was also considered the most beautiful; but that had been in her day, and her day had reached its zenith toward the finish of the Second Empire. A portrait painted in 1863 by Amaury Duval, pupil of Ingres, and ultimately bequeathed to the Louvre by Jules Lemaître shows her in early romantic bloom, hair center-parted above a cameo brow, huge limpid eyes toning in color with the bunch of Parma violets which was always tucked into her waist. The violets were a sort of permanent prop for the sentimental adorers who called her "La Dame aux Violettes." Her body was trim and tiny, her voice a gentle contralto. She had a lovely ease which put everyone else at theirs, a disarming honesty and the great gift of sympathetic listening. Never in a hurry, yet never vague, with a quick but kindly wit, this little female for some forty years made a career of pleasing men spiritually, intellectually and . . . well, she knew how to please in that way too.

By the 1890's Jeanne de Loynes's beauty had understandably faded. A garish coating of rouge and white powder had replaced the early bloom and a henna dye had made harsh the brown hair of the young lovely in the Duval portrait beneath which, with surprising candor, she continued to sit while receiving guests. But the eyes were still magnificent, the voice as melodious as ever and the charm irresistible.

The actual dates of her life remain indefinite. She neither gave them out nor made any pretense of being younger than she was. She admitted with pride to having known some of the great men in Louis Napoleon's time and would speak of being present during the Siege of Paris, the Prussian Invasion and the flame-filled horror of the Commune. Gustave Flaubert wrote *Salambô,* of which she was rumored to have been the inspiration, in 1862 and Sainte-Beuve who was her early literary guide died in 1869. And now during the '90's, at an age about which it would be unkind to speculate, she was the adored mistress of Jules Lemaître who was twenty years her junior. It was a deep and abiding love on both sides. Aurélien Scholl with typically barbed indulgence remarked, "Dear Jules! To him she will always be sixty!"

Jeanne Detourbey was born of low stock in Reims, where she started out earning a living first as a woolpicker in a factory, then as a bottle washer in a champagne house. But she quickly rose from these squalid beginnings and what made her rise was an inborn intelligence and a calculating evaluation of her own beauty and God-given charm. She came to Paris determined to succeed and remained to conquer. An early conquest was Marc Fournier, director of the Porte Saint Martin theatre who tried her out on the stage, but the girl's talents didn't lie in that direction. Her next "protector" . . . to make respectable the term . . . was Emile de Girardin who has been called the "master of French journalism." He inaugurated the first cheaply priced newspaper with *La Presse* and he founded *La Liberté,* both of which are hoarsely hawked on the streets of Paris to this day. He was also a periodic member of the Chambre des Députés and a passionate patriot who had ill-advisedly advocated the fatal war with Prussia. It was Girardin who started Jeanne on her lifelong interest in politics and journalism. It was also he who first gave her the idea of conducting a salon, for he'd bring any number of the important men of the moment for evenings of discussion in the apartment in which he had installed her and she was quick to listen and learn.

One of the men she met through Girardin was Prince Napoleon, son of King Jérôme, brother of Princesse Mathilde, known to his intimates by the skittish name of Plon-Plon. Although a direct heir to the Bonaparte succession, he was a member of the National Assembly and, surprisingly enough, a supporter of the liberal party. Jeanne took leave of Girardin and took up with Plon-Plon. This glittering liaison with a prince of the realm gave the young bottle washer from Reims a definite boost in the *monde* even though it was the *demi-monde.* The liaison was brief. Plon-Plon walked out on Jeanne and into the notoriously open arms of Cora Pearl, a luscious morsel of mid-century dalliance. Cora, whose real name was Emma Crouch, daughter of the Irish bard who foisted "Kathleen Mavourneen" on a lachrymose world, was a wench not of easy virtue but of absolutely none. After an apprenticeship of Dublin streetwalking, she made her way . . . and most of that on her back . . . to Paris where she became a leading cocotte. Her chief claim to posterity was the grand finale of a young clubmen's banquet in the "grand seize" private dining room of the Café Anglois when four lackeys staggered in to a fanfare of music bearing an immense covered serving dish, plopped it onto the center of the table, removed the lid and revealed Cora like a big pink salmon, stark naked and blowing kisses.

Jeanne Detourbey was the complete antithesis of this type of daughter of Eve. If she was frankly a kept woman (and she was shrewd enough to see to it that she was well-kept) she was also an innate lady. An exquisitely discreet demi-mondaine with a bourgeois concern for respectability, she was less a *déclassée* than an *"un-classée."* Having acquired a taste for journalism and politics through Girardin and Prince Napoleon, she felt she needed an education in those subjects, along with a fundamental schooling in literature and history. This may have been due to the eager curiosity of an intelligent girl, although it was probably more the foresight of a clever and seductive woman, ambitious to please the politicians, journalists and writers who were beginning to worship at her minute feet.

One of the early worshipers was Alexandre Dumas *fils*. He was young then and broad-shouldered, with just enough of the tarbrush inherited from his Negro grandfather to make him fascinating. Dumas' plays were bringing in fat returns from the box offices of every capital in Europe and he was in a position to keep his mistress in style. How lavish the style was, there's no telling. The third of the successful writing dynasty was notoriously tight-fisted and George Sand referred to him as the "far from prodigal son." Jeanne's love affair with Dumas *fils* was broken off but not her friendship. One of her extraordinary qualities was the ability to retain former lovers as lifelong friends. Both Dumas and Girardin were frequent guests at her subsequent salon and even her relationship with Prince Napoleon was one of affectionate friendship, for when with the downfall of the Empire he had to go into exile with the rest of the Bonapartes, she offered to place a large portion of her fortune in his cause. It is quite likely that friends meant more to Jeanne than lovers. Loyalty to them was a passion with her and she would never hear of the faults of any of them.

This woman had perhaps only two great loves in her life. The final one, when she was well past fifty, was for Jules Lemaître. The first, when she was in her late twenties, had been for a wealthy and brilliant young man named Ernest Baroche who had made a fortune in the Malfidano Mines. They were madly in love and Baroche was willing to marry her but she was hesitant, fearing the disillusionments of domesticity. During her hesitation, the 1870 War broke out and Baroche had to join the regiment he commanded. At Le Bourget, in a last cartridge attempt to keep the Prussians out of Paris, he met the glorious death of a hero. What was pretty glorious also was the fact that he left his adored one his fortune, his bank securities, his interests in the Malfidano Mines and the ownership of a sugar refinery at Seine-et-Marne. The person in charge of the refinery was a young Comte de Loynes. A friendship sprang up between Jeanne and the count through a mutual mourning over Ernest Baroche. Friendship ripened into love on the part of the count, and, on the part of Jeanne, knowing a good thing when she saw it. The two were married in a civil service. The Loynes parents, duly horrified, refused to acknowledge a daughter-in-law from the demi-monde, snatched away their recreant son and made arrangements for an immediate annulment. Jeanne relinquished the count but clung tenaciously to the coronet. From then on, the life she wanted was hers. She was a wealthy heiress and, in the eyes of the law, a bona fide countess. Within record time, the Loynes crest appeared on everything from her largest silver platter to her wispiest chemise.

It would have been easy for the Comtesse de Loynes to have turned the new and elegant house she quickly acquired into a place of frivolous rendezvous, but she wanted none of that. This former bottle washer graced with the coronet, this courtisane turned respectable, was determined to have one of the most distinguished salons in all of Paris. And that she had. André Maurel in his memoirs writes that from 1870 to 1908 "all that was eminent and celebrated of Paris sat at her table and submitted to the charm of her sweetness, her reserve, her finesse, her irresistible attraction." At the start, she set out to be an intellectual of sorts . . . the sort being a woman who could hold her own with the genuine intellectuals. For this she needed a higher education and the one she received really came from the heights. During her days with Girardin she had known Sainte-Beuve, failing in health, tortured by pain, always shivering despite the long woollies hand-knitted for him by Princesse Mathilde. The great critic had been her early guide in literature. For her flyer in history and philosophy she chose . . . and captured . . . the two experts in those fields, Hippolyte Taine and Ernest Renan.

Both men, like all men, were charmed by the countess. Renan especially. As he grew older, Renan had become more and more a familiar figure in the Paris salons. Anatole France said that "his old age was a pleasant comedy. In society, surrounded by pretty women, sunk into a big chair, he resembled a Prophet of the Old Testament who, in his last days, has become a blackguard and a libertine." Renan himself spoke of his late-in-life frivolity in his admission speech at the Academy saying, "One arrives in your Assembly at the age of Ecclesiastes, a charming age, most proper to serene cheerfulness, when after a laborious youth one begins to perceive that all is vanity, but that a vain thing ought to be enjoyed." Renan was well aware of the futility of Parisian life but considered it "a good furnace in which to burn the surplus of life which philosophy and science have not absorbed." Renan the great iconoclast still remained a highly spiritual man. In the preface to one of his last works he wrote, "Let us not renounce God the Father," a quiet protestation of his broad idealism. Maurice Barrès, who was also a devotee of the Loynes coterie, wrote snortingly in the *Figaro:* "Monsieur Renan likes to have it said that he acknowledges God the Father; the better to strangle God the Son." The day before his death in 1892, Renan sat in an armchair, his wife's hand in his. "Courage!" he said, "we all depart, the skies only remain," and a moment later he said, "I die in the holy communion of humanity and the Church of the future."

How much actual instruction the little countess received from these two giants is debatable. But their talk, their mere presence was for her as good as a course at the Sorbonne and she was quick to assimilate. If she could never hope to become an expert on a diversity of subjects, she could learn enough to touch gracefully upon most and steer the true experts into doing the talking. It was an irresistible form of flattery which earned her a reputation for learning which she didn't at all deserve. She made no pretense of being a bluestocking. She was first and foremost an enchantingly feminine creature and she once asked Clemenceau if it were necessary to have read Spinoza in order to make out a laundry list.

In earlier days she had learned about poetry through Théophile

Gautier. He was a constant caller and would talk to her for hours
about the clear, cool ways of the Parnassian school. If in her
culture-seeking she had felt no hesitancy in going to the right
source for instruction in appreciation of poetry, she did the same
in regard to the best of prose . . . meaning automatically French
prose (it was Oscar Wilde who said, "we cannot go to war with
France because her prose is perfect"). With calm assurance she
had sought out the unquestioned master of French prose, Gustave
Flaubert. Flaubert was also her master and she his mistress for
a brief time. He was a vividly attractive man. James Gibbon
Huneker recalling Paris days gives a flash impression of him:
"My most cherished recollection is the glimpse I had of Gustave
Flaubert, huge, a veritable Viking . . . a magnificent man. He
was hurrying through the rue Saint-Lazare . . . Solitary, his
brain filled with dreams, Flaubert went his way." Flaubert had
a boundless zest for life. He adopted Goethe's motto which he
carried with him engraved on his watch, "memento vivere," to
remind himself to "keep his eye incessantly open on the things
of this world. This spectacle is big enough to fill all souls."

The Flaubert-Loynes affair was not of steady or long duration.
The author was in Paris only occasionally and briefly, for Gustave
Flaubert belonged to Rouen as James Joyce belonged to Dublin.
To be more geographically precise, Flaubert belonged to Crois-
set, an outlying suburb where, in a house bordering the Seine,
he worked night and day the clock around. Sun-dabbled ex-
cursionists on boating parties would watch this giant striding
up and down his terrace in his dressing gown, deep in some book
of reference, and midnight bargemen would set their courses by
the lamp which glowed till morning in his study window.
Flaubert had no patience with the least inaccuracy of detail in
his writing and the amount of research which went into every
one of his books is scarcely to be believed. It is said that "he

chopped down an entire forest in order to produce one perfect wooden box." As an example of his zeal, when writing *Salammbô,* his superb novel of ancient Carthage, before undertaking a description of the cypresses in the Temple of Astarte he read through the four hundred pages in fine print of a treatise on the pyramidal cypress in a horticultural publication. When such relentless work would finally get the better of his stupendous endurance, he'd fly the gray respectability of the Madame Bovary province and escape to Paris for a few weeks of the literary scene of which he was passionately fond. He was a vital addition to the Magny dinners, those weekly gatherings of congenial writers whose number included Taine, Daudet, Zola, the Goncourts and occasionally Henry James as well as their one woman member, George Sand. Occasionally he'd drop in at the palace on the rue de Courcelles to pay his respects to the Princesse Mathilde — but his court he paid to Jeanne. That she meant a great deal to him is doubtful, for he once told Edmond de Goncourt that all the women he ever possessed were no more than the mattress for another woman he dreamed of. Flaubert, at all events, must have been amused by the pretty countess's interest in authors and their works and he'd occasionally bring to call a young disciple whose short stories were beginning to attract considerable attention. Anatole France said of them that they "epitomized the three great qualities of the French writer . . . first of all, clarity, then again clarity, and lastly, clarity." The young disciple was Guy de Maupassant.

Jeanne de Loynes's appreciation of fine poetry and great prose was secondary to her appreciation of the poet or the writer. The same attitude was true in regard to music; she admired the composer even though her musical knowledge was limited. One of her good friends was Gounod, patriarchal and blandly receptive to the national and international incense rising in clouds at his

feet. The opening night of his opera *Mireille* he brought to her
box the Provençal poet Mistral who had written the words.
Mistral fell instantly in love with the lady and begged her to
let him stay in Paris and live with her forever. She told him
gently, "You're a big child whom I love and admire. Go back
to your Provence, keep singing about it and don't come back
until your heart has white hair." A less awesome master of
music than Gounod was Jules Massenet, a youth of gentle goodness and affable humor. After *Thaïs* and *Manon* had skyrocketed
him to fame, he never lost his smiling simplicity, even during
the tensions of conducting. During a rehearsal of *Manon* with
the chorus singing and acting as listlessly as only an opera
chorus can, he tapped his baton and cried out plaintively, "Brother
and sister artists! Come! Sing it like an encore! As though the
audience had applauded!"

Mme. de Loynes's acquaintance with painting came through
Jean Louis Gérôme, dean of instructors at the Beaux Arts, whose
own creations were somewhat on the order of theatre curtains.
His immense canvases "The Death of Caesar" and "The Departure for the Masked Ball" are frightening examples of the
Academy taste of his day. Gérôme, who looked like a grand old
imperialist with waxed mustachios and hair severely en brosse,
was a kindly and well-loved instructor and students fought for
enrollment in his classes. He presented Jeanne with one of his
sculptures, a life-size figure of a Tanagra which looked as though
it had been carved out of lard. The lady, whose artistic sensibilities were purely Second Empire, thought it was just lovely
and proudly installed it in the foyer of her house. This was a
heavy, mid-century mansion filled with horrendous mausoleum-
like furniture, suffocating draperies, shiny portraits like enlarged
daguerreotypes and ghastly little souvenirs of the Exposition
of '78.

The salon of the Comtesse de Loynes was largely a political one, but politics kept under tactful control. Georges Clemenceau was a faithful and indulgent friend and so was Paul Déroulède, Clemenceau's fiery opponent. Their cautious hostess took care that they called on different days. The most colorful of politicos was Henri de Rochefort, an intriguing and wildly misdirected firebrand who looked like Don Quixote. His white hair stood up like a clown's top knot and Jules Renard called it the paper frill on a *gigôt d'agneau*. Being an Orleanist nobleman, he reacted with abhorrence to anything Napoleonic. During the Second Empire he had published a caustic little weekly so anti-government, that he'd been forced to flee for his life to Belgium. Here he continued to publish the seditious pamphlet, printed on revolutionary red paper, and took care to post copies to the Tuileries every week. After Sedan and the ousting of the Empire, Rochefort returned to Paris during the Commune, that holocaust of hell and bloodshed in which twenty thousand Parisians perished without exactly knowing why. For some flamboyant reason, this unpredictable "aristo" sided with the Communards. His role was that of a reporting observer, his most gleeful observation being that of watching the wrecking of that monument to Napoleon and the Grande Armée, the Vendôme Column. Writing it up for his radical paper, he headed his article "A Columnicide, or the Extraction of the Giant Molar." With the victory of the Versailles government and the establishment of the Third Republic, the mad marquis was arrested along with other communard leaders, tried and sentenced for deportation to the penal colony in New Caledonia. Along with a crowd of convicts, he was jammed into a foul cage below the heaving decks of a prison frigate. The voyage was stormy and Rochefort was violently seasick. However, he kept up his spirits and those of his companions and, between bouts of nausea, apologized saying, "Forgive me, but I'm throwing up all the bile the Second Empire has caused me." Once arrived in New Caledonia, he managed three times to escape from the misery of the roofless bagnio and three times was caught. After a fourth attempt, he was pardoned ... it seemed to the authorities the easiest solution. He returned to Paris more or less of a hero ... nobody quite knew why. His first dinner upon his return from Nouméa was with Mme. de Loynes. His subsequent career was one of arrests, deportations, minor triumphs in society, politics and literature and a duel fought with Paul de Cassagnac over an article about Joan of Arc. He founded the still popular paper *l'Intransigéant* and in the late '90's he wrote *The Adventure of My Life* which appeared in five racy volumes. Jules Lemaître summed him up as "an espouser of colorful and idiotic causes."

It would be gratifying to think that the political members of the Loynes coterie were among the more liberal thinkers of the country, but such was far from the case. Most of them leaned at a giddy angle to the extreme Right, which could mean anything from blind pro-monarchism to savage anti-Semitism; and all too frequently the two movements went hand in hand. If the countess herself was a Royalist, she was a levelheaded one. She would never have dreamed of going about wearing one of the Royalist Movement buttons adorned with a picture of "Our Young King" (probably because they were unbelievably hideous) and she only smiled when one evening at her house a group of enthusiasts speculated upon how the youthful monarch would make his triumphal entry into the capital ... in open landeau like President Carnot, or would the Royal Coach be rolled out of the Carnavalet Museum, refurbished with plumes and fleur-de-lis'd banners and hitched to three pairs of prancing grays? She knew better than to hope for an immediate Restoration, but she did throw her cap in for what seemed the next best hope, a brief allegiance to General Boulanger.

The rise and fall of an obscure and utterly absurd cavalry

officer named Georges Boulanger was a phenomenon which could only have sprouted from romantic soil in a climate of conflicting loyalties. France at all times has admired the *beau geste*. Furthermore the country had become accustomed to *coups d'état*. The first Napoleon's was a matter of not too ancient history and that of his nephew, a matter of personal memory. It was not surprising that in 1889, a third was almost successfully brought off. Boulanger was a military career man who endeared himself first to the army by bringing about certain reforms. The reforms were hardly of world-shaking importance. One was the addition of codfish to the soldiers' mess, another, the painting of all sentry boxes tri-color, a third, the allocation of a horse to every captain and . . . most rapturously appreciated of all, permission for privates to wear beards. When he turned to politics and became minister of war, he endeared himself to the French people, who were still licking their wounds received at Sedan, by advocating a policy of militant Revenge against Germany. Handsome, blond-bearded, a magnificent rider, impeccably clad in tight-fitting uniform dazzling with medals and augmented by a red carnation (symbol of the Boulangist Party) he embodied the dash and bravura of the Grand Army prior to 1870. Paris fell in love with this comic opera hero as a girl might lose her head over a second officer of Hussars. It has been said that it is useless looking at Boulanger except through the eyes of a woman. Every scrawny factory girl, every footsore midinette gazed at his picture on a three-sou postcard stuck in the cracked mirror of her attic bedroom and society women, flaunting the red carnation, dreamed of luring him into their scented boudoirs.

His vanity was preposterous. When one palpitating female complimented him on the shapeliness of his hands, he added to her raptures by saying "Ha, madame! But you should see my feet!" When, on his black charger, he caracolled down the

Champs Elysées, there were cries of "Vive Boulanger!" and a few alarming shouts of "Vive l'Empereur!" Aristocratic hostesses swore allegiance to him and as intelligent a woman as the Duchesse d'Uzès gave him considerable funds, for she saw in him a leader who would effect a restoration of the monarchy.

Fortunately for the Third Republic, Boulanger was no leader but merely an absurd show-off . . . "a Bonaparte without a victory to his name," as André Maurois calls him. One of the first to see through his sham was Clemenceau, who had him removed from office and sent to command a garrison in Clermont-Ferrand. When the general set off, crowds mobbed the station to prevent his departure, emotional admirers swarmed through his car, climbed all over the train and one or two desperadoes flung themselves onto the tracks ahead of the engine but jumped nimbly aside when finally it started to move. After a few weeks, Boulanger broke orders and returned to the capital flagrantly AWOL. The Paris mob went wild. They pelted his carriage with flowers and hailed him as the new Man of Destiny. A summary dismissal from the army merely added to his popularity and when he had the gall to stand for a seat in the Chamber as deputy for the North, he won by an overwhelming majority. His cheering supporters looked to the glorious moment when they would bear him on triumphant shoulders to the Elysée Palace itself.

A number of anti-Boulangists failed to share this enthusiasm. Among these were the university students who regarded this as a fine opportunity for indulging in their favorite pastime of rioting. A large and noisy delegation marched in protest to the house of Charles Floquet, President of the Chambre. Floquet received them cordially, shook their hands, told them to study diligently and never make fun of their professors, then sent them back to the Left Bank completely happy. Actually Floquet, a dedicated radical, was all on their side. Like Clemenceau he saw through the bogus nonsense of Boulanger, and the day the general made his initial entrance into the Chambre, Floquet cried out, "Sir, at your age Napoleon was dead!" This resulted in a duel in which the chocolate soldier was slightly wounded and that added fuel to the popular blaze. The Leftists began supporting him as being "for the people," whatever that meant. The Right saw in him a crusader for the monarchy and even the Comte de Paris wore the red carnation. The Bonapartists went blithely along because this was the sort of melodrama they enjoyed and Boulanger reminded them of their two emperors, whom he resembled at least to the extent that he all but pulled off a third *coup d'état*.

Two things saved France from another dictatorship. One was a clever move by the Liberals to try Boulanger for treason. The other, in keeping with the times, was an affair of the heart. The general had a mistress, a quiet lady who went by the engaging name of Mme. Bonnemain. In 1891 this Mrs. Goodhand died in Brussels and her heartbroken lover, who with his treason trial pending had fled the country, committed suicide on her grave. A stone still stands in the Belgian cemetery bearing simply the epitaph "Marguerite et Georges." Back in France, the Byronic gesture caused sentimental consternation among the general public, although the aristocracy considered it to be in bad taste as a painful offense to the general's widow and Clemenceau dismissed the whole opéra bouffe affair with the terse obituary: "Boulanger died as he had lived . . . a young second lieutenant."

Mme. de Loynes wasted no time in mourning the demise of the hero of the hour. The red carnation was quickly discarded for her habitual Parma violets and she turned full attention on her salon. At the time she was busy changing its locale from the rue de l'Arcade to 152 Avenue des Champs Elysées. In making the move, she took with her all her monumental furniture, her cumbersome draperies, her bibelot hideosities because, as she explained, her friends were used to them and any change of décor might prove distracting. The conversation begun in the rue de l'Arcade continued without interruption in the Champs Elysées.

Nor did the move alter her manner of dress which remained romantically Winterhalter. When Léon Daudet first called upon her, he found her wearing a quilted tea gown of dusty rose trimmed in black Alençon lace, fluttering an eighteenth century fan, surrounded by a bevy of little poodles who whenever their mistress laughed . . . and when she did, she had a habit of flinging her round arms joyously above her head . . . would jump about and yap hysterically. Physically frail as a flower and afflicted to an abnormal degree with the national aversion to drafts, she kept a log burning the year round in her fireplace and never sat more than a few feet away from the intense heat.

And yet this woman must have had a formidable inner strength, for her daily routine and the constant demands made upon her called for tireless and self-renewing energy. Every afternoon from five to seven she was at home to callers, and they called in a steady stream. She would also set aside private appointments during the day for persons who sought her advice. Her advice was usually good and her capacity for sympathetic listening even better. It was mainly for the latter that men sought the advice. They knew the beautiful woman would hear them out to the end and in future would never betray a confidence.

In addition to her daily "at homes" and private confessionals, she gave two carefully planned weekly dinners, one every Friday, the other every Sunday. Sunday was for her intimate friends whom she called her "family." Friday was the evening for feeding her lions. And she fed them royally, for her table was one of the best in Paris. She supervised every detail of her cuisine. She knew the most excellent brands, patronized the best delicacy shops, drove with her chef to outlying markets for the freshest vegetables. She had an Escoffier sense of cooking and whenever she dined out well, never returned home without a new recipe she'd wheedled from the maître d'hôtel tucked into the palm of her tiny kid glove.

Cost was no problem and she imported her game, fish and fruit from the right provinces in the right season. Her fowl came from Bourg en Bresse with an occasional present of pheasant or grouse sent by a poacher she knew, hams from Luxeuil, and the only fish allowed into her kitchen had to be freshly dripping with brine from the Brittany coast. Fruits were served at lush prime . . . peaches and pears from the Gironde, apples from Normandy. Once François Coppée bit into a melon which wasn't quite ripe and it caused an intra-salon scandal that lasted for years. The Loynes wine cellar was famous and the service generous. Before each guest stood a glass for sherry, a glass each for white and red Bordeaux, one for Burgundy, another for Château Yquem and a goblet for champagne. It was sufficient to satisfy even the novelist Xavier de Montépin, an unquenchable drinker who, whenever offered a choice of two wines, would hold up a glass in either hand and say "Volontiers!" Meals were served with perfect timing and no dish ever arrived cold.

Dinner was announced on the dot of seven by an ancient maître d'hôtel who had the mournfully impressive manner of a sacristan at the Madeleine and Madame and her guests went straight to table never waiting for any latecomer. The meal lasted just two hours. From nine on, after-dinner guests would drop in with the latest news from the Chambre, the most recent gossip from the Boulevards. The talk was always gay, stimulating

and easy, but evenings never lasted long. At eleven, Mme. de
Loynes's companion, Mlle. Beer, would come in quietly, undo
the countess's hair which fell in two long, thick tresses down to
her knees, and start arranging it for the night. This was the
signal for guests to depart . . . which they all did within
twenty minutes. The guests were mostly men, although one
or two special wives were allowed in on sufferance. There was
an atmosphere of easy grace to these evenings, of gaiety and
warm intimacy. It was the hostess who created the atmosphere
. . . not because of her literacy or political perception. She was
no genuine intellectual and her politics were naïvely childish.
It was her tact, her unbelievable charm, coupled with a simplicity
which made her treat celebrities and ordinary persons like close
friends. One was never aware that she was running a salon.
She seemed more to be presiding over an affectionate foyer. She
disciplined conversation gently but definitely, never allowing
discussion to heat up into argument. A delicate touch on the
arm and a quiet "One moment, Rochefort, let's hear Maurice
Barrès opinion," a gesture to impose respectful attention when
Renan wanted the floor or a whispered "Sh, mon ami, Sardou is
talking about his new play."

Victorien Sardou was in a position of authority to talk about
plays and playwriting and to talk with style and brevity. "A
well-contrived play," he said, "like a good novel, can be told
about in three minutes. One minute for the subject, one for
action and plot and one for the denouement." Certainly *Tosca,
Fédora, Mme. Sans-Gêne* and those other highly successful creations of overtheatricality which Bernard Shaw called "sheer Sar-
doudledum" are masterpieces of sleek compactness. Léon Blum,
the future Premier, who during the '90's was dramatic critic
for *L'Humanité,* said, "There are, in the mere first act of *Di-
vorçons,* my entire two big volumes on marriage."

Sardou was a frequent guest at the Loynes Friday dinners. He used also to visit her by private appointment to pour his personal problems into Madame's receptive little ear. He called her his "supreme consolatrice," although what Sardou, luxuriating in his fat royalties, had to be consoled about is hard to conjecture. He owned a house in Paris, a farm outside Nice, as well as his Villa Théodora on the shores of the Mediterranean. As if such an accumulation of real estate were not sufficient, he acquired a Louis XIV château at Marly. It was approached through huge wrought-iron gates and up a magnificent avenue which was flanked on either side by a row of rose-colored granite sphynxes that had been the sensation of the Exposition of '67. The château itself was a treasury of Beauvais tapestries, a collection of ancient firearms, priceless documents pertaining to the French Revolution and a library of over twenty thousand books. Sardou was an omnivorous reader and a genuine scholar when it came to research for correct details in his historical dramas. The period of the French Revolution fascinated him as much as the Civil War intrigues our modern afficionados. The fate of the Royalists during the Terror appealed to him chiefly because of its dramatic possibilities. His romantic drama *Thermidor,* originally called *The Last Tumbril,* was withdrawn from the Comédie Française and all other government-owned theatres because President Carnot thought it too eloquently sympathetic to the royal martyrs. It is gratifying to learn that during the shocking hysteria of the Affair, Sardou was openly on the side of Dreyfus . . . which cannot be said for all the members of the Loynes circle.

At the height of his success as a dramatist, Sardou was also at the height of an affair with his great interpreter, Sarah Bernhardt. Each play he wrote was practically tailor-made for her. "Sardou et Sarah," they were known in the theatre world as "The

two S's." For every production they launched together they
had the Midas touch. Their joint venture with *Théodora,* with
incidental music by Massenet, grossed over two and a half million francs on its initial run at the Odéon. All of this was on
the professional side. The personal one may well have been less
felicitous. Love affairs with Sarah were always tempestuous.
Perhaps that was why he needed consolation.

One characteristic he and his "supreme consolatrice" had in
common was a terror of drafts, almost to panic degree. Winter
and summer, Sardou went about swathed in a voluminous muffler with a Kronstadt hat jammed down over his brow. Even
indoors, he was never without a beret. Michel Georges-Michel
would come across him in the Pâtisserie Favart on the Boulevard
des Italiens, bundled in innumerable wrappings and avidly devouring mille-feuille pastry. "Saperlipopette!" It was Sardou's
pet expletive. "Eat pastries, young man!" Such was his advice
to young writers. "They rejuvenate one. At least that is the
opinion of old men who were deprived of pastries in their youth.
Others make the same silly mistake with love." According to
Michel Georges-Michel, it was actually a draft which caused his
death. He had been asked to preside at the unveiling of Rodin's
statue to Henry Becque. A bitter, wet wind swirled about the
speakers' platform and Sardou, sneezing and coughing, went
miserably through the ceremonies, then hastened home to bed
and a case of pneumonia from which he never recovered. An
ironic spirit of his phobia must have hung about after his death,
for when a subsequent memorial statue was erected to him it
was first installed in the *carrefour* of the Madeleine where at
all seasons, day and night, there blasts a continual windtunnel
from the rue Royale and the two boulevards. As Michel Georges-
Michel put it, the statue succumbed to the drafts and was thought-
fully transferred to the more salutary air of the Boulevard Suchet.

Another playwright friend of Jeanne de Loynes, and a vastly entertaining man, was Adolphe-Philippe d'Ennery. He was a prodigally prolific writer with over three thousand plays to his credit, an output to compete with that of Lope de Vega in number if not in quality. D'Ennery was the perpetrator of that hardy perennial *The Two Orphans*. When he wasn't turning out originals, he was dramatizing the books of popular novelists. Jules Verne was one of his steady collaborators and between them they launched the stage version of *Around the World in Eighty Days*. Spectacular melodrama with preposterous plots, they were known as the "delight of the concièrges" and they ran for months, sometimes for years. D'Ennery quite frankly wrote his "janitorious" plays for the crowd who lapped them up. The crowd still does some periodic lapping when that thundering museum piece *Michael Strogoff* is resuscitated at the Châtelet . . . that theatre having a stage large enough to accommodate the massive sets, snowstorm machinery, sleighs, Tartars, Russians and a pack of ravening wolves. D'Ennery had the mercantile instinct of the practical businessman. In the phrase of the day, he "turned his windmill in the direction he knew the breezes would blow" and his profits were immense. The cheaply popular caliber of his plays never in the least shamed him. They constituted his livelihood. The enjoyment of that livelihood was another matter.

It is not as a playwright that D'Ennery is to be remembered but as an art connoisseur who left his rare Oriental collection to the city, as a delightful host in his house on the Avenue du Bois and especially as a quick and engaging wit. Every afternoon found him at his special table at the Café Saint Martin playing dominoes and tossing off the *mots* which gained him the name of the King of the Boulevard Saint-Martin. Aurélien Scholl once asked him why he never wrote any of his native wit into his plays and was told, "I wouldn't want to upset my public. They'd think someone else wrote them."

Adolphe D'Ennery was a happy man and one who had an appearance of being eternally young in spite of the fact that since early youth his hair had been snow-white. "It's a misfortune to be prematurely white," he told Jeanne de Loynes. "I'm old before my time." Then he added brightly, "So you see? I'll never age any further!"

In 1882, D'Ennery married Gisette Desgranges. She had been his mistress for years, and before that she'd enjoyed a highly successful amorous career. In fact, she and Jeanne, when the latter was still Mlle. Detourbey, were on the Second Empire town at the same time. The Goncourt brothers, who seem to have known her well, for their journal is filled with items about her, remonstrated with her over not only her promiscuity but over her choice of what seemed to them inferior lovers. Gisette laughed away their concern. "Que voulez-vous?" she said, "It's been raining and I've been bored." After Gisette's marriage to Adolphe D'Ennery, she quieted down but still kept a spirit of independence. Seeing her starting out from home one evening, her husband asked her where she was going.

"Where I like" she retorted.

"When will you be back?"

"When I like."

"Good," he said "But no later, please."

Edmond de Goncourt had met Gisette in her earlier days at a party of some friends and later took her back to her house in a fiacre. He gives an accurate report of their conversation which bears repetition:

GONCOURT: What if you came to see my "monsters"?*

GISETTE: Well maybe, some day.

* A term for etchings.

GONCOURT: No. Tell me what day. I'll tell you why. So that I can dust them.

GISETTE: Then, *your* day. I'm always free. I belong to no jurisdiction.

GONCOURT: Free, yes; but vacant?

GISETTE (after a brief pause): No. (another pause) Here I am at four in the morning with Monsieur de Goncourt, a man I've always been mad to know.

GONCOURT: Et ça roule?

GISETTE: Ça roule. Just the same I'll admit I've never read a single book of yours. I don't know if you've got any talent.

GONCOURT (solemnly): I have a great deal. (further badinage) Do you know our conversation is as tiring as a Beaumarchais comedy. Here we are, the two of us and a thousand things might happen. May I suggest one? If and when I make love to you, supposing that I succeed, we'll end up by quarreling, then we'll hate each other. Shall we make a treaty? Shall we become old friends? We'll reciprocally speak well of each other. We'll defend each other when people talk against us. We'll share our enemies.

GISETTE: And where will that lead us?

GONCOURT: That will lead us never to become annoyed with each other, to dine together once a year and to know each other without ever bearing any sort of grudge. Till Thursday! (kissing her hand before her door) This is very solemn!

The Ennerys were a happy couple. Years of lively marriage went by and Gisette's once toothsome figure plumped out into overgenerous proportions. One Tuesday night at the Française, she had gone up the stairs ahead of her husband while he loitered below chatting with a friend. Hearing the warning bell for the rising curtain, she paused on a step and called down for him to hurry. As he continued to delay, she stamped her foot in exasperation and muttered, "Vieux cocu!"* Adolphe glanced up tenderly at his wife's middle-aged posterior and called back gaily, "Not any longer, ma chère!"

The Ennerys were lifelong friends of the countess. They were always a part of her "family" Sunday dinners, along with Jules Verne and other intimates. Ennery was always gay, always with a bite to his wit. One day, discussing an aging actress named Zulma Bouffer who was booked to play too young a role in a play at the Ambigu, his wife said the opening was Wednesday. He said no, that it was Tuesday. She insisted it was Wednesday. "Impossible!" he said. "Wednesday, Zulma will be too old."

Gisette D'Ennery was the first to die. Adolphe was stricken with sorrow over her loss and soon went into a decline. Mme. de Loynes put herself out to take care of him and to nurse him herself. When he finally died, she was holding his hand and gently stroking his forehead.

A third successful playwright friend of the Comtesse de Loynes was Henri Lavedan. It was largely through her influence that he was elected to the French Academy at the remarkably youthful age of thirty-nine. Other writers had made their way to the coveted chair under the Cupole through her quiet but powerful guidance and her salon has been called a "veritable factory of Academicians." Every writer of stature was at some time stricken with what was called the "green fever," the feeling that he owed it to himself and posterity to put on the green-trimmed uniform and take his place amid the forty Immortals. As Ludovic Halévy pointed out to Anatole France, who was hesitant about

* Old cuckold.

putting himself up as a candidate, "One *must* be a member! And besides, *Membre de l'Academie Française* looks so well on the cover of a book!" Jeanne de Loynes knew its importance to an author's career. She was personally acquainted with a number of the grand old Immortals themselves. Whenever she read that death had made a vacancy in their Elysium, she was quick to pick a possible replacement from her circle of friends and start grooming him for the ordeal which lay in wait for him. There has always been something Molièresque about the complicated and humiliating business of getting oneself elected to the Academy . . . a sort of do-it-yourself immortality. First of all, the initial letter of application must be a gem of fine prose and brevity. Then come the weeks of personal soliciting for votes when the wretched candidate, bearing credentials like a servant with letters of reference, must go to pay a formal call on every accessible Academician. One can imagine the strained assumption of easy charm, the self-conscious offhand display of  intellect, the ghastly efforts to please without fawning and the further indignities attendant upon making it into the world's most civilized frat house.

Little Mme. de Loynes knew all the ropes and enjoyed telling her candidate how to pull the right one at the right time — which of the great men he should approach first and what he should talk about. Being a mortal woman, she sensed that these Olympians must get fed up with their particular subjects. She knew that Leconte de Lisle, the Master of Parnassian verse, would far prefer to discuss the charms of the Luxembourg Gardens where he walked every day than accept stilted homage for his poetry. Louis Pasteur found little relish in chatting about rabies or anthrax if he could be led into a discussion of the beauties of catholicism. As for the Duc d'Aumale, one could far more rapidly cut the royal ice with him by bringing up the name of some

reigning demi-mondaine than by asking him about his art collection at Chantilly.

If, which rarely happened, for the countess was cagy on
backing an Academy winner, one of her candidates were turned
down on his first attempt at admission, she was firmly insistent
that he make a second. "After all," she would say, "Voltaire
had to try three times before he made it." And if, which was
even more rare, her aspirant failed altogether, she would console
him with the reminder that Balzac never did get in. But her
protégé usually did make it and her reward was his Reception
Day when she took her place in the Visitors' Gallery under the
great Cupola which, according to Goncourt — who himself
never made the steep grade — shed a light "gray as the literature
encouraged beneath it, falling cold and mournful on the cra-
niums below." The pretty ladies on these reception days in their
tulle scarfs and great hats must have looked like gay flowerpots
in the ancient balcony. Jeanne gave little thought to the dingy
light or the academic dust. Her proud moment was when her
winner made his initial entrance, wearing for the first time his
frog-footman uniform with its palm-embroidered jacket, satin
breeches and the unaccustomed sword batting nervously against
a silk-stockinged leg, spoke his acceptance speech then, at the
finish, sank gratefully into his appointed chair . . . one of the
historic fauteuils once occupied by who knows which master . . .
Musset? La Fontaine? Voltaire himself? Of these revered armchairs Prosper Mérimée once impiously remarked that they were
the requisite for that assemblage in which "we are paid eighty-
three francs a month to sleep during sessions . . . but not to
snore, that is expressly forbidden."

Somnolence among the Immortals was a standard joke. There
was the one about a man meeting his academician friend on
the Pont des Arts and asking him where he was going. "To the

Academy," says the friend. "Whatever for?" asks the man. "To catch an hour's sleep." "Ah yes. The sleep of the gods!" But for all the derision, admission to this high court of scholarship was the undisputed stamp of prestige and Mme. de Loynes knew it. As her friend Paul Bourget wrote, "The French Academy represents along with the Vatican and the House of Lords one of the three pillars of civilization." Ernest Renan took a more moderate view of his predecessors. "Don't say they have done nothing, these devotees of culture who spend their lives investigating the credential of words and weighing up syllables. They have produced a masterpiece . . . the French language." Undoubtedly Jeanne de Loynes's proudest moment in the Visitors' Gallery was on January 16, 1896, when Jules Lemaître gave his "Discours de réception" and took his seat amid the famous Forty. Lemaître was comparatively young to be an academician, only forty-three, and an observer noted "his April contrasting sharply with the December of the other members." But Lemaître was already a leading theatre reviewer, a first-rate playwright and the best literary critic since Sainte-Beuve. His ironic essays in the ten volumes of his *Les Contemoprains* even now are well worth reading. The Comtesse de Loynes was justly proud of his laurels, or rather his Academic palms. She had worked for him to receive them, more diligently than for any of her other candidates. Jules Lemaître was her last and greatest love and the final years of her life were entirely dedicated to him.

They had met ten years previously. She was over fifty and he barely thirty-three. The setting for the meeting was like something created by Dumas *fils* in his early hearts-and-flowers period. It was in a conservatory at a masked ball given by Arsène Houssaye, author of long forgotten novels and onetime director of the Théâtre Français. Houssaye had been quite a gay blade in his day. Toward the end of the Second Empire, he used to give lavish bachelor parties for which he'd import the leading cocottes of the season; each of them was brought to the festivities in a sedan chair, borne by liveried flunkeys. In later years, Houssaye liked to get dressed up in historical costume, hire an orchestra and invite his friends to attend a party in similar historical costume if with less enthusiasm. Jeanne de Loynes's concession to costume that evening had been a Venetian tricorne hat, a mask and an enveloping domino of purple to match her violets. What Lemaître was wearing is not recorded . . . what any wretched man is obliged to wear at any fancy-dress function is usually mercifully forgotten. The two were introduced in the conservatory and the tactful host left them to talk for two hours straight in the romantic atmosphere of flowers, ferns, damp earth and dripping water pipes. Lemaître was completely captivated by her manner, her graceful choice of words and the warm beauty of her voice. She, delighted by his youthful intelligence and obvious ardor, rather capriciously refused to divulge her name. Eventually she rose, still wearing her mask, and asked him to see her to her carriage. "I'm home every afternoon from five to seven," she whispered as she swept into her waiting brougham. A footman slammed the door and hopped onto the box, the coachman cracked his whip and Lemaître, like a moonstruck schoolboy, stood listening mutely to the diminishing clatter of hoofbeats on damp cobbles. Next morning, in a whirl of infatuation, he called up Henri Houssaye, the son of Arsène (Lemaître and Henri Houssaye were among the moderns who owned telephones) who said, "Stop by for me tomorrow and I'll take you there."

When they arrived next afternoon at 152 Avenue des Champs Elysées, Madame was holding her usual daily court. Maurice Barrès was there and Ludovic Halévy, co-author of *La Périchole* and *La Belle Hélène*. An important senator was just taking his leave, Boni de Castellane was paying his elaborate respects and before long, Ernest Renan lumbered in. The distinguished company impressed young Lemaître. But what impressed him most was his remarkable hostess who, seemingly unconcerned about her own fading looks, sat beneath the Duval portrait of herself, dispensing tea and irresistible charm. If her advancing years caused her secret distress (and what aging beauty does not go through such private hells?) they were of no consequence to her gentlemen callers, who continued to adore her. As one of them, Arthur Meyer, remarked, "She knew how to discourage age so as not to sadden the old friends who looked at her." Lemaître, the new friend, also looked at this lady, his senior by two decades, and found her lovely and completely desirable. He couldn't have failed to notice the contrast with the young beauty of the Duval portrait but, as André de Fouquières put it, "he must have dreamed of that young woman as one dreams of what cannot exist, of a person in a novel he might have written, of the image of a past which perhaps it was well he never knew." The next day he called again, and the following one, and for the next twenty years not a single day went by in which he did not see her.

The literary set was rather astonished over the Loynes-Lemaître affair; not all of them were kind about it. Henri Becque, whose tongue could be as caustically sharp as his social perception, said, "Jules Lemaître is now working in demolition." Such comments didn't bother the lovers. From the moment she first received Jules, Jeanne ran her salon and her life exclusively for him. She recognized the high quality of his talents and she knew the people who could further his career. To watch it grow was the only reward she wanted. The great happiness of her later years, as she told Arthur Meyer with disarming candor, was to find herself the mistress of this young intellectual. "I am rewarming myself with his youth" were her words. Lemaître, for his part, became her lover not in order to advance himself but because, quite simply, he adored her and because, no matter what her age, she was all grace, all gentle response, all woman. It was his midsummer love affair and her blazing autumnal one, profound and tender on both sides.

Although they never stayed in the same house, he living in the rue des Ecuries d'Artois which was nearby, there was a marital quality to their relationship. At the weekly Friday dinners she reigned as hostess at one end of the table, he at the other end acted as host. For the Sunday "family" meals, his place was as head of the household although he sometimes took a Sunday off to see the Strauses, Princesse Mathilde or his friend the dramatic critic Ganderax. All other evenings, the two ate tête-à-tête in a small, intimate dining room. Afterward they'd play a game or two of billiards at which the lady always won. He would leave early because, for all her boundless energy, she fancied her health as being delicate and would have to get to bed.

Lemaître brought new blood into the salon, new people, new interests. Among the newcomers was Maurice Donnay, later to become a stylish playwright but then a popular *chansonnier* of Montmartre where he was producing the beguiling shadow plays at the Chat Noir which were attracting Tout Paris. He'd bring his guitar and sing his latest songs, being warned by his hostess that they must not be bawdy, for this courtisane-countess was insistent at all times on strict respectability. Or Donnay would strum a muted accompaniment while Lemaître, who had a fine speaking voice, would read from the early poets — François Villon, Clément Marot and the Renaissance nightingale Pierre de Ronsard. His mistress would listen with eyes half closed and at the finish sigh softly, "Ah, my friend! If Ronsard could have heard you read that!" Sometimes Donnay and Léon Daudet would join in duets . . . ancient ballads or marching songs of the Chouans, the royalist army of the Vendée. Léon Daudet was a belligerent monarchist. He was also a snob and an anti-Semite to the degree that he'd all but leave the room upon the arrival of Arthur Meyer. Instead he took out his venom in his memoirs, which make for shocking reading.

Arthur Meyer had started out as secretary to a celebrated Second Empire courtisane named Blanche d'Antigny who, it was said, took daily baths in champagne. He emerged from this exotic milieu to go into journalism, making his way to the conservative top when he became editor of the *Gaulois,* an openly royalist paper which dealt less with world news than with social reportage. Meyer was pretty much of a snob himself. An accepted member of the smart set, a renegade Jew, converted Catholic, he never, according to Léon Daudet, "forgot that he was of Jewish origin, but did everything in his power to make others forget it." He was cowardly, overly ingratiating, and his appearance didn't add any further prestige; he looked very much like one of Forain's vicious cartoons, big paunch, large pink nose and watery eyes, head almost bald except for a white fringe at his fleshy neckline, which along with his Dundreary mustachios he had curled daily by a coiffeur. He cultivated only the upper echelons of the *gratin* and any encounter with royalty sent him into a tailspin of excitement. Calling one day on Boni de Castellane, he walked in to find that the Infanta Eulalie of Spain was also present. In his rapturous confusion, Meyer nodded cheerily to the Infanta and with a low bow kissed Boni's hand instead of hers. The story went the rounds of the clubs and the Jew baiters were delighted.

Poor Meyer! Those were harsh times in which to be a Jew, and to be an absurd one was fatal. The fact that he proclaimed himself as violently anti-Dreyfus merely added to the absurdity, for everyone saw through the subterfuge including Mme. de Loynes, who tried nevertheless to be a loyal friend. The one unkind remark ever attributed to her was when, during a discussion of duty to one's country, Meyer blustered that at the first sign of danger to the Patrie he would rush for the border, and she slyly inquired "Which border, my friend?" Arthur Meyer's worst humiliation came about when Edouard Drumont, author of *La France Juive* and editor of the anti-Semitic daily *La Libre Parole,* after merciless insults managed to goad Meyer into a duel. Meyer, who couldn't have fought a duel with little Lord Fauntleroy, shaking from head to foot, met his opponent on the island of the Grande Jatte. The choice of weapons was swords and when the call to start sounded, Meyer, his right arm paralyzed with terror, lifted his unarmed left hand and grabbed Drumont's brandished blade in a grotesque gesture of self-protection which resulted in a spurt of blood and the intervention of the surgeon. The affair of honor was declared finished, but not the gossip. Exaggerated accounts of the ludicrous incident were repeated in the boulevard cafés and the columnists wrote it up under the heading of "La Gauche Célèbre!"

The Comtesse de Loynes had too many good Jewish friends ever to be an openly declared anti-Semite. Loyalty to friends with her was a deep emotion. But loyalty to country was a passion which went to the degree of blind chauvinism. For all her remarkable qualities, the lady was not a profound thinker. Once while discussing the wave of anti-clericalism which was sweeping the country, an ardently Romanist guest declared that when it came to his loyalties, he was a Catholic before he was a Frenchman. "Catholic before being French?" she exclaimed. "Oh happy the man who has been baptized before being born!"

The friends who surrounded the countess during the latter '90's influenced her political thinking . . . if thinking it can be called. During the Dreyfus case, a hysterically patriotic organization which called itself La Ligue de la Patrie Française was more or less formed in her salon. This body, according to the *Oxford*

*Companion to French Literature,* "typified all that was bigoted, anti-Semitic and reactionary in public life." It was an offshoot of the Nationalist Movement and, of all persons, Jules Lemaître was chosen for its president. This seems incomprehensible when one recalls that Lemaître had started out as a bourgeois liberal and ardent Republican. But gradually he had gone conservative, then reactionary. The Panama scandal with its sordid political shenanigans had disgusted him with the existing government and the League appeared to him as a shining hope for a corrupted nation. What started out as a mere propaganda committee developed into a contending political party with high hopes of succeeding to power. After all, one more political party in France was rather like one more religious cult in California. Paul Déroulède lent his endorsement, fiery old Henri de Rochefort was wildly active in the cause and even cheerful, easygoing Alfred Capus became a Leaguer because, he said, "Pacifism is the art of adapting oneself to defeat." The Ligue de la Patrie Française grew. Its members began to feel confident of winning a victory in the Chambre. All the important meetings of its leaders took place in the Loynes salon, and public rallies were held in hired halls in which Lemaître turned from writing to oratory. So did François Coppée. It was said that the two of them "drenched all of France with the torrent of their oratory." Election night, the countess sat with Lemaître, Coppée, Maurice Barrès, Brunetière and the rest of the misguided patriots in the Café de la Paix, where announcements of the returns were periodically delivered to them. With each announcement, their hopes dwindled. When defeat was certain, she somewhat sententiously, quoted Tacitus, saying, "It is not necessary to succeed, but to persevere."

However, instead of wasting time in persevering over a dead and buried cause, she went back to running her drawing room in the old manner. To quote Jules Bertaud: "The thunder of political strife echoed no longer within those gracious walls, and when at last she died, it seemed as though a peculiarly French tradition of culture had passed away forever." She died in 1908 . . . quietly and without inconveniencing anyone.

Lemaître, when he heard the news, hid his sorrow by remarking, "Sweet darling! We shall meet her in a better *demi-monde*." But poor old Arthur Meyer came closer to summing her up when he said that her tombstone should read simply: "Here lies Charm."

# 8

## THE GRAND HORIZONTALS

ON ANY fine afternoon of spring, the stroller under the chestnuts of the Champs Elysées might have caught sight of a
debonair phaeton amid the more conservative vehicles out on
the Avenue, its harness gleaming conspicuously, cockades of pink
carnations on the horses' bridles and on the driver's and footman's
hats, and lolling back on the satin upholstery a ravishing creature
of insolent beauty. Her dress would have been as smart as that
of any society lady but more flamboyant, her immense hat would
have been preposterously trimmed into a flowerstand of roses or
a veritable aviary of bird wings, and her parasol would have had
several additional flounces of frilling. In a day when a respectable
woman would as soon have walked naked down a street as to
appear with make-up on her face, the creature's mouth would
have been crimson with rouge, her eyes rimmed with kohl, and
while young matrons of the *gratin* exhibited their jewels sparingly
and only in the ballroom or the opera box, the beauty's diamonds,
flashing in the sun, would have semaphored the word "Courtisane" for all the world to see and rich men to take note. For this
would have been an "eight-spring luxury model," out to make a
pleasurably shocked world aware of her existence. She was a
member of that high-priced hierarchy known as the "Dégrafées"
(the Unbuttoned) or, more graphically, "The Grand Horizontals"
. . . as undisputed a part of the Paris scene as the aristocracy, the
Army or the French Academy. The leading cocottes were in an
upper echelon not to be spoken of in the same breath as the

status of an ordinary prostitute. They were celebrities as firmly established as the top stars of the theatre. They were the talk of the smart set. *Boulevardiers* quoted their bons mots (for these great dolls were clever as steel traps and terrifyingly witty). Even the press rated them as important news. The respectable *Figaro* devoted columns to descriptions of their jewels, their furs, their rampant aigrettes and cascading birds-of-paradise. The *Echo de Paris* printed accounts of their activities, insofar as they were printable, and one issue of the literate *Gil Blas* had a full-length article on a litter of puppies born to the prize poodle of Marthe de Kerrieu. Daily papers and weeklies were blatantly frank in regard to their alliances and ruptures, never hesitating to give names, and the public lapped it up as avidly as a shopgirl of today devouring the latest Hollywood scandal.

These queens of the demimonde made no attempts to be accepted by polite society, knowing it to be impossible. Yet they also knew that their presence was tolerated, even actually expected in certain settings that were the prerogative of the privileged class. They joined the upper crust carriage parade during the "Hour for the Bois," they mingled with the blue-bloods at Auteuil and Longchamps, they sat alongside of the high nobility at Bagatelle to watch the polo. They wandered about exclusive art exhibit openings and they added a colorful touch of sin to charity bazaars. Afternoons between five and seven, they turned up at the Palais de Glace where, at sight of them, English governesses hustled away their young charges while respectable skaters lingered on for a few more figure eights and a few surreptitious glances. Mondays at the Opéra and Tuesdays at the Française, they brushed powdered shoulders with duchesses, and at the after-theatre restaurants they sat on banquettes beside high-born hostesses who focused their lorgnettes to study their gowns and jewels, not without a certain envy.

They were star performers in the late-supper scene at the Café

de la Paix, Durand's, the Café Riche. And they were seen at
Paillard's, favorite restaurant of the Prince of Wales.

The midnight resort par excellence for the Horizontals was, of
course, Maxim's, for "What Sainte Clothilde was to the *monde,*
Maxim's was to the demi-*monde*." Few society ladies would have
dared to be seen within the art nouveau interior of that naughty
place, with some emancipated exceptions such as Princesse
Caraman-Chimay, née Clara Ward from Detroit, Michigan, who
eventually ran away with the violinist Rigo and appeared at the
Folies Bergère in pink tights and a series of "Plastic Poses." The
masculine clientele of Maxim's was composed chiefly of members
of that rich and exclusive coterie the French call "le High Life,"
pronouncing it "Hig Leef," rhyming with "fig leaf." The feminine clientele was made up of ladies of easy virtue and expensive
vice. For at Maxim's the courtisane was queen and it was one of
her regal duties to be seen there night after night at the same table,
drinking the same vintage champagne, toying with the same
fresh caviar, listening to the same selections from *Froufrou* played
by Boldi's orchestra. Blazing with jewels, trailing yards of chinchilla and clouds of ylang-ylang scent like puffs from a censer,
she'd wind a haughty way to her special table past the staring
diners, her sinuous movements reflected in the lotus-bordered
mirrors, her bare shoulders made more appetizing by the dim,
iridescent glow from the Lalique glass roof . . . while in her wake
would follow the adorer who was to pay for the champagne, the
caviar and the voluptuous etceteras. And pay he did . . . through
the nose . . . for some of these exquisite wages-of-sin earners
demanded as much as twenty-five gold louis "and," as one of
them stipulated to a prospective patron, "not by the hour, but by
the quarter of the hour."

Such a running price (if "running" may not be the exact
word) could be demanded only by those who had reached the

top of the demimondaine ladder. It had been an arduous and tricky climb for most. Daughters of shopkeepers, cabdrivers, country clerks, God knows what, they had started out honestly enough as nursemaids, artist's models, milliner's assistants, but their beauty and love of a good time had led them to the more enjoyably profitable primrose path. They had to be clever and levelheaded at gathering the primroses. They had to be up to date on the smart world, to acquire elegant manners and more than a smattering of education, to be skillful not only in the bedroom but in conversation at a restaurant table, they had to acquire a sense of timing, when to be voluptuously abandoned, when to be lightheartedly gay and when to be a sympathetic companion. It took intelligence, style and perseverance for an ordinary *demoiselle* to promote herself into the extraordinary position of *grande courtisane.* Once she'd achieved the promotion, she was inclined to adopt some heraldic name preceded by a "de" . . . Liane de Pougy, Clémence de Pibrac, Nelly de Neustraten, Emilienne d'Alençon and further *noms de guerre* culled from the pages of the Almanach de Gotha.

They earned prodigal amounts of money and spent it prodigally. In his Journal, Edmond de Goncourt reports with much irritation that his maid had given notice saying she preferred to work for a *grande cocotte.* The surroundings were more luxurious, the food richer, a poor honest girl received lovely cast-off clothes and got taken to swank watering resorts. Their extravagance was in the classic prostitute tradition of absurd gesture. Emilienne d'Alençon, in a fit of petulance at a lover, flung the matchless pearl necklace he'd just given her out of a third-floor window (one assumes she noted where it landed). In an earlier generation, La Païva, a Second Empire *horizontal* (her palatial house is now the Travellers' Club), stipulated to a wealthy and ardent banker that the price of her favors would be twenty bank notes of a thousand francs each which he must burn one by one during the amatory session. The banker brought the notes, but the sight of them going up in flames was so harrowing that he couldn't accomplish his part of the session. "However," he later confided to a fellow clubman "the notes were all counterfeit." One expensive beauty demanded that her lover, Monsieur de Gramont-Caderousse, give her at Easter the largest and most costly Easter egg there was in town. Easter morning she looked out her window and saw an immense ovoid, gilded and gaily decorated. When opened, it contained an elegant victoria, her coachman and footman and two horses!

The men who footed the cost of these exuberant acts were a variety of Maecenases, wealthy aristocrats, members of the Bourse, successful bookmakers, Argentine millionaires, certain acceptable Americans and a few of the more frivolous crowned heads. One or two of the crowned heads spent so much time in Paris they seem part and parcel of the local scene, Leopold of Belgium, Alfonso of Spain and of course the Prince of Wales who loved Paris gaily and seriously, a city which respected his anonymity where, as he said, "Everybody recognizes me and nobody knows me." The other crowned heads were usually in the French capital on visits of State . . . to attend military reviews or open pavilions in expositions or to endure the excruciating honor of standing beside Monsieur le Président during receptions at the Elysée Palace. They were lucky if they could escape to spend an hour or so at Maxim's, or better still the Café Anglais where on the second floor was the "Grand Seize," a famous and rather notorious private dining room reserved exclusively for royalty, tastefully done in white, gold and red, a sofa discreetly placed in an alcove and a door which locked on the inside. It was none too easy for these royal visitors to slip away from stern public functions to tender private pastimes. André Germain, whose book

*Have Kings the Right to Love?* presents the problem in the very
title, says that their excuse was a visit to the President of the
Senate, "the most useless personage in the Republic who un-
wittingly furnished their alibi." The curious hours these kings
and princes selected for visiting the President of the Senate must
have struck their retainers as rather odd, but nobody commented.

"Gay Paree" and Maxim's are synonymous and under a late
and unusually heavy barrage of the popping of champagne corks,
Maxim's could become very gay indeed. There were times when
guests behaved less like sophisticated men of the world than like
college sophomores. Arnold de Coutades, known to his friends as
Coco, ended up one heavy night, fully dressed, silk-hatted, in
one of the Place de la Concorde fountains, declaiming a gallant
speech to the bronze lady who was dousing him with a steady
stream of water. Maxim's was the perfect setting for cham-
pagnized exuberance and Cornuché the manager had to be the
diplomatic genius that he was to know just how far to let the
gambols go. When Maurice Bertrand, who was known as "le
Monsieur de chez Maxim's," a clubman who was plastered every
night of his life, leapt onto Boldi's music platform and started
conducting the orchestra with a stalk of asparagus, Cornuché
let it pass. And it was not too bad when a Dutch baron named
Paland started juggling plates, five at a time, at his table. But
when Baron Paland brought in a procession of sandwich men
whose billboards advertised a patent medicine for kidney com-
plaint, Cornuché had to call a halt. When the same baron imported from the Cirque d'Hiver a troupe of American Indians in
war paint and feathers and treated them to cigars and champagne,
Cornuché had to evict them before they started scalping the
clients. One evening Maurice Bertrand entered the main dining
room in deep mourning. He was followed by six professional
pallbearers carrying a genuine coffin. Wiping his eyes with a

black-bordered handkerchief, he asked the stunned assembly if they'd care to view the remains. Cornuché's horror was somewhat mollified when the lid was lifted and the remains found to be magnums of champagne from which everyone was invited to drink the proprietor's health. In a book of memoirs, Hugo, who for years was the formidable headwaiter, tells of an evening when a patron whom he tactfully refers to as Mr. F. conducted a blasphemous ceremony he called "The Liturgy of the Golden Calf." After lining up all the waiters, captains and busboys, Mr. F. passed before them with an ecclesiastical plate piled high with gold coin. Pausing before each one, he told him to stick out his tongue, placed a coin on it and made a sign of the Cross with his left hand.

The squandering of money at Maxim's was limitless. Hugo amassed a fortune in gratuities and Gérard the doorman (he served as model for Yves Mirande's play *Le Chasseur de chez Maxim's*) was able to retire to a château in the Pyrenees on the tips he'd saved up. James Gordon Bennett, proprietor of the *Paris Herald,* paid the flower girl five hundred francs for a bunch of country violets and on one expansive occasion a Mr. Todd from New York tossed out fistfuls of louis d'or. They landed all over the room, rolled under tables, fell into wineglasses, hit a few people in the eye and during the merry romp, the queens of the demimonde scrambled, dived, grabbed, kicked and clawed over them like street urchins over pennies.

The tossing of gold coins at Maxim's got to be almost as much of a convention as the tossing of confetti at *Mi-Carême.* When the restaurant was renovated in 1932 and the old raspberry-colored banquettes taken out to be reupholstered, several hundred louis d'or were unearthed from the cracks and crevices into which they'd fallen forty years before.

The wildest of the coin tossers were the Russians. Visiting

grand dukes, princes, Imperial Army officers, the town was over-run with them. They were popularly known as the Boyars and when any of them went into Aristide Bruant's cabaret in Montmartre, the famous *chansonnier* would yell out, "Here come the Cossacks!" Their wealth knew no bounds and neither did their behavior, but they were eagerly catered to because, at the moment, the country was in a state of elation over the Franco-Russian Alliance. The French fleet had put in at Kronstadt, the Russian fleet had returned the call at Toulon, the Tsar and Tsaritza had made an official tour of France, and President Faure had been received at St. Petersburg, secretly chagrined that his position as president of a republic precluded his wearing Court costume. Paris went joyously Rooski. The birth registrars of those years record any number of little Ivans, Dimitris, Olgas and Serges. In Paris, the Boyars were out for a whirl and more than ready to pay. Grand Duke Wladimir added a number of unmounted gems to the gold coin tossing at Maxim's and Grand Duke Serge presented Augustine de Lierre with a twenty-million-franc necklace of pearls tastefully served on a platter of oysters. The professional beauties who reaped the profits of such ducal extravagances often as not earned their rewards, as these titled Tartars could go to eccentric lengths for what they considered to be a whirl. Their antics in the privacy of a *cabinet particulier* could turn into sadistic orgies. One particular count was partial to making pincushion designs with a sharp-pronged fork on a woman's bare bosom while Prince Nicolaevitch and his fellow officers played an interesting little game with loaded revolvers. They'd turn off all lights, then fire in every direction. The extent of the human damage was hushed up but the material damage was stupendous, and their equerries paid royally for the frolic.

In addition to the visiting Slavs there were a few resident ones who preferred the Right Bank of the Seine to either bank of the

Neva. Grand Duke Alexis lived at 38 Avenue Gabriel. Back in his native land he had been Admiral of the Imperial Fleet in charge of the budget. He had handed in reports for vast expenses and demands for reimbursement without showing evidence of having ordered the construction of a single battleship or even a light cruiser. His mistress was an actress named Baletta and after Russia's defeat by the Japanese at Port Arthur, the Moscow and St. Petersburg public referred to her diamond necklace as "The Pacific Fleet." Alexis found life easier in Paris.

Another expatriate was Prince Orloff who had moved to Paris after an incident that cost him his position in the Tsar's army. He and a German officer had had a quarrel resulting in the challenge to a duel. The weapons were neither swords nor pistols but liqueur glasses of Cointreau. They started drinking early in the evening. The German, after the eightieth round, threw up the sponge . . . which wasn't the only thing he threw up . . . and passed out. Orloff kept on until he'd downed one hundred and twelve glassfuls, then rose and walked away seemingly fresh as a daisy. The next day he came down with an all but fatal liver attack and orders of exile which was spent in the not too harsh severity of a palace on the rue Saint-Dominique, a château near Fontainebleau, the position of Secretary to the Russian embassy and an uninterrupted series of love affairs.

If grand ducal behavior could on occasion be appalling, grand horizontal behavior could match it. It was nothing for La Belle Otero, the Spanish dancer, to jump up onto a table at Maxim's and go into a writhing fandango so sensual that every man in the room felt she was making love to him. Watching her, Sem the cartoonist said, "I feel that my thighs are blushing." Cornuché knew Otero to be such a drawing card to his establishment that he never restrained her. But he did some restraining at his Casino in Deauville when a less talented miss named Régine de Fleury sprang onto the pastry sideboard, pulled up her skirts to reveal a pink bottom and sat down on a pile of ices and cream puffs. La Belle Otero had a blatant altercation with the Russians themselves the evening at the Comédie Française when she was ousted from her seat because of the unexpected arrival of the Tsar and his retinue. Striding in magnificent fury toward the exit, she paused for a moment before His Imperial Majesty's box and shouted in her voice of Andalusian brass, "All right, I'll leave! But from this day on, I'll never again eat caviar!"

Such irreverence for royalty was in the Grande Cocotte tradition.

Emilienne d'Alençon had her own high-handed way with Leopold of Belgium. Playing a page in a revue at the Folies Bergère, she attracted the attentions of that wicked old monarch — who added her to his amorous stable.* When Leopold called on her one morning, she sent her maid to give him the peremptory message that she received no one before eleven. The king had the good humor to say: "Let her sleep. I'll come back after Mass and take her out to lunch." It is reassuring to realize that Belgium's king observed his religious devotions before such a rendezvous.

Emilienne d'Alençon was a sugary blonde who, according to Jean Lorrain, looked like a raspberry ice. She was all rosy dimples and pink taffeta with lace frills and occasionally she'd add the surprising note of a monocle. She started her career of what the ever chivalrous French call "galanterie" at the age of fifteen when she ran away from home with a gypsy violinist. A year or so later, fired by aspirations for the stage, she managed to get into the Conservatoire. How she managed may have been the not unusual method of first getting into cozy relations with a senator

---

* It was Emilienne d'Alençon and not Cléo de Mérode, as has been incorrectly rumored, who was for a time one of Leopold's Paris loves.

who "had influence." She never completed her course at the Conservatoire but left after a year. It is doubtful if the move cost France another Bernhardt, for Emilienne's thespian gifts were less adaptable for the House of Molière than for the Cirque d'Eté where she appeared in an act with trained rabbits. Later she and her talented troupe were booked at the Folies Bergère and were much applauded. The rabbits were tinted bright pink and wore paper ruffs. She loved them dearly and toted them along with her everywhere, even to supper at Maxim's where she'd entrust them to the indulgent care of Ursule the lavabo woman.

Among Emilienne's early "protectors" . . . another chivalrous term . . . was the youthful Duc d'Uzès, then barely nineteen, and not yet finished with his education. As Elisabeth de Gramont put it, "he went from the skirts of his professor-priest to the under-skirts of a cocotte." Young Uzès all but ruined himself over this blond lady of the rabbits. His family, desperately concerned, had him shipped off to a regiment in Africa where the poor lad came down with violent dysentery and died at the age of twenty. Shortly after this tragedy, the duchess his mother discovered the loss of a family heirloom, an emerald necklace valued at a million francs. Guessing where it might be, she wrote to Mlle. d'Alençon who dutifully returned it, and the duchess, who was known to be the best sportswoman in France, sent her in exchange a magnificent diamond solitaire. Absurd as she was, Emilienne d'Alençon had a kind heart, a rare quality for anyone in a profession in which a certain amount of bitchiness of nature is almost a requisite. She gave readily to charity and was generous with handouts to friends who were down on their luck. She adopted a bastard child, not her own, and took him wherever she traveled, including a short stay in England. There she passed herself off as a Comtesse de Beaumanoir and the child as heir presumptive to the title. The London ladies were charmed by her manners, which were of crooked-little-finger refinement, and the London gentlemen were allured by her candy-box looks. As she spoke no English and they very little French, her mental powers were not put to any severe test and everything went off swimmingly. Like most of the Horizontals, she'd make her presence known on the Riviera in winter and the beaches in summer, where she startled the bathers with her black silk tights and close-fitting suits. In her spare time, she instructed young debutantes of the demi-monde in what they should know about the banking aristocracy and the ramifications of the Almanach de Gotha.

She almost made the Gotha herself, for she married a titled army officer and for a time could call herself a countess. During this interlude, she became more refined than ever. She wrote a book of poems called *The Temple of Love* . . . at least her name was signed to it, and she made gallant efforts to run a salon specializing in guests who were members of the Academy, or at least candidates for that Institute. It was all on a commendably lofty level. The salon didn't last long. Neither did her marriage. She later took up with a jockey named Alec Carter who was killed in the 1914 war, after which she ended her days in drugs, poetry and lesbianism.

One ramification of the demimonde, and almost a genteel one, was the category of hetairas that were known as the *demi-castors*. *Castor* is French for *beaver* and the term "semi-beaver" would seem bewildering until one considers the manner in which the beaver puts the finishing touches on its house. These were clever and beautiful women, often of good background, who through some breach of the moral code or the scandal of divorce had been socially ostracized but had managed to turn the ostracism into profitable account. Cultivated, endowed with civilized graces, they were frankly — kept women, but kept by one man only, or, at any rate, by one man at a time. The keepers were bankers, diplomats, noblemen, successful men of letters. Each supported his *demi-castor* in a style to which she became willingly accustomed, in a handsome, well-staffed and exquisitely equipped apartment or *hôtel privé*. The lady usually ran her domicile perfectly and her protector would bring his men friends to luncheon or dinner, confident of good food, excellent wines and entertaining conversation. There was an atmosphere of innuendo about these gatherings that the guests found more than agreeable ... the expensive furnishings and rare objets d'art which they knew to have been paid for by their friend ... the intimacy of manner between him and their hostess, an inadvertent term of endearment, a door left accidentally ajar affording a glimpse of a great double bed in an inviting tumble of satin pillows and Valencienne lace spread.

A really distinguished *demi-castor* was Laure Hayman. Born in the foothills of the Andes of a Creole mother and a British father, a direct descendant of the painter Francis Hayman who had been Gainsborough's master, Laure Hayman was a woman of taste and refinement. If she was regarded as a courtisane, she was a very choosy one. Among her choices had been Karl Egon Fürstenberg, the King of Greece, the financier Bischoffsheim, Prince Karageorgevitch and the young Duc d'Orléans, although in 1891 he had just come of age and she was over forty. She was also the mistress of Marcel Proust's Uncle Weill — a liaison which profoundly shocked the other members of the respectable Proust family. Proust used her as a partial model for his Odette de Crécy. The playwright Lavedan had her in mind for certain of his leading roles and Paul Bourget deliberately chose her for the prototype of his heroine Gladys Harvey. When that novel was first published, Laure sent Proust a special copy bound in a piece of iridescent silk from one of her petticoats, and she wrote on the flyleaf, "Never meet a Gladys Harvey." She dressed with quiet elegance, wore her well-earned jewels with discrimination, rode horseback like an amazon, set one of the best tables in Paris and ran a brilliant salon to which men of letters and the arts flocked. She spoke English fluently, and another of her protectors was Michael Herbert, the secretary of the British embassy. She dropped Herbert and for some reason took up with Charles de la Rochefoucault, a rich baron and prominent sportsman but not too bright intellectually. Laure was a person of education and Rochefoucault's use of incorrect language was in her eyes deplorable. He wrote her from Biarritz, "We're having a torrential heat wave," to which she tartly replied, "Don't complain, we're in the midst of a torrid downpour." Some hidden and terrible sorrow suddenly made Laure Hayman decide to go into retirement. It was like the retirement of a great actress or singer. The youthful Proust wrote her a tender letter of farewell in ornithological terminology, comparing her to a "swallow for grace, a bird of Paradise for beauty, a wood dove for faithful friendship, an eagle for courage and a homing pigeon for sure instinct."

If the "semi-beavers" remained in discreet semi-obscurity, not so the unabashed Horizontals. The three top members of this brazenly spectacular coterie were Emilienne d'Alençon, Liane de Pougy and La Belle Otero, a trio known as "Les Grandes Trois," of which Liane de Pougy was the undisputed star. A cool beauty with perfect proportions, classic features and the flawless skin of a white camellia, she was spoken of as "Notre courtisane nationale," with the deference the French pay to any of their national institutions. In addition to her more sultry attractions, she had style, a regal poise, what today would be called "class," and her manners were impeccable when she wanted them to be. She played the piano well and the guitar even better, she spoke English and Spanish and she rode a horse with dash.

Born Anne de Chassaigne, the daughter of an army officer and his bourgeois wife, she was educated at the Sacred Heart in Rennes, then married off to a navy officer at the age of nineteen. But she cared neither for marriage nor for the navy officer and almost immediately brought suit for divorce. The navy officer protested and expressed his dissent by firing two bullets into her shapely thigh where they lodged without further damage. In later years Liane was fond of telling the story and would wind up, "If anyone doubts me, he can feel the bullets." Most gentlemen couldn't wait to doubt. After breaking off this marriage, she supported herself for a time giving piano and English lessons. When or how she gave up this humdrum employment for a more lucrative living is indefinite . . . at least the *when* is. She first attracted the public's attention as she rode with the Marquis MacMahon in an open landau to watch the Grand Prix and shortly after that, the Folies Bergère booked her as a show girl to appear somewhat statically in a short skit where her acting ability would not be put to any severe test. The Prince of Wales happened to be in Paris at the time of her opening. Liane had never met him, but she felt no compunctions about writing him: "Monseigneur, I am about to make my Paris debut. I would be consecratedly yours if you would come and applaud me." Edward, amused by such naïve gall, did go along, taking with him some friends, prominent members of the Jockey Club, and overnight Liane de Pougy became a celebrity if never a very good actress.

Adorers started flocking and she started reaping the profits. Houses, driving equipages, jewels and works of art were showered upon her by bankers, crowned heads, rich men-about-town and even Pierre de Nolhac, curator of the museum of Versailles and member of that august body, the French Academy. She was worshiped by the librettist Henri Meilhac, who in collaboration with Ludovic Halévy turned out the books for so many operettas

. . . *La Belle Hélène, La Périchole* . . . Meilhac was old by then and usually went around trailing one long shoestring because he was too fat to lean down and tie it up. To what degree of fulfillment his worship got him one doesn't know but Edmond de Goncourt, that "sublime old gossip," wrote in his Journal (May 11, 1894) of the rumor going the rounds that Meilhac had signed over to her eighty thousand francs worth of bank notes for the mere privilege of seeing her naked. Meilhac's fellow academicians worried about the old boy's health under this amorous strain. They banded together to write him a letter of warning, imploring him to remember that nobody wanted an empty chair in the Academy just then.

Liane was a safe gamble for the luxury trade. When she took a trip to Russia, a country whose court circles were always good for business, her Paris jeweller found it worth his while to travel along with a few priceless items, most of which ended up on her. Her flawless beauty inspired poets, Catulle Mendès and Robert de Montesquiou dedicated sonnets to her and when she arrived in Italy, D'Annunzio spread a gold chasuble sprinkled with rose petals at her feet.

Her staunchest champion among the newspaper men was Jean Lorrain, whose brilliant column called "Pall Mall," a combination of charming *belles lettres* and blatant scandal gossip, was an important feature of *Le Journal*. He was her devoted slave. His devotion must have been purely platonic, for Lorrain was a screaming homosexual. His torso, big as that of a porter from the Halles, was held in by a corset so tight it gave him a bosom. His hair, which he wore in bangs and a pompadour, was dyed a peroxide blond. With his cheeks garishly rouged, his eyes heavily made up, he looked like a Place Pigalle streetwalker. His first meeting with Liane de Pougy had been through a chance encounter in the Bois when the lady, infuriated over some rudeness he'd written about her in "Pall Mall," whaled him with a riding crop, an introduction which blossomed into a beautiful friendship. From then on, Lorrain wrote only the most glowing things about her. He also wrote a Folies Bergère act for her called "L'Araignée d'Or" in which as a golden spider, clad in a few scant wisps of metallic lace, she writhed prettily in the center of an immense wire web in whose cruel meshes were entangled her hapless male victims elegantly dressed in white tie and tails. The opening night of this theatrical gem, Lorrain, fearful that someone might hiss the act or his beloved Liane, bought seats throughout the house for fifty Montmartre thugs with orders to leap upon and silence any catcallers. Nobody catcalled but the reviews were tepid and a day or so later — this again is an item from the Journal of the erudite Edmond de Goncourt — Lorrain received an anonymous letter containing the corpse of a flea and the message: "Killed on the naked stomach of Liane de Pougy. For Jean with love."

Liane had a pair of fine carriage horses which one night were stolen from her stable. The shock was so great that she took to her bed and was unable to attend the police investigation. When summoned she wrote to the Prefect of Police, "I am confined to my bed, but if Monsieur le Prefet choses to come to me, I am prepared to give him every satisfaction compatible with my condition."

It was practically against the rules of their trade for these amatory professionals ever to fall in love themselves. However, a few of them were frail enough to lose their hearts to the men who supplied their caviar ticket. When Lucette de Varenne poisoned herself because her wealthy lover refused to marry her and when Léontine de Courcy turned off similar despair by turning on the gas, a gossip writer remarked, "In former days one didn't die of love. We have to reach this epoch to see ladies of love die from what furnishes their livelihood." Liane de Pougy's search for oblivion came out somewhat differently. She bade farewell to her maid, wrote a note to her mother which she signed with her childhood name, lifted a bottle of veronal to "those lips that had done such lucrative business" and drank the contents. The dose put her to sleep for forty-eight hours. When she came to, she had a series of vomiting attacks which cleared her system and she emerged frail and lovelier than ever. As Georges Montorgueil, writing it up in "Minutes Parisiennes," commented, "Suicide has an excellent effect upon these delicate natures. They don't die, but they do purge themselves."

Liane's beneficial suicide was over a Dr. Robin. He had been her favorite lover for a time and she fancied herself seriously in love with him. She was jealous of his home life and would never allow him to speak of his wife and child, insisting that he refer to them, if he had to, as "the monster" and "the little monster." One evening he canceled a rendezvous with Liane on the pretext of having to attend a medical meeting. Subsequently she found out that instead he had dined with a former mistress. In a fury of spite, she took up with the painter Jean Béraud, and therewith Docteur Robin gave Mlle. de Pougy the air. There was a midnight scene outside the Robin domicile with Liane screaming up at Mme. Robin, demanding her husband, and Madame screaming back that she had no intentions of giving him up, after which, Liane rushed back to her bed and her bottle of veronal. Jean Lorrain was present the morning of her recovery. She vowed amid floods of tears and bouts of nausea that from that day forth she'd take on only lovers she didn't like.

The Grand Horizontals had a way of getting religion in later life and retiring to a convent after they had retired from the turf . . . if "turf" may serve as a synonym. Liane de Pougy was the exception who saw the light in her middle thirties, at which youthful age she became a postulant at a Dominican order in Lausanne, adopting the not inappropriate name of Sister Mary Magdalene of the Penitence. Her penitence lasted only a year or so, then she shed her veil and habit for her former aigrettes and chinchilla. However, she continued to profess a spirit of devoutness and always kept a copy of *The Imitation of Christ* with marginal notes by Lamennais on the night table by her bed as a pious reminder to herself and, one assumes, whoever might be sharing the bed.

Whether or not she remained true to her vow of taking on only lovers she didn't like, she eventually took on a husband whom she not only liked but loved. He was a Rumanian nobleman, Prince Ghika of Moldavia, nephew of the Queen of Greece. His aristocratic family were horrified by his marriage to a courtisane and cut him off without a sou. Nothing downhearted, he and his bride repaired to a country cottage and twenty-seven years of marital bliss except for a brief interlude of divorce when the prince fell temporarily in love with his secretary. But he soon fell out of love and he and Liane were reunited to live happily forever after until his death. His widow, who by then was aged seventy, returned to the convent in Lausanne and again put on her habit of Sister Mary Magdalene of the Penitence.

During Liane's days of triumph her only rival, and she was a formidable one, was the Spanish dancer Caroline Otero, known the gay world over as La Belle Otero. The most colorful encounter of the two rivals took place one evening at Maxim's when Otero, in a carefully contrived plot to outdazzle Pougy, made a startling entrance wearing an evening gown as décolleté as the law allowed and her entire collection of jewels. They blazed at her neck and ears, in her hair, on her bosom, her arm, hands and waist, and one or two sparkled on her ankles. A few minutes later Liane, who had been tipped off by a friend, made her own

EDMOND DE GONCOURT
*"That sublime old gossip"*

Photo Nadar, Collection Yvan Christ, Paris

MME. DE LOYNES

*Most feminine and Parisian of all the great hostesses*

JULES LEMAÎTRE
*Distinguished literary critic, academician and Mme. de Loynes's*
*last and fullest love*

Photo H. Manuel, Collection Yvan Christ, Paris

HENRI DE ROCHEFORT
*"Espouser of colorful and idiotic causes"*

Photo E. Pirou, Collection Yvan Christ, Paris

VICTORIEN SARDOU
*Highly successful dramatist, omnivorous reader and genuine scholar*

Photo Nadar, Collection Yvan Christ, Paris

EMILIENNE D'ALENÇON
*Charmer of men and trainer of rabbits*

Photo Reutlinger, Collection A. Jakovsky, Paris

LA BELLE OTERO
*The Spanish dancer in her Russian period*

Photo Reutlinger, Collection A. Jakovsky, Paris

LIANE DE POUGY
*Undisputed star in the top trio of grand horizontals*

Photo Walery, Collection A. Jakovsky, Paris

startling entrance wearing a white gown of classic purity, her only jewel a single diamond drop at her perfect throat, but she was followed by her maid bearing a large velvet cushion on which was piled in a glittering mound the remainder of her mistress's invaluable collection.

Among the treasures Otero wore that evening were three pearl necklaces, one the former possession of the Empress Eugénie, another that of the Empress of Austria and a third which had once belonged to Léonide Leblanc. Eight bracelets, a dazzlement of rubies, emeralds and sapphires jangled on her wrists. Ten cabochon ruby clips outlined her bosom, a superfluous note of emphasis, and a pearl and diamond tiara crowned her blue-black hair. About her middle was her famous diamond bolero, a masterpiece by Cartier who, before parting with it, placed it on display in their window for three weeks, virtually stopping all traffic on the rue de la Paix. It was valued at 2,275,000 gold francs, kept in the vaults of the Crédit Lyonnais, and whenever she wanted to wear it for a turn on the stage it was brought in an armored coupé by two armed gendarmes who stood guard in the wings.

Caroline Otero, like all gypsies, was avaricious for money, but she liked jewels even better and she'd play with her collection like a child playing with toys. She had the gypsy's love of tinsel and gewgaws and often, along with her real gems, she'd wear theatrical jewelry. One evening onstage during a particularly lively ballet number her genuine pearl necklace broke and the pearls flew in every direction. Otero was at the height of her popularity then and a sympathetic audience demanded that the show be stopped until each pearl had been recovered. Stage hands, dressers, extras scurried about picking up the precious beads. It happened that one or two fake pearls had also dropped off her costume. Seeing this, a rival dancer, Valentine Grandais, pounced upon one, walked down to the footlights, bit it and showed the audience the broken halves. A musician in the orchestra pit had found three of the real ones and had put them in his pocket but after seeing Grandais' little act of bitchery, he thought they were fake too and threw them away.

Otero's chief jewelry supplier was a hideous German baron named Ollstreder whom she'd captured when she danced in Berlin. He was a horrible old lecher who never confused love with lovemaking. There was never any romantic courtship, or subtle buildup, to his attentions. Any evening that he wanted Caroline's services, he'd send her a box from Cartier's containing some costly item and his calling card. "On such a basis," Otero told her maid, "one can't call a man ugly."

The baron didn't care whether she thought he was ugly or not. He was content to show her off in public as a purchased possession. She saw to it that he paid for the exhibit. It was from him she extorted Eugénie's pearl necklace along with a pair of earrings to match. One night at the opera, the baron left her for a few minutes to go speak to a pretty countess he knew. Otero, who could be insanely jealous, tore off one of the earrings, hid it in her bosom and dashed away to the cabaret where they usually had supper. The baron came puffing after to find her in a wild Spanish fury. "When one has the honor of being with la Belle Otero," she screamed (she had a way of referring to herself in the third person like royalty), "no one else exists!" and she blamed him for the loss of her earring. Ollstreder promised her a new pair. She made sure the missing one was still safely in her bosom, then relented a bit but demanded, by way of reparation to her outraged sensibilities, the diamond *rivière* of Marie Antoinette. She got it.

In such maneuvering she was following out the advice she once gave the youthful Colette. "Remember, little one," she said, "that there's a moment in the life of every man when he opens wide his palm."

"The moment of passion?" asked Colette wide-eyed.

"No!" laughed Caroline. "The moment when you twist his wrist!" and she made a gesture which, Colette wrote, would have squeezed an entire grapefruit or broken a number of bones.

Caroline Otero was a magnificent animal, of a beauty which today would seem too much like that of a Senorita on a cigar box. She moved with the grace of a panther and her entrance into any restaurant or public place had all the brio of the overture to *Carmen*. Born in Barcelona, the natural child of a Greek nobleman and a Cadiz gypsy, she started her dancing career at the age of twelve and her other career at the age of fourteen. At Oporto she was kidnaped by the Chief of Police who was madly in love with her, rescued by a rich youth whose family, in order to keep him from marrying her, had her put in jail. By fifteen, she had acquired three Andalusian grandees and an Italian husband "who was," she wrote in her memoirs, "as handsome as Bizet's Toreador." He was also as brainless as Wagner's Parsifal and young Caroline skipped off to Marseilles, shedding her husband on the way. In Marseilles, she found a job dancing in a waterfront *caf'-conce'* where she bewitched the male clientele and roused the jealousy of the resident *demoiselles,* one of whom picked a quarrel with her which Caroline settled by felling her with a cast-iron chair. She made her way to Monte Carlo where, wandering into the Casino one evening, she startled the Casino habitués by the youthful assurance with which she walked calmly up to the gaming table and, although she'd never before set eyes on a roulette wheel, played four single winning numbers in turn, placing her accumulating winnings back on the table each time, and all but broke the bank. Her naïve ignorance of the game became self-evident when she started to walk away without cashing in her chips or even gathering them off the table. The astonished *croupier* called her back and she held out her skirt as he dumped into it the equivalent of a hundred and fifty thousand francs. With this loot, it wasn't any problem to travel to Paris and set herself up in style. In '89 she danced at the Cirque d'Eté, and drew the attention of various impressarios who booked her for turns in music halls and *café-concerts*. By 1892, La Belle Otero had come into her own at the Folies Bergère and was the furore of Paris.

It was during the music hall period that Colette knew her. The authoress, then a slip of a girl, was doing her own time as a pantomimist on the circuit, and when they appeared on the same bill Otero would sometimes invite her back to her house for supper along with some of the girls from the show. In her enchanting memoirs *Mes Apprentissages* Colette writes of those evenings when Lina, as she called her, would slip out of her fine clothes and into a loose robe, shout that food was ready and everybody would fall to.

> I've always liked to eat [Colette says], but what was my appetite compared with Lina's! . . . When finally she pushed her plate aside, it would be after it had been emptied four, even five times . . . She'd let her robe fly open, her chemise slip down. In the brown cleavage between two curiously shaped breasts like elongated fruit, firm and raised at the points, would sparkle carelessly a single diamond, a row of radiantly pink pearls or a bit of theatrical jewelry.
>
> "To the piano, Maria! The rest of you shove the hell this table out of the way!"
>
> It had hardly struck ten. Till two in the morning, Otero danced for her own pleasure. Throwing her robe aside, she danced in her chemise and swirling silk petticoat. The sweat ran down to her thighs. She'd grab a sauce-spotted napkin from the table and wipe her face, her neck, her armpits. Then she'd dance again and again.

During her peak years, Otero lived on what used to be the rue Georges Bizet but since has, for some unexplained reason, been changed to the rue Peter the First of Serbia, in a magnificent house run by fifteen servants and a private secretary who was a Spanish grandee and the former consul at Lisbon. On fine afternoons, she'd station herself to wait for her carriage on a second-floor balcony dressed in loud colors, gaudy sequins and make-up to match. Her carriage was an eight-spring landau upholstered in blue satin and pulled by four black horses. Her entrance through the gates at the races must have had all the subtlety of a circus parade.

There was a certain naïveté to her very vulgarity. Whenever she wore her diamond corselet in the theatre, before making her whirlwind entrance, she'd resort to an extraordinary muscular trick of swelling her bosom up and out to a degree that only a fortuitously placed gem on either side discouraged the points from popping forth. She considered this a brilliant accomplishment and would roar with delight over any observer's astonishment. Caroline's moods could change like patterns in a kaleidoscope. At one moment, she'd be possessed of all the demons in a Spanish hell, the next, she'd become an angel of sweetness and generosity. Only her brash self-assurance remained constant. Aside from her extraordinary gift for dancing she had neither vocal nor acting ability and yet her reputation was blazing enough to prompt Carré, the director of the Opéra Comique, by way of a stunt, to put her on in a one-hour version of *Carmen*. It must have been both funny and painful. The *habañera,* which was mainly danced, came off well enough. As Otero couldn't sing "Au Clair de la Lune," what her singing of the *seguidilla* was like, staggers the imagination. Regular artists of the Comique were stationed in the wings to give her the correct cues and to hum the note they trusted she'd start on and at the finish of a performance that must have had Bizet whirling in his grave, she had the gall to complain that the orchestra wasn't in time.

It was with characteristic bravado that Otero wrote her own somewhat improbable autobiography. According to her, all men fell dead over her. Actually a few of them did . . . and by their own hand. Comte Chevedolé, a prominent member of the Jockey Club, blew his brains out after he'd squandered his fortune on her. An explorer named Payen offered her ten thousand gold francs for one night of her lavishments and when she turned him down, put on a similar brain-blowing performance in the Bois outside the Chinese Pavilion where they'd first met. When she journeyed to New York to appear at the Eden Musée, she was billed as "The Suicide Siren." As her ship came into the harbor, it was met by a chartered yacht on which were forty men-about-town each wearing a yellow rose and a red carnation in homage to her and to Spain. They waved and blew kisses and she writhed an appreciative fandango on the top deck. In America, she is said to have made a mint of dollars which, after she'd converted them into francs, were lost on the tables of Monte Carlo. Jurgens, the manager of the Eden Musée, with whom she lived during her New York engagement, filched what was left of receipts in the box office to follow her back to Paris. Vanderbilt, she claims, offered her a yacht, Dion an automobile, D'Annunzio wrote her a poem, Renoir painted her portrait and the statesman Briand went clear down to Cannes for the sole and laudably respectable purpose of wishing her a happy birthday. When she appeared in Berlin, Kaiser Wilhelm commissioned a pantomime to be written in which she performed at the Wintergarten. It was a colossal hit . . . or rather La Belle Otero was a colossal hit (this is still according to her own colossal memoirs). After the opening, she was mobbed by handsome and titled wooers who offered her jewels, schlosses on the Rhine, purebred horses and, one surmises, assurances of suicide. Out of these knight pursuants she chose hideous old Baron Ollstreder.

Her diamond-blazing travels took her on to Moscow and St. Petersburg where she credits herself with having inflamed practically every male member of the Imperial Court. Prince Peter, she tells us, cried out in amorous anguish, "Ninouchka, ruin me, but never leave me!" Grand Duke Nicholas, it would seem, had less suppliant tactics. He had her abducted by force and placed in a second-floor room of his palace where she kicked up such a ruckus, screaming and beating him with her fists, that the duke decided to give her time to cool off so he calmly walked out carrying her sable cloak and locking the door behind him. Thereat she flung open a double window and leapt down into a snowbank. The thermometer registered twenty below zero and the Spanish *femme fatale* was in a ballgown and satin slippers. But lo! a kindly moujik happened by in his sleigh, rescued her out of the drifts, wrapped a filthy fur rug about her bare shoulders and drove her to safety . . . safety being the palace of the more docile Prince Peter. After this she came down with pneumonia, from which she made an uneventful but dramatic recovery.

During her mid-forties, La Belle Otero gave up her public career. "I wish to retire in full beauty," she stated to the press. The vast fortune she'd garnered had long since vanished on the green baize cover of the roulette table. The diamond corselet was sold at auction and broken up into lesser works of the jeweler's art. Her other gems and pearls dwindled away one by one into pawn receipts at the Mont de Piété. Her furniture was sold along with the portrait painted by Franck which Kaiser Wilhelm had commissioned. She went to live in Nice . . . in a small, one-room apartment on the rue d'Angleterre, not too far from the palatial hotels of the Promenade des Anglais which she used to patronize. As far as I know, she still lives there. Anne Manson, who wrote about her in Guilleminault's *La Belle Epoque,* went to call on her in 1948 and found a fat, elderly woman who looked like a Spanish shopkeeper. However, there still remained something of the flair, something uniquely of a vanished era. "When Otero departs," Mademoiselle Manson writes, "there will depart with her the last symbol of an epoch, superficial, light and at the same time virtuous and cynical, covetous toward others yet madly extravagant in its pleasures, full of faults but not without its splendor."

# BIBLIOGRAPHY

# BIBLIOGRAPHY

Achard, Marcel. *Rions avec eux*. Paris: Arthème Fayard, 1957.

Auriol, Georges. *Histoire du rire*. Paris: Marpon et Flammerion, [1893?].

Barrès, Maurice. *Mes Cahiers*. Paris: 1929.

———. *Les Déracinés*. Paris: Plon, 1937.

———. *Huit jours chez Monsieur Renan*. Paris: E. Paul, frères, 1913.

Barry, William. *Ernest Renan*. New York: C. Scribner's Sons, 1905.

Bennett, Arnold. *Paris Nights*. New York: George H. Doran Co., 1913.

Bergerat, Emile. *Souvenirs d'un enfant de Paris*. Paris: Fasquelle, 1911–12.

Bernard, Jean-Jacques. *Mon Père, Tristan Bernard*. Paris: Albin Michel, 1955.

Bernard, Tristan. *Auteurs, Acteurs, Spectateurs*. Paris: Lafitte, 1909.

Bibesco, Marthe Lucie. *La Duchesse de Guermantes, Laure de Sade, Comtesse de Chevigné*. Paris: Plon, 1950.

Billy, André. *L'Epoque 1900*. Paris: Editions Jules Tallardier, 1951.

———. *Les Frères Goncourt*. Paris: Flammarion, 1954.

Bled, Victor du. *Le Société française depuis cent ans*. Paris: Bloud et Gay, 1923.

Brisson, Adolphe. *Nos Humoristes*. Paris: Société d'Edition Artistique, 1900.

Brogan, D. W. *The French Nation*. New York: Harper and Bros., 1909.

Brousson, Jean-Jacques. *Anatole France en pantoufles*. Paris: Les Editions G. Crie et Cie., 1924.

Burnand, Robert. *La Vie quotidienne à Paris*. Paris: Hachette, 1947.

———. *Paris 1900*. Paris: Hachette, 1951.

Chastenet, Jacques. *La France de Monsieur Fallières*. Paris: Libraire Arthème Fayard, 1959.

Carco, Francis. *La Belle Epoque au temps de Bruant*. Paris: Gallimard, 1954.

Chevalier, Haakon. *The Ironic Temper, Anatole France and His Time*. New York: Oxford Press, 1932.

Chevassu, Francis. *Les Parisiens, portraits d'aujourd'hui*. Paris: Alphonse Lemerre, 1892.

Clermont-Tonnerre, E. de Gramont. *Memoirs, au temps des equipages*. Paris: Grasset, 1928.

———. *Robert de Montesquiou et Marcel Proust*. Paris: Flammarion, 1925.

———. *Souvenirs de la Tour Eiffel*. Paris: Grasset, 1937.

Clergue, Helen. *The Salon, A Study of French Society and Personalities in the Eighteenth Century*. New York: G. P. Putnam's Sons, 1907.

Colette. *Mes Apprentissages.* Paris: Ferenczi, 1936.
———. *La Vagabonde.* Paris: Albin Michel, 1950.
Dabot, Henri. *Calendriers d'un bourgeois du Quartier Latin.* Paris: Peronne, 1905.
Daudet, Ernest. *Les Coulisses de la société française.* Paris: Paul Ollendorff, 1893.
Daudet, Léon. *Salons et journaux.* Paris: Nouvelle Libraire Nationale, 1917.
———. *Souvenirs autour d'un groupe litteraire.* Paris: Bibliothèque Charpentier, 1910.
Deschamps, Gaston. *La Vie des lettres.* Paris: Armand Colin et Cie., 1894.
Donnay, Maurice. *J'ai vécu 1900.* Paris: Arthème Fayard, 1950.
Dorgelès, Roland. *Portraits sans retouche.* Paris: Albin Michel, 1952.
*Le Figaro Illustré.* Paris, 1890's.
*Le Figaro Salon.* Paris, 1890's.
Fouquières, André de. *Cinquante ans de panache.* Paris: Pierre Horay-Flore, 1951.
———. *Mon Paris et ses parisiens.* Paris: Pierre Horay-Flore, 1953.
Goncourt, Jules et Edmond de. *Journal des Goncourt.* Paris: Fasquelle et Flammarion, 1956.
Gourmont, Remy de. *Le Livre des masques.* Paris: Société du Mercure de France, 1896.
———. *Promenades Littéraires.* Paris: Société du Mercure de France, 1929.
Gregh, Ferdinand. *L'Age d'or.* Paris: Grasset, 1947.
Gramont, Elisabeth de. *Marcel Proust.* Paris: Flammarion, 1948.
Guilleminault, Gilbert. *Le Roman vrai de la troisième république.* Paris: Denoël, 1958.
Hermant, Abel. *Souvenirs de la vie mondaine.* Paris: Plon, 1935.
Hervieu, Paul. *Peints par eux-mêmes.* Paris: Alphonse Lemerre, 1893.
Huddleston, Sisley. *Paris, Salons, Cafés, Studios.* Philadelphia: J. B. Lippincott, 1928.
Huneker, James Gibbon. *Egoists.* New York: C. Scribner's Sons, 1909.
———. *Essays.* New York: C. Scribner's Sons, 1929.
———. *Steeplejack.* New York: C. Scribner's Sons, 1920.
*L'Illustration.* Paris, 1890 on.
Keim, Albert. *Le Demi-siècle.* Paris: Albin Michel, 1950.
Lauwick, Hervé. *Le Merveillieux humeur de Lucien et Sacha Guitry.* Paris: Librairie Arthème Fayard, 1959.
Lemaître, Jules. *Les contemporains.* Paris: H. Lecène et H. Oudin, 1889.
Lorrain, Jean. *La Ville empoisonnée.* Paris: Jean Crès, 1936.
Mauduit, Jean. *Maxim's.* Monaco: Editions du Rocher, 1958.
Maurois, André. *A History of France.* New York: Farrar, Straus and Cudahy, 1948.
———. *Le Monde de Marcel Proust.* Paris: Hachette, 1960.
———. *A la Recherche de Marcel Proust.* Paris: Hachette, 1949.
Meyer, Arthur. *Ce que je peux dire.* Paris: Plon–Nourrit et Cie., 1912.
———. *Ce que mes yeux ont vus.* Paris: Plon–Nourrit et Cie., 1911.

Morand, Paul. *1900*. Paris: Les Editions de France, 1931.

Otero, Caroline. *Le Roman de la Belle Otero; sa vie intime, ses amours, ses succés racontés par elle-même*. Paris: Editions "Le Calame," 1926.

*Paris Almanach*. Paris, 1895.

Poniatowski, André. *D'un siècle à l'autre*. Paris: Presses de la Cité, 1948.

Pouquet, Marie-Jeanne. *Le Salon de Mme. de Caillavet*. Coulommiers: P. Brodard, 1926.

Régnier, Henri de. *De mon Temps*. Paris: Société du Mercure de France, 1933.

Renard, Jules. *Journal* (29th Edition) Paris: Gallimard, 1935.

*La Revue Blanche*. Paris, 1891-1903.

*La Revue des Deux Mondes*. Paris, 1890's.

Ritz, Marie. *César Ritz, Host to the World*. Philadelphia: J. B. Lippincott, 1938.

Robertson, W. Graham. *Life Was Worth Living*. New York: Harper and Bros., 1931.

Roman, Jean. *Paris fin de siècle*. New York: Arts, Inc., 1960.

Rostand, Maurice. *Confession d'un demi-siècle*. Paris: Jeune Parque, 1948.

Rothenstein, William. *Men and Memories*. New York: Coward-McCann, Inc., 1931.

Sarcey, Francisque. *Quarante ans de théâtre*. Paris: Bibliothèque des Annales politiques et littèraires, 1900–1902.

Scholl, Aurélien. *L'Esprit du boulevard*. Paris: Victor-Havard, [nd].

Spencer, Philip. *Flaubert*. London: Faber, 1952.

d'Uzès, Duchesse. *Souvenirs*. Paris: Plon, [1939].

Verneuil, Louis. *Rideau à 9 heures*. New York: Editions de la Maison Française, 1944.

Vollard, Ambroise. *Souvenirs d'un marchand de tableaux*. Paris: Albin Michel, 1937.

Walkley, A. B. *Drama and Life*. New York: Brentano's, 1908.

Wilson, Barbara. *The House of Memories*. New York: Dial Press, 1929.

Wilhelm, Jacques. *La Vie à Paris sous le deuxième Empire et la troisième République*. Paris: Arts et Métiers Graphiques, 1947.

# INDEX

# INDEX